JUSTICE IN
THE UNITED STATES

JUSTICE IN THE UNITED STATES

Human Rights and the U.S. Constitution

JUDITH BLAU
AND
ALBERTO MONCADA

ROWMAN & LITTLEFIELD PUBLISHERS, INC.
Lanham • Boulder • New York • Toronto • Oxford

ROWMAN & LITTLEFIELD PUBLISHERS, INC.

Published in the United States of America
by Rowman & Littlefield Publishers, Inc.
A wholly owned subsidary of The Rowman & Littlefield Publishing Group, Inc.
4501 Forbes Boulevard, Suite 200, Lanham, Maryland 20706
www.rowmanlittlefield.com

PO Box 317
Oxford
OX2 9RU, UK

British Library Cataloguing in Publication Information Available

Library of Congress Cataloging-in-Publication Data

Blau, Judith R., 1942–
 Justice in the United States : human rights and the U.S. Constitution /
Judith Blau and Alberto Moncada.
   p. cm.
 Includes bibliographical references and index.
 ISBN-13: 978-0-7425-4559-5 (cloth : alk. paper)
 ISBN-10: 0-7425-4559-8 (cloth : alk. paper)
 ISBN-13: 978-0-7425-4560-1 (pbk. : alk. paper)
 ISBN-10: 0-7425-4560-1 (pbk. : alk. paper)
 1. Human rights. 2. Constitutional law. 3. Human rights—United States.
 4. Constitutional law—United States. I. Moncada, Alberto, 1930– II. Title.
 III. Title: Justice in the U.S. IV. Title: Justice in the United States.
 K3240.B59 2006
 341.4'8—dc22
                                                                    2005024803
Printed in the United States of America

∞™ The paper used in this publication meets the minimum requirements of American
National Standard for Information Sciences—Permanence of Paper for Printed Library
Materials, ANSI/NISO Z39.48-1992.

For Harold and in loving memory of Theda

Para Esther, con el cariño de siempre

Contents

꿈

Preface

Our goal is two-fold: first, to engage readers' interests in human rights, and, second, to encourage American readers to examine the U.S. Constitution from a critical and comparative perspective. Global justice and peace are thwarted so long as the most powerful nation defies international laws and treaties, and the well-being of Americans is compromised by an inadequate Constitution. The constitutions of most countries are evolving in harmony with international human rights standards, but this process has not yet begun in the United States.

Revising a constitution ought to be an intense and inclusive process, involving the grassroots (in classrooms and community meetings), local and national committees, as well as legal and other experts. The democratization of this process is increasingly possible with electronic technologies. Our own attempt in chapter 10 is a textbook exercise to illustrate that it can be done, and because this exercise is a cautious one, we also suggest in the satire in chapter 9 that there may be alternatives to state-capitalism and indirect, representative government. The international arena is fast-paced and much can be gleaned about new forms and methods of democratic governance from current developments that build on the United Nations World Summit on the Information Society and UNESCO's e-governance programs.

What are the origins of ideas found in books? Students and classroom discussions matter a great deal, perhaps the most. And, for their lively and provocative discussions, we thank our colleagues in Sociologists without Borders and Sociólogos Sin Fronteras. An inspiration for this volume is Bereket Selassie, who *did* write a constitution and is a colleague at the

University of North Carolina. We also thank Berhane Araia, Heather Kane, Andres Unger, and Vickie Wilson for their assistance with tables and manuscript preparation. We feel especially fortunate to have had the Rowman & Littlefield team with us: Alan McClare, Jason Proetorius, and Luann Reed-Siegel. Our thanks!

Abbreviations

AFDC	Aid to Families and Dependent Children
ASEAN	Association of Southeast Asian Nations
AU	African Union
EAFT	European Association for Free Trade
ECHR	Egyptian Center for Housing Rights
ECSC	European Coal and Steel Community
ECU	European Currency Unit
EDC	European Defense Community
EEC	European Economic Community
EPA	Environmental Protection Agency
ERATOM	European Atomic Energy Community
EU	European Union
GDP	Gross Domestic Product
GM	genetically modified
HDI	Human Development Index
ICCPR	International Covenant on Civil and Political Rights
ICESCR	International Covenant on Economic, Social, and Cultural Rights
ILO	International Labour Organization
INGO	international nongovernmental organization
IRIN	UN Office for the Coordination of Humanitarian Affairs
Mercosur	Mercado Comun del Cono Sur/Southern Cone Common Market
NEPAD	New Partnership for Africa's Development
NGO	nongovernmental organization

NRPB	National Resources Planning Board
OCHA	Office for the Coordination of Humanitarian Affairs
OECC	Organization for Economic Cooperation in Commerce
OECD	Organization for Economic Cooperation and Development
OSHA	Occupational Safety & Health Administration
PAC	Policy of Common Agriculture
PLO	Palestine Liberation Organization
PSOE	Partido Socialista Obrero Español
TANF	Temporary Assistance for Needy Families
UDHR	Universal Declaration of Human Rights
UNDP	United Nations Development Programme
UNESCO	UN Educational, Scientific, and Cultural Organization
UNICEF	United Nations Children's Fund
UNIFEM	United Nations Development Fund for Women
WB	World Bank

The Idea of Rights 1

W hen it comes to having rights and freedoms, Americans are re-
grettably at least a quarter of a century behind most everyone
else in the world. In this chapter we explore the historical roots
of American rights and freedoms. This is a tale told often, but our emphasis
is different owing to our interest in human rights, not simply political and
civil rights. To propose revisions to the U.S. Constitution, we need to lay
out the framework of the current Constitution. In this chapter we review
features of the Declaration of Independence, constitutional provisions for
rights and freedoms, court interpretations of the rights of corporations,
and the premises of liberal law. We also introduce human rights to clarify
how they are different from what Americans emphasize, namely, individual rights.

The Declaration of Independence

On June 7, 1776, Richard Henry Lee rose to his feet at the convening of
the Second Continental Congress, to declare a motion for independence.
It passed, and the members of a small committee, headed by Thomas Jefferson, sequestered themselves to prepare the document. Two days later,
the committee presented the Declaration to Congress and proclaimed the
right of revolution. The philosophical grounding of this right to revolt is
important, but just as important is what Jefferson deemed to be rights.
Paragraph 2 begins thus:

> We hold these truths to be self-evident, that all men are created equal, that
> they are endowed by their Creator with certain unalienable Rights, that
> among these are Life, Liberty and the pursuit of Happiness.—That to secure

these rights, Governments are instituted among Men, deriving their just powers from the consent of the governed.[1]

Jefferson deliberately misquotes John Locke, who wrote instead, "Life, Liberty and Pursuit of Property." All the Framers of the Constitution believed that property was a right, as we will later describe, but we charitably speculate that the reason why Jefferson substituted "Happiness" for "Property" was because property in the colonies included slaves, and although having human chattel may have been acceptable, it probably was not comfortable to celebrate.

The "self-evident" truths about equality and rights also requires some explanation. For Jefferson "self-evident" did not imply some democratic ideal whereby ordinary men would see the justification for the revolution. Instead, it is an elitist term that goes back to the Stoics' conception that a tribunal of wise men could weigh the options and arrive at good ethical judgments.[2] It was "self-evident" in this hypothetical and philosophical sense.[3] Additionally, the arguments of the Declaration draw from a long line of writers, including Saint Thomas Aquinas, the Enlightenment philosophers—especially the French *philosophes*, Voltaire and Jean-Jacques Rousseau—but mainly the English philosopher John Locke.[4] The lines of the Declaration, as Brian Orend points out, could have been written line for line by Locke, with the exception of the substitution of "Happiness" for "Property."[5]

Nor is Jefferson completely original about connecting rights to political action. The English barons had demanded concessions in the form of the Magna Carta from King John in 1215, and in the same century, King Magnus of Norway was pressed to issue the Magnus Lagaboters Landslov, which promised all equality before the law.[6] Additionally, in the sixteenth century, there had been upheavals for the advance of liberties and freedoms, and royalty in France, Holland, Spain, and England had been forced to make major concessions, relinquishing their own powers and extending rights to property holders and sometimes others as well. Following decades of civil war in England, the Levellers, in the mid-seventeenth century, demanded guarantees of the peoples' "native rights," including legal rights, and the right to life, property, and the exercise of free speech and of religion. This culminated in the passage of the Habeas Corpus Act of 1679 and the Bill of Rights in 1689, which together greatly advanced peoples' freedoms and democracy. Their provisions included trial by jury, prohibitions against cruel and unusual punishment, security of law and person, representative government, and free elections.

Although in 1776 the French Revolution was more than a decade away, Rousseau and others were thinking much along the same lines as the British colonists, and in 1789 the French Assembly proclaimed rights and freedoms in the Declaration of the Rights of Man and of the Citizen. All this does not diminish the philosophical and political importance of the Declaration of Independence. Its arguments about inalienable rights, equality, the possibility of universal reason, and the will of the people were specially crafted for the American context, and it is a stunning document, cited still as a justification for revolution.

The Declaration provides a set of *philosophical* reasons why the colonists should raise up and rebel, and Jefferson provides a list of "the causes which impel them to the separation." Yet Jefferson did not need the Stoics and a "tribunal of wise men" for a justification. He simply could have looked out the window and onto the streets. The insurrection had started more than a year before, on April 18, 1775. However, instead of praise and support for their idealism—and, yes, wisdom, as Jefferson later said—the colonial Congress responded to the peoples' insurrection by sending King George an apology in its Olive Branch Petition. And, months before Jefferson penned the Declaration, about February 1776, Thomas Paine's pamphlet *Common Sense* hit the streets of colonial towns. Written in England and shipped to America, it presented many of the ideas that inform the vision behind the Declaration. Historians Samuel Eliot Morison, Henry Steele Commager, and William E. Leuchtenburg describe its great importance: "Within a month this amazing pamphlet had been read by or to almost every white American. It rallied the undecided and the wavering."[7]

The Idea of Rights

Thus, while the Declaration was not all that novel, and derived much from John Locke, it also rubber-stamped a revolution that had already begun, and was immensely helpful in spurring efforts to establish rules and procedures for governance well before the war was over. Individual colonies formed their own governments beginning in 1776, with a resolution by Congress, and each of their constitutions included a Bill of Rights, placing democratic control of government in the hands of the sovereign people (that is, those who held property). Thus, Jefferson's Declaration was like a cueing card for everything that came next—independence, writing a constitution, and setting up the machinery of governance. The last land battle of the War of Independence was mid-November 1782, and the Peace of Paris was signed later that month.

We will be emphasizing throughout this book that *ideas* about rights are extremely powerful on their own, since they find expression in constitutions and charters, but to matter at all, these ideas need to appeal to peoples' common sense (as Thomas Paine recognized) and relate to their understandings and experiences. We wish to emphasize here that Thomas Jefferson's ideas about "rights" are different from what we now term "human rights," although it has been Jefferson's (as well as James Madison's, Alexander Hamilton's, and the other Framers') conception that have dominated American political culture for over two and a quarter centuries. One important difference between early American rights and human rights is practical coverage. Only white males held rights in the new republic, and for purposes of political participation, only white males who owned property. (Popular political participation was not introduced until the Jacksonian era.[8]) In contrast, the contemporary term *human rights* refers to all human beings in their fulsome sense, and to social, economic, and cultural rights as well as political rights. The colonial rebellion that culminated in national independence was for political freedom; today there is much more at stake because people share the world in ways that were unimaginable in the late eighteenth century.

We can say now that the freedoms spelled out in the Declaration were inadequate even for their times, most egregiously so regarding slavery, but also in the abominable treatment of indigenous groups and the disenfranchisement of males without property and of women.[9]

It makes sense to consider that individual political rights were prioritized in the context of the War of Independence and in the period of early nation building. But economic rights became an easy analogue to political rights as the new nation began to industrialize. Bit by bit, Americans adopted the idea that they had individual economic rights as well as political rights, but the form these rights took was not the right to economic security, but the right to ownership. Capitalism was beginning to bloom precisely at the time America gained its independence, and individual economic rights became increasingly salient, without much public debate. The white, male American citizen had as much right to get rich as he had to go to church. Especially in rural New England, new industries sprouted everywhere—sawmills, grain mills, paper mills, factories for iron production—and with these new industries came, inevitably, a class division.[10] Critics at the time, most especially Karl Marx, further contended that capitalist production not only leads to the impoverishment of workers but to their dehumanization and devaluation as well, owing to the ways that production estranges the workers from "their own nature and essence," and from what they produce, and from their relationships with other human be-ings.[11] But few, if any, were reading Karl Marx in nineteenth-century America.

In the twentieth century, socialist societies responded in a forthright way to the viciousness of capitalism, while imperiling the political free-doms of their citizens, while Europeans adopted cushions in the form of welfare capitalism.[12] Celebrated too in Europe was an extension of politi-cal freedoms, namely the idea of social rights, which, as elaborated by T. H. Marshall, included some sort of economic welfare and security.[13] Why welfare capitalism was less successful in the United States than in all other industrialized countries will be addressed later, but a short answer is that welfare capitalism penetrates through all social classes in European countries especially, and Britain to some extent, but in America, welfare was for the poor and divided Americans instead of unifying them around a sense of reciprocal responsibility (the exception, of course, being inter-generational responsibilities of Social Security and Medicare). It would not be an exaggeration to say that the United States wanted no part of social and economic rights—these were "socialist"—but the Soviets believed that civil and political rights would evolve when people were properly fed and housed. Over this difference the Cold War was waged.

Much has changed since the end of the Cold War, most notably pene-tration of all societies and nations, and even most communities, by capi-talist enterprise and capitalist commodities. This has threatened and desta-bilized most of the world's population and will continue to do. A response to these threats has been for states to bolster or revise their constitutions, hefting up the human rights provisions that enable them to move forward with new programs, new laws, and new practices that will protect the social fabric and the well-being of their populations. Most countries have revised their constitutions within the last two decades, as appendix 1.1 shows. This appendix is a list of all state constitutions available in English and the dates of current constitutions, and, in some cases, dates of earlier constitutions. This offers striking evidence of the extent to which countries —both new and old—are revising their constitutions in response, we ar-gue, to increasing global interdependencies. We will later show that these changes are in large part to bolster human rights provisions.

The United States has the oldest constitution in the world, nothing to be proud of. Its provisions for the well-being of the citizenry are negligi-ble, and even though laws exist pertaining to, for example, labor rights and social security, laws, without constitutional backing, are extremely easy to change. What we want to stress is that human rights or *derechos humanos* or *droits de l'homme* are very different from Jefferson's "rights," the long intellectual tradition from which he drew, and also different from rights in contemporary America. This is not to imply that the elements of Jefferson's vision—equality, liberty, and the inalienability of persons from their rights—are displaced by human rights, but that the American liberal tradition defines rights in a very partial and particularistic way. It is useful to consider that for Jefferson and the French *philosophes*, people were the *objects* of rights bestowed by the nation-state, whereas from the human rights perspective, human beings are the *agents of their own rights*. Human rights are deeply embedded in society, accompanying rights as well as responsibilities.

By examining the document that best embodies this American tradition, namely, the Bill of Rights and additional amendments, it will be clearer why we juxtapose political and civil rights with human rights. Here we point out that we are dealing with human rights, not crimes against humanity, which are defined by international criminal law.[14]

Bill of Rights and
Other Constitutional Amendments

Whereas Lockean Jefferson highlighted people's inalienable rights, it was the vision of the Hobbsian Federalists that prevailed in the Constitution. The Constitution puts constraints on peoples' democratic rights. It does so by diluting voters' influence through the electoral system, but also because power is divided between states and the federal government; the people are marginalized by the tensions between the competing jurisdictions. True, the system of checks and balances has been relatively successful in deterring would-be tyrants, but the same system provides disincentives for citizen involvement in governance. However, we are not concerned with the nature and structure of governance, but rather with constitutional provisions for individual rights, which are laid out in the ten 1791 Amendments (The Bill of Rights), and in a few important subsequent amendments. Although they are well known to Americans, it is useful nevertheless to again examine the constitutional amendments that are related to rights and freedoms. They are reproduced in appendix 1.2.

The important First Amendment states peoples' rights as they relate to religious freedom, and freedom of speech, of the press, the right to assemble, and to petition government. The wording is important: "Congress shall make no law"; which is to say, in colloquial, but apt terms, "just watch your back, because the State may sneak up and take those freedoms away."

In the language of Isaiah Berlin, these are negative freedoms, liberties held defensively against the state.[15]

The controversial amendment on the right to bear arms (sometimes interpreted as the rights of the individual states to keep militia) is stated in Amendment II, and Amendment III offers qualified privacy protection to citizens when soldiers want access to their homes. The important provisions ensuring legal rights—for protection against unreasonable search and seizures; protections against illegal imprisonment, double jeopardy and self-incrimination; due process; trial by jury; protections against excessive bail—are all spelled out in Amendments IV through VIII, with IX stating the coherence of rights. Amendments X and XI specify that the national government is supreme only within its own sphere, and that individual states have their own sovereign power. Amendment XII clarifies that electors vote, not persons.

Enactment of Amendment XIII declared about three million slaves to be free. But not free in any modern sense: as Frederick Douglass stated at the time, "the black was free from the individual master, but a slave of society. . . . He was turned loose, naked, hungry, and destitute to the open sky."[16] No constitutional amendment was ever proposed that would give African Americans full equality. The Civil Rights Act, a piece of legislation that addresses discrimination (again, in the negative sense of rights) and not full rights, does not. Besides, like any piece of legislation, it can be repealed just as it was passed into law.

Southern states did everything in their power to circumvent the 1865 Thirteenth Amendment, leading to the enactment of the Fourteenth Amendment in 1868. It overrides the power of individual states to abridge the rights of citizens, to uphold due process and equal protection of the laws. As we will elaborate below, it subsequently became the basis of the legal doctrine of corporate personage rights. Ratification of the Fifteenth Amendment in 1870 was presumed to guarantee black suffrage, but was sabotaged by states that rushed to impose poll taxes and other restrictions to limit the black franchise. It was not until nearly a century later, in 1964, with the ratification of the Twenty-Fourth Amendment, that the Constitution expressly prohibited states from imposing poll taxes. Women achieved the vote with the ratification of Amendment XIX, in 1920.

Amendments XVI, XVII, XVIII, XX, XXI, XXII, XXIII, XXV are not of particular interest here. Amendment XXVI lowers the voting age to eighteen, and XXVII prohibits members of Congress from giving themselves a raise, at least during the current session of Congress.[17]

We argue that the freedoms laid out in the Constitution are not human rights. They are political and civil rights, but not human rights, at least in the contemporary sense. (To clarify, political rights are the individual rights of liberal democracy, including the right to vote, to hold office, and to participate in governance. Civil rights are more complex, but essentially involve the protection of the person's existence,[18] and include freedom of thought, opinion, and religion; right to recognition before the law; right to a fair trial; freedom of movement; and right to a nationality.)

They are not human rights, and, moreover, they can undermine human rights because they exclusively focus on individual rights and thereby sever humans from their societies, social networks, and communities. They do nothing to promote solidarities, but instead promote the defense of personal rights as opposed to the rights of others, thereby impairing peoples' understanding of the importance of society and of the complex interdependencies within communities, societies, states, and, now the globe.

Corporate and Property Rights

The rights of corporations have a complex but fascinating relationship to the U.S. Constitution, and although we will discuss the Beard thesis later, which traces the implied importance of property rights in the Constitution, it is useful here to summarize why corporations have quasi-personhood rights. It is an interesting story because it was never a court interpretation; corporations' rights trace back to a simple error, and once publicized, entered into judicial precedence.

In the 1886 case *Santa Clara v. Southern Pacific Railroad*, Chief Justice Waite asserted in an oral argument that "[t]he court does not wish to hear argument on the question whether the provision in the Fourteenth Amendment to the Constitution, which forbids a State to deny any person within its jurisdiction the equal protection of the laws, applies to those of corporations. We are all of the opinion that it does."[19] And what is the precedent for this? In an earlier case that year, *Southern Pacific Railroad 118 US 294*, a court stenographer had made an error in transcription, giving Southern Pacific the rights of a person—immunity from a state's authority—and when discovered by a newspaper report word was flashed to many newspapers via the telegraph. Whatever their reasons, the justices did not revoke the error, and embraced it as their own.[20]

Corporate personhood rights are extensive: (1) corporations and shareholders are immune from persecution; (2) corporations are offered some First Amendment rights;[21] (3) under the Fourteenth Amendment corporations may establish a business anywhere they want and have considerable power over citizens' groups that wish to protect endangered natural habitats; (4) under the Fifth Amendment, they may hire real persons who will protect their rights against self-incrimination;[22] (5) under the Fourth Amendment's search and seizure provisions, they are protected against surprise visits by government officials, such as Occupational Safety and Health Administration inspectors,[23] and (6) under its due process provisions, they are protected in courts.[24] Moreover, (7) they have the right to airtime to lobby against legislation that they perceive as harmful to them; [25] (8) under the Sixth Amendment, they have the right to trial in criminal cases.[26] Because in a famous 1886 case the U.S. courts rejected the idea that corporations and businesses were a matter of "special privilege" and instead a matter of "general utility with certain person-age rights," corporations and businesses have been shielded from considerable regulation and control by state authorities ever since.

Corporate rights, according to Carl Mayer, dramatically expanded in the 1990s, as the Supreme Court further elaborated corporations' personhood rights, while their responsibilities to workers, communities, consumers, and the environment shrank.[27] Additionally, as Anthony Ogus explains, the U.S. Constitution is moot on contract rights, and that is why there are virtually no constitutional cases dealing with contracts of, for example, sale, credit, housing, and, most significantly, employment. This makes the United States virtually unique in matters of contract law, as other countries especially recognize labor contracts, and instead gives business entities and corporations unusual power.[28]

We highlight these issues here because the media, as well as elected officeholders, have been less than forthright with the American public about the extent to which corporations' rights have been expanded while those of American citizens have not.

The Federalist Papers

It was Jefferson's hand that penned the Declaration, but not the Constitution. The Constitution is largely based on *The Federalist Papers*, written by Alexander Hamilton, James Madison, and John Jay as serialized papers published between October 1787 and August 1788. What has become known as the "Beard thesis" is based on Charles A. Beard's close reading and interpretation of these papers and his conclusion that property interests played a large role in the thinking of the Framers. What the U.S. Constitution and early national laws accomplished, according to Beard, was to pave the way for the advance of capitalism.[29] (Georges Lefebvre makes this case for the French constitution.[30])

Very specifically, Beard concludes that the Framers, especially Alexander Hamilton, felt that political power ought to expressly flow from a strong economic system.[31] Public policy, according to Hamilton and the other Federalists, ought to promote economic growth, while curbing the excessive self-interest of fledgling industrialists and planters. It was Hamilton who proposed measures that would promote economic self-sufficiency and prosperity, through tariffs on imported goods and an excise tax on certain goods produced domestically. John Adams likewise agreed in his contributions to the *Federalist* that a main task of government (led by men of superior wisdom and capabilities) would be to protect the propertied and financial interests of the nation.

Thus, from the very beginning of the nation's history, economic interests played a major role in the nation's legal and political climate, even if these interests were not spelled out explicitly. Instead the overt emphasis, at least for public consumption, was on equality and its justification by an unseen natural law and secular justifications having to do with the social contract between ordinary citizens and the state. Far more public attention was given to the relationships between individual states and the national government than to the relationships between government and economic interests.[32] Analyses of debates carried out in the drafting of the constitutions of individual states tend to support this conclusion.[33]

Alan Pendleton Grimes draws from *The Federalist Papers* in his analysis of the drafting of the U.S. Constitution and arrives at the same conclusions that Beard had. Additionally, he argues that constitutional interpretations during the Reconstruction period drew heavily on Manchester Liberalism, an ideology of the supremacy of the values of capitalism and economic values. As Grimes states, in the decades following the Civil War, "The greatest good of the greatest number was, therefore, interpreted to mean the greatest acquisition for the greatest number of people." Furthermore, "Equal opportunity gave way to each man an equal chance to prove the extent of his inequality. In a pecuniary value scheme, it was evident that not all men were worth the same."[34]

In sum, the political culture in which the Constitution has been applied has always supported economic rights of property holders, although the Constitution says very little about property rights per se, and the legal culture in which the Constitution has been interpreted has always supported corporations, although the Constitution says nothing about corporations. Yet we do not want to convey the idea that the Constitution is merely a

vehicle for property rights and the rights of corporations; we wish to further show how capitalist ideals were confounded with political ones in the
eighteenth century.

Freedoms and Liberties

"Life, liberty and the pursuit of happiness," especially in the context of the
American Revolution, would have been understood by colonists as freedom from the British and, likewise, as personal freedom. Thomas Paine,
who was avidly read by the colonists, describes freedom as individuals having autonomy and independence. To illustrate his point, he wrote that the
servant accepts servitude in looking after the interests of his or her master,
but when the servant "encounters the world, in [his or her] own persons,
they repossess the full share of freedom." Thus, freedom is something that
all freemen inherently possess even if in their society their station in life
conceals it. Yet he went on to explain that freedom is possessive: "I consider freedom as personal property . . . wherever I use the words *freedom* or
rights, I desire to be understood to mean a perfect equality of them."[35]
Clearly, Paine did not mean that only holders of property had freedom,
since servants have freedom—even though it may not be apparent—but
what he did want to convey, according to Eric Foner, is that holding freedom is like holding property insofar as it secures one's autonomy.[36]

An interesting aspect of Paine's thinking that he shared with Locke was
his conception of property rights. Within natural rights theory generally
(although not for Jefferson), property was a natural right of free people before they founded governments. According to Locke, in the state of nature,
property was a natural right because after eating the apple and falling into
sin, "men employed their labor," and acquired rights to property (the trees,
land, and so forth), and when they founded a government, it became the
government's responsibility to help individual men protect their natural
right to it.[37] The difference between Locke and Paine, on the one hand,
and Jefferson, on the other, is really like splitting hairs, since Jefferson believed that property was a means to happiness and ought to have all the protections of civil law.[38]

When "freedom" hit the ground, so to speak, in the newly independent
nation it was put to immediate, practical use in laws protecting the freedoms of commerce, trade, and property holders. The greatest beneficiary
by far of freedom was capitalism. Writes Zygmunt Bauman:

> The capitalist economy is not only the territory where freedom may be
> practiced in the least constrained fashion, uninterfered with by any other

social pressures or considerations; it is also the nursery where the modern idea of freedom was sown and cultivated, to be later grafted on other branches of increasingly ramified social life.[39]

Thus, the term *freedom* in the United States so confounds capitalists' freedom with individuals' political freedom, that when Americans embrace the latter they only serve to reinforce the former.

Human Rights in Today's Context

The Indivisibility of Human Rights

In the phenomenological sense of reflective interpersonal interactions, human rights cannot be distinguished from the origins of humans. Archaeologists infer that human rights oriented humans' behavior as early as Paleolithic times, when men and women began to forge and hunt together in groups and to establish settlements.[40] Recognizing and regarding the rights of others, including others in future generations, distinguishes humankind from other animals. We feel this is important to emphasize because human regard for other humans is the anchoring principle of human rights. It becomes complicated when people have no interaction with one another, or they are different from one another in ways that matter deeply to them.

The waiter in Borneo, the stock analyst in Boston, and the Polynesian fisher all share a conception of human rights and, in the abstract, they all want it for the others. In practice, the waiter, the stock analyst, and the fisher privilege the human rights of their own kin and neighbors, but it is easy to imagine that they give scant attention to advancing the human rights of others. As it turns out, that is not quite the case. People have an amazing empathy with others they do not know when they learn about them and about their dire predicaments. Westerners' responses to the human suffering caused by the Asian tsunami in 2004 illustrate the capacity that people have for empathy with others who are distant and come from very different cultures and circumstances.

However, such empathy is short-lived. We will argue that what is required is a shift in consciousness, so that it becomes automatic to think and act in ways that take collective well-being into account. The prime mover for this shift in consciousness is globalization that impels interconnectedness among humans never imaginable before, and, in turn, the knowledge and a consciousness of others' predicaments as well as of one's own privileges. This is not as complex as it might seem because the rights of humans are not discrete and partial, but come in one package, or, rather, follow holistically from a clear assumption that humans are both different and equal.

The Vienna Declaration

To introduce the principles of human rights, we draw from the Vienna Declaration and Programme of Action, or, simply, the Vienna Declaration.[41] It has worldwide backing. Delegates from 171 states, as well as representatives from 840 international nongovernmental organizations (INGOs), unanimously approved it at the World Conference on Human Rights, held in June 1993. We reproduce portions of the Vienna Declaration in appendix 1.3, excluding sections that have to do with implementation, the role of parties (states, regional alliances, and INGOs and NGOs), and sections pertaining to the rights of specific groups.

Especially important is the leading phrase: "human rights derive from the dignity and worth inherent in the human person" and that the human person "should be the principal beneficiary and should participate actively in the realization of these rights and freedoms." Explicit here is the warrant of all humans to respect and dignity, and an affirmation of their agency in securing and holding these rights. However, the protection and promotion of human rights are the "first responsibility of Governments," and states have the responsibility for promulgating the universal norms for human rights (Article 2), in accordance with their frameworks (Articles 5 and 36). In other words, universally held principles are equally valid across all societies, even though they have different traditions, customs, religions, and legal systems. Nevertheless, there must be vigorous efforts to promote women's equal rights (Article 18), to combat discrimination and racism (Article 15), to protect minorities (Article 19), to ensure safe havens for asylum seekers (Article 23), and to alleviate extreme poverty (Article 25). Extraordinary violations of human rights demand a swift international response (Article 28).

Human rights are promoted within contexts, and the Vienna Declaration underscores that there are reciprocal relations involving the flourishing of human rights, democratic governance, economic and social development, and social progress. Civil society enters into this dynamic ("tolerance and good neighbourliness"), and so do economic actors and the state (Article 8). This is one of the clearest statements about the relationship between human rights and development; humans are the "subject of development," and have the right to self-determination (Article 2) and to develop (Article 10). Furthermore, human rights are not achieved in the absence of democratic structures, and more than that, structures that provide citizens with opportunities to have "full participation in all aspects of their lives" (Article 8).

In the context of global interdependencies and extraordinary inequalities, the Vienna Declaration makes it clear that it is the responsibility of the entire international community to uphold human rights standards, through promoting "peace, democracy, justice, equality, rule of law, pluralism, development, better standards of living and solidarity" (preamble). Finally, while human rights are subjectively experienced by humans, and holistically so, they are also objective, and inseparable (e.g., Article 5).

Thus, the international community laid out, with unanimous agreement, the principles for human rights, and during the decade of the 1990s, many states revised their constitutions in ways that reflected the principles of the Vienna Declaration. New global interdependencies and the intensification of global capitalism made clear that the advance and protection of human rights must be an international mandate. Corporate actors, polluters, terrorists, media, drug traders, financiers, and tourists have little respect for state borders, making international agreements on human rights all the more important. The rapid diffusion of consumer capitalism and wage labor through all countries in a very short period of time destabilized local economies, spurred migration, created staggering problems for families, and often fueled ethnic antagonisms. Environmental decline and destruction take an immense toll on peoples who depend on the sea or forests for their living.

Of course, none of these things are new, but the acceleration of global capitalism after the early 1970s compounded problems for people, locales, and states in novel and intense ways that were never before possible. We can consider the Vienna Declaration as the international affirmation that humans (not impersonal economic actors) are the subjects of development and ought all be buffered against the ill effects of global capitalism and all benefit from economic growth. Especially important to note is the coupling throughout the document: "human rights and fundamental freedoms." Thus, we might surmise that the two are reciprocal and reinforcing, with human rights supporting people's freedoms and, likewise, when people have their freedoms they can realize their human rights. We return to this later to see if we can avoid the tautology, but this conception, as it stands, can usefully be compared with the eighteenth-century American conception that persists in spite of its being outmoded.

Freedom in Today's Context

The general themes that dominated early American ideas about freedom—the rights of enterprises and corporations, people's autonomy and nonrestraint, and distrust of democracy—are strikingly different from the themes of the Vienna Declaration, which instead takes the idea of freedom and links it to human rights, democracy, and society. It appears that we are in two discursive realms when we consider "rights" in the American tradition and "human rights" in contemporary times. That is nearly correct, but not entirely so. The human rights tradition grows partly out of the early American and European experiences with civil and political rights. Moreover, a long, long history of ideas, much of it Western, plays a vital role in the way that we think about human rights, including Immanuel Kant's ideas about conscience, Rousseau's understanding of human altruism, and Locke's and Jefferson's conceptions of rationality.

However, if contemporary human rights thinking does not prioritize corporate or property rights, and does not valorize autonomy to the extent that the American rights tradition does, how does it consider freedom? Generally, the human rights advocate considers freedom, at least analytically, in two senses. First, civil and political freedoms involve freedom of religion, speech, and assembly, and of conscience and ideology. This is freedom conceived in exactly the same way as it is in the U.S. Constitution's Bill of Rights. In fact, human rights law provides for *more* freedoms in this particular sense than the Bill of Rights does. Besides those listed above, international human rights provisions often specify additional freedoms, such as freedom of movement, freedom to speak one's native language, freedom to privacy, freedom of conscience, freedom of communication, and the right to an ideology. In other words, civil and political freedoms relate to the protections that individuals have as free agents, and, if anything, they have been expanded since the U.S. Constitution was written.

To elaborate even further and suggest how the context of freedom has changed, we might contrast Jefferson's phrasing regarding human freedoms as "life, liberty and the pursuit of happiness," with the phrasing in the 1948 Universal Declaration of Human Rights (UDHR):

> Whereas recognition of the inherent dignity and of the equal and inalienable rights of all members of the human family is the foundation of freedom, justice and peace in the world.[42]

Interesting here is the organic conception of the inalienable rights of all humankind as being the foundation of freedom, justice, and peace. The UDHR does include all of the individual rights that the U.S. Constitution does (e.g., the right to a fair trial), but it does so from the premise of inclusiveness and universality, and less from the premise of autonomous human beings.

The second conception of freedom from the human rights perspective links individual freedom with the developmental freedoms of the community, society, and state. This view has been best articulated by Amartya Sen.[43] These mutualisms depend on opportunities to exercise freedoms—opportunities for an education, for raising children, and for employment—and clear ways of harmonizing the capabilities, needs, and talents of individuals with the collectivity. Sen clarifies the important role that a great variety of institutions play in supporting these mutualisms, notably economic ones, but also legal, social, cultural, and political ones.[44]

Thus, the very conception of freedom has grown, matured, blossomed in today's world and has done so in spite of the obvious fact that there are fewer resources to go around today than there were two centuries ago. A key aspect of the concept of "freedom" that has changed is the recognition that freedom is not zero-sum. Rather, the more we share our freedoms, the more there are to go around. Today we consider human rights—not simply rights—to mean interconnected freedoms and opportunities. To illustrate, there are now international agreements about the following fundamental rights: food security; housing; education; health care; social security; employment; leisure, freedom of expression; freedom of movement; privacy; political freedoms; civil rights; freedom from discrimination, freedom to join a trade union; freedom to marry; protections for children; protections for the elderly and disabled; rights to a cultural, racial, or ethnic identity; protections for minority and indigenous populations; language rights; freedom from discrimination; and environmental rights.

Liberalism

Liberalism is a confusing term in America, making sense only in the context in which it is used.[45] In political discourse, it is used by those on the Left to refer to people who advocate tolerance and compassionate for the underprivileged, and is used derogatively by those who want to trim government spending for domestic programs. We will refer to liberalism as a widely shared set of assumptions among white native Americans about the importance of individual freedoms, which becomes elaborated to refer to autonomy, individual achievement, individual competition, and the deserved nature of work and merit. We intend to suggest that liberalism and libertarianism—namely, the absence of constraints and an exclusive emphasis on individual rights—are, at least within realms of personal consciousness and social discourse, widely embraced by white Americans, both Democrats and Republicans. We are, after all, a nation that was in the vanguard of neoliberal economic practices and in our social programs emphasizes the individual over the group—for example, means testing and affirmative action.

Liberal Law

The predominant emphasis that Americans give to liberal justice over collective justice is consistent with Americans' emphasis on procedural law over substantive law and on political and civil rights over economic, social, and cultural rights. Although both sets of rights can be codified, they are rooted in fundamentally different sets of implied societal relationships, different forms of legitimacy, and different kinds of institutions. Political and civil rights, as we have emphasized, comprise something like a contract between the nation-state and each and every citizen. Among the most important provisions of this contract are standards protecting citizens against possible abuse by the state itself. The language that is used throughout the amendments to the Constitution conveys this fundamental right. For example, "Congress shall make no law" (Article I); "no Soldier shall, in time of peace be quartered in any house" (Article III); "the right . . . to vote shall not be denied or abridged by the United States or by any State" (Article XV).

We want to stress here that liberal law and the liberal state are not *alternatives* to state arrangements that prioritize the collective welfare through provisions for economic, social, and cultural rights. Governmental structures are more or less the same throughout the world. In spite of variation between, for example, the presidential and prime minister models, countries distinguish among the executive, judiciary, and legislative branches of government.[46] In addition, all constitutions have provisions for elections. All constitutions provide protections for citizens regarding their civil and political rights, such as rights to a fair trial. The American Civil Liberties Union has suggested that liberal rights of citizens are better protected in 118 countries than in the United States, in the specific sense that they have abolished the death penalty whereas the United States has not.[47]

The defense of the liberal state is that constitutions will secure private liberty—and free commerce.[48] Civil and political freedoms *were* very important rights in the eighteenth century when they were articulated and codified as rights. Yet they are *not* rights in the contemporary sense of the term. Indeed, they are negative rights to protect individuals from arbitrary power. In conventional contemporary usage, these are not human rights but instead considered immunities.[49]

The American liberal legal system evolved with the liberal nation-state, open to the rights of equal, sovereign American citizens but indifferent to the importance of pluralism, cultural identity, the prior rights of humans—such as those of economic well-being, health care, and leisure—and social institutions and civic society. The great strengths of the U.S. Constitution lie in the civil and political freedoms it accords citizens, not in defending their basic human rights, not in its organic relationship to changing society,[50] but all early constitutions did have provisions for these rights.

The United States is host to fifty-one sovereign constitutional traditions, and while the traditional view has been that this political pluralism is a hedge against tyranny,[51] it also undermines the rights of citizens who can be caught in the middle of competing interpretations of the law and inconsistencies across jurisdictions. The recent emphasis has been to harmonize laws across jurisdictions, giving provincial or regional courts given powers and reserving to the national courts all others. Finally, other nation-states are looking outward, not inward, to form regional alliances that will protect individual nation-states and their citizens from the increasing economic and environmental turbulence and from the power of multinationals. While the United States fortifies its borders with fences and a powerful military presence, other states are opening their borders in the interest of cooperation around jobs and migrations, as well as around matters pertaining to cultural, environmental, scientific, and technological exchanges.

Another way of considering liberalism is that by emphasizing the individual it underplays the importance of groups, both as drawing from their own distinctive cultures, and as having rights as groups that are equal to those of majority groups. In the United States, there are legally mandated mechanisms to promote opportunities. They are geared to individuals who fall within designated categories—the disabled, minorities, women—but they fall short of affirming equality. Because of their narrow, targeted focus they are stigmatizing, and because they depend on inscrutably precise legal interpretations, they invite contention. All national policy regarding the rights of minorities and women rests on the interpretation of a single piece of legislation, the Civil Rights Act of 1964, and because it highlights the contrast between the advantaged and disadvantaged, it fails to underscore the importance of diversity and pluralism.

We can make another distinction between liberal rights and human rights. Liberal rights have been defended on utilitarian grounds—namely, that granting individual liberties benefits the economy and the state as well as individual happiness. On the other hand, human rights rest on a teleological premise, namely that from the granting of broad rights there will evolve unexpected solidarities and the progressive development of society. Liberal rights are rights of the unattached and decontextualized person, whereas human rights are embedded in society.[52]

Democracy and Human Rights

It is safe to say that deeply penetrating democracy enhances human rights—just as human rights enhance deeply penetrating democracy—because collaborative efforts greatly enhance respect and understanding of others. As Mary Robinson, former United Nations high commissioner of Human Rights states, "global civil society is emerging that accompanies more connections between individuals, economies and cultures that is creating more participation at the grassroots level, at the state and regional levels."[53] Joseph Stiglitz is more specific but comes to a similar conclusion when he advocates development strategies for labor and the importance of labor's role in civil society, the public sector, and government.[54] Workers, he concludes, must play an increasingly vital role in ownership and governance. In a later chapter, we will be developing this theme. We briefly note here that states are increasingly embracing broader conceptions of democracy, including direct democracy in the workplace and in governance. An interesting recent example of such a commitment occurred at the 2004 conference of the Arab League.[55] Participants agreed to a range of principles on democracy and human rights, and the importance of participatory governance. As we shall later show, this is not exceptional. What is exceptional is the American tradition of limited democratic rights, and its failure to recognize fundamental human rights.

Implications

To clarify some of the points we have merely implied, appendix 1.4 provides illustrative empirical evidence of contemporary inequalities in America, a consequence of the valorization of individualism and of the failure to provide mechanisms that promote genuine opportunities. It is true that emerging economies exhibit such extreme inequalities as these, but no other industrialized nation does. The United States is the richest country in the world, but its people are the worse off among all the affluent countries.

Thus, capitalism generates high levels of economic inequality, never antici-pated by the Founding Fathers. These inequalities are of such magnitude that they threaten the social fabric, impair human relations, threaten peo-ple's well-being, and degrade human dignity, because they lead to great dis-couragement about the unfairness that generates such economic disparities. Paradoxically, what stifles dissent is liberalism itself—people feel that they only have themselves to blame if they are poor.

Americans cannot protest when they lose their jobs, become homeless, have no health care, cannot afford higher education for the children, lose their pensions, and go hungry. They cannot protest because the U.S. Con-stitution fails to give them rights to housing, a job, an education, food se-curity, health care, and so forth. The United States has not signed the international treaties that make states responsible for upholding the rights of their citizens. As we will show, virtually all constitutions do stand by these rights. Increasingly, economic actors benefit from American free-doms, not ordinary people.[56]

Notes

1. Thomas Jefferson, Declaration of Independence (July 4, 1776), www.law .indiana.edu/uslawdocs/declaration.html

2. Thomas Jefferson, "Letter to Richard Henry Lee, 1825," quoted in *American Political Thought*, by Alan Pendleton Grimes (New York: Henry Holt, 1955), 88–89.

3. The core premise of the American Declaration—"that all men are created equal" with "unalienable Rights"—and of its near contemporary, the French Declaration on The Rights of Man and Citizen—"men are born free and equal in rights"—goes back a long, long way. It is possible to trace the central idea back to the Egyptians, Greeks, and Romans, as well as to Chinese, Islamic, and Hindu philosophers. For example, remarkable ancient Egyptian texts refer to the equality between "the son of any of importance and any of humble origins." The formal-ization of the principle of equality started as early as the first century C.E. with Marcus Tullius Cicero and then later continued in the seventeenth century in the works of Hugo Grotius, a Dutch jurist. This detailed account can be found in Paul Gordon Lauren, *The Evolution of International Human Rights: Visions Seen* (Philadel-phia: University of Pennsylvania Press, 2003), esp. 11–14. Also see: Grimes, *Amer-ican Political Thought*, 88–92; Stephen Eric Bronner, *Reclaiming the Enlightenment: Toward a Politics of Radical Engagement* (New York: Columbia University Press, 2004), 56–59.

4. A sudden burst of writing exploded on the French scene in the eighteenth century, all devoted centrally to the idea that all members of the entire human race are equal and all have rights and obligations. These authors were known as the

philosophes: Voltaire, Baron de Montesquieu, Marquis de Condorcet, and, especially, Jean-Jacques Rousseau, who wrote on rights, and especially on political rights in his *Contract social, ou Principes du droit politique* (1762). Jefferson's greatest debt, which he acknowledged, was to John Locke, who wrote in the *Second Treatise* that we all have natural rights to life, liberty, and property, and any government that violates these rights may be overthrown, by force if necessary. See John Locke, *Second Treatise of Government* (Indianapolis, Ind.: Hackett Publishing, [1690] 1980), esp. 107.

5. Brian Orend, *Human Rights: Concept and Context* (Orchard Park, N.Y.: Broadview Press, 2002), 202.

6. Lauren, *The Evolution of International Human Rights*, 18.

7. Samuel Eliot Morison, Henry Steele Commager, and William E. Leuchtenburg, *A Concise History of the American Republic* (New York: Oxford University Press, 1983), 80.

8. Judith R. Blau and Cheryl Elman, "The Institutionalization of U.S. Political Parties: Patronage Newspapers," *Sociological Inquiry* 72 (2002): 576–99.

9. Ellen Carol DuBois, *Feminism and Suffrage: The Emergence of an Independent Women's Movement in America, 1848–1869* (Ithaca, N.Y.: Cornell University Press, 1978).

10. See Walter Licht, *Industrializing America* (Baltimore: Johns Hopkins University Press, 1995).

11. Karl Marx, "Economic and Philosophic Manuscripts of 1844" (Moscow: Foreign Languages Publishing, 1961), 81.

12. Gøsta Esping-Anderson, *The Three Worlds of Welfare Capitalism* (Cambridge: Polity Press, 1990).

13. T. H. Marshall, *Citizenship and Social Class, and Other Essays* (Cambridge: Cambridge University Press, 1950). Also see: Asbjørn Eide, "Economic and Social Rights," in *Human Rights: Concept and Standards*, ed. Janusz Symonides, 109–74 (Burlington, Vt.: Ashgate Publishing, 2000).

14. This is somewhat arbitrary since human rights and humanitarian law stem from the identical conception of human agency, dignity, and rights, but humanitarian law deals with atrocious violations and is accompanied by formally constituted international courts and tribunals, which handle cases such as genocide, the inhumane treatment of prisoners of war and war criminals, and the forced removal of populations. (See Geoffrey Robertson, *Crimes against Humanity* [New York: New Press, 1999].) A major difference is that international humanitarian law refers to objective law, which requires testamentary and evidentiary proceedings, whereas human rights depend on subjective recognition of shared experiences, practices, and conditions.

15. Isaiah Berlin, *Four Essays on Liberty* (Oxford: Oxford University Press, 1969).

16. Quoted in Morison, Commager, and Leuchtenburg, *A Concise History of the American Republic*, 326.

17. Why there has been no constitutional amendment of any substance since the ratification in 1920 of Amendment XIX (the rights of women to vote) is a puzzle. The proposed Equal Rights Amendment, first proposed in 1923, and sent to the states after congressional approval in 1972, was not ratified. See: www.equalrightsamendment.org/era.htm. We suspect that contentiousness over this proposed amendment has been a deterrent to subsequent attempts to amend the Constitution. It must be stressed that the U.S. liberal tradition considers the Constitution as a hermetically sealed document that is inseparable from the nation's founding.

18. Manfred Nowak, "Civil and Political Rights," in *Human Rights: Concept and Standards*, ed. Symonides, 69–108.

19. See Doug Hammerstrom, "The Hijacking of the Fourteenth Amendment" (2002): reclaimdemocracy.org/personhood/fourteenth_amendment_hammerstrom .pdf

20. The 1886 case of *Santa Clara v. Southern Pacific Railway* became the key precedent for subsequent decisions. With that, corporations became legal persons in the United States, and gained the ability to challenge regulatory actions. In 1893, corporations won a major victory in the case of *Nohle v. Union River Logging*, which gave them Fifth Amendment due process rights against the federal as well as state governments.

The Fourth Amendment right against search and seizure has been used by corporations to avoid having to open up their books. Furthermore, Fourth Amendment protections require inspectors from the Occupational Safety & Health Administration (OSHA) and the Environmental Protection Agency to produce a warrant in advance of an inspection, giving companies an opportunity to whisk irregularities out of sight. Many First Amendment free speech protections apply to corporations. See www.reclaimdemocracy.org

21. *National Bank of Boston v. Ebellotti* (1978); *Pacific Gas & Electric Co. v. Public Utilities Commission* (1980). See Carl J. Meyer, "Personalizing the Impersonal: Corporations and the Bill of Rights," 1990: www.reclaimdemocracy.org/personhood/ mayer_personalizing.html

22. *Hale v. Henkel* (1906).

23. *Hale v Henkel.*

24. *Noble v. Union River Logging R. Co.* (1903).

25. William Myers, "The Santa Clara Blues," Redwood Coast Alliance for Democracy: www.iiipublishing.com/alliance.htm.

26. *Armour Packing Co v. United States* (1908).

27. Mayer, *Personalizing the Impersonal*; also see Jan Edwards, "Challenging Corporate Personhood," *Multinational Monitor* 23, nos. 10 and 11: www.multinationalmonitor .org/mm2002/02oct-nov/oct-nov02interviewedwards.html

28. Anthony Ogus, "Property Rights and the Freedom of Economic Activity," in *Constitutionalism and Rights: The Influence of the United States Constitution Abroad*,

ed. Louis Henkin and Albert J. Rosenthal, 125–50 (New York: Columbia University Press, 1990).

29. Charles A. Beard, *An Economic Interpretation of the Constitution of the United States* (New York: Macmillan, 1913).

30. Georges Lefebvre, *The French Revolution, Vol. II* (London: Routledge & Kegan Paul, 1964), 359–60.

31. Beard, *An Economic Interpretation of the Constitution of the United States.*

32. For a recent assessment of Beard's interpretation see: Shlomo Slonim, *Framers' Construction/Beardian Deconstruction: Essays on the Constitutional Design of 1787* (New York: Peter Lang, 2001).

33. Jonathan Eliot, *Debates in the Several State Conventions on the Adoption of the Federal Constitution,* ed. James McClellan and M. E. Bradford. (Cumberland, Va.: St. James River Press, 1989); quoted in Grimes, *American Political Thought,* 115.

34. Grimes, *American Political Thought,* 291.

35. Quoted in Eric Foner, *Tom Paine and Revolutionary America* (London: Oxford University Press, 1976), 143.

36. Foner, *Tom Paine and Revolutionary America* 143.

37. John Locke, *Second Treatise of Government,* ed. C. B. Macpherson (Indianapolis, Ind.: Hackett, 1980), 30, 61.

38. H. A. Washington, *The Writings of Thomas Jefferson, Vol. VI* (New York: Riker, 1853–1855), 24.

39. Zygmunt Bauman, *Freedom* (Minneapolis: University of Minnesota Press, 1988), 45.

40. William H. McNeill, *The Rise of the West* (Chicago: University of Chicago Press, 1963), 5.

41. For a summary of the context of the Vienna Declaration see: www.un.org/rights/HRToday/declar.htm

42. Universal Declaration of Human Rights: www.un.org/Overview/rights .html

43. Amartya Sen, *Development as Freedom* (New York: Knopf, 1999).

44. So concluded Bertrand Russell as well. See: Bertrand Russell, *Human Society in Ethics and Politics* (London: Routledge, 1954).

45. European liberalism is quite different, and we touch on this in Judith Blau and Alberto Moncada, *Human Rights: Beyond the Liberal Tradition* (Lanham, Md.: Rowman & Littlefield, 2005).

46. See: S. E. Finer *Five Constitutions* (Brighton, Sussex: Harvester Press, 1979).

47. Amnesty International, November 2004 Report: www.amnestyusa.org/ abolish/index.do; membership in the European Union requires such abolition: europa.eu.int/comm/external_relations/human_rights/adp/

48. Bruce Ackerman, *We the People: Foundations* (Cambridge, Mass.: Belknap, 1991).

49. Louis Henkin, "Introduction," in *Constitutionalism and Rights: The Influence of the U.S. Constitution Abroad,* ed. Louis Henkin and Albert J. Rosenthal, 1–18 (New York: Columbia University Press, 1990).

50. See Matthew J. Moore, "Revisiting Constitutional Interpretation," *Studies in Law, Politics and Society* 28 (2003): 3–31.

51. James T. McHugh, *Es Uno Plura: State Constitutions and Their Political Cultures* (Albany: State University of New York Press, 2003).

52. Sen, *Development as Freedom*; Jack Donnelly, "Ethics and International Human Rights" in *Ethics and International Affairs: Extent and Limits,* ed. Jean-Marc Coicaud and Daniel Warner, 135 (Tokyo: United Nations University Press, 2001).

53. Mary Robinson, "Can Globalization Work for the World's Poor?" address to the Fifth CIVICUS World Assembly, March 24, 2004, Botswana: www .eginitiative.org/

54. Joseph E. Stiglitz, "Democratic Development as the Fruits of Labor," address to Industrial Relations Research Association, 2000: www.globalpolicy.org/socecon/bwi-wto/wbank/stigindx.htm

55. Arab League, Sana'a Inter-Governmental Regional Conference on Democracy, Human Rights, and the Role of the International Criminal Court, January 2004: www.arableagueonline.org/arableague/english/details_en.jsp?art_id= 2641&level_id=239).

56. Robert Albritton, "Socialism and Individual Freedom," in *New Socialisms: Futures beyond Globalization,* ed. Robert Albritton and Richard Westra, 17–32 (London: Routledge, 2004).

Appendix 1.1
Dates of Constitutions for Contemporary Nation-States

Name of Country	Year of Current (and Recent) Constitutions
Afghanistan	2004
Albania	1998
Algeria	(1976), 1996
Andorra	1993
Angola	1992
Antigua and Barbuda	1981
Argentina	(1853), 1994
Armenia	1995
Australia	1900
Austria	(1920), 1929
Azerbaijan	1995
Bahamas	1973
Bahrain	(1973), 2001
Bangladesh	(1974), 2004
Barbados	1966
Belarus	(1994), 1996
Belgium	(1970), 1994
Belize	1981
Benin	1990
Bhutan	2004 draft
Bolivia	(1967) 1994
Bosnia and Herzegovina	1995

(continued)

Name of Country	Year of Current (and Recent) Constitutions
Botswana	1965
Brazil	1988
Brunei Darussalam	1959
Bulgaria	1991
Burkina Faso	1991
Burundi	2004 subject to referendum
Cambodia	(1993) 1999
Cameroon	(1972) 1996
Canada	1982 and unwritten customs
Cape Verde	(1982) 1999
Central African Republic	(1995) 2004 subject to referendum
Chad	1996
Chechnya	2003
Chile	(1980) 1997
China	1982
Colombia	1991
Comoros	2001
Costa Rica	1949
Croatia	1990
Cuba	1992
Cyprus	1960
Czech Republic	1992
Congo–Brazzaville	2002
Congo–Kinshasa	(1967, 1997) 2003
Denmark	1953
Djibouti	1992
Dominica	1978
Dominican Republic	(1966) 2002
Ecuador	1998
Egypt	1971
El Salvador	1983
Equatorial Guinea	(1991) 1995
Eritrea	1997
Estonia	1992
Ethiopia	1994
Fiji	1997
Finland	1919
France	1958

Appendix 1.1 (*Continued*)

Name of Country	Year of Current (and Recent) Constitutions
Gabon	(1961) 2003
Gambia	1997
Georgia	1995
Germany	(1949) 1990
Ghana	1993
Greece	(1975) 2001
Grenada	1975
Guatemala	(1985) 1993
Guinea	(1990) 2001
Guinea-Bissau	1984
Guyana	1980
Haiti	1987
Honduras	(1982) 1999
Hong Kong	1990
Hungary	(1949, 1989) 1990
Iceland	1874
India	1950
Indonesia	1945
Iran	(1979) 1989
Iraq	2004 provisional
Ireland	1937
Israel	none
Italy	1948
Ivory Coast (Cote d'Ivoire)	1960
Jamaica	1962
Japan	1947
Jordan	1952
Kazakhstan	1995
Kenya	1963
Kiribati	1979
Korea, North	(1948, 1972) 1992
Korea, South	(1948) 1987
Kuwait	1962
Kyrgyzstan	1993
Lao People's Democratic Republic	1991
Latvia	1991
Lebanon	(1926) 1990

(*continued*)

Appendix 1.1 (*Continued*)

Name of Country	Year of Current (and Recent) Constitutions
Lesotho	1993
Liberia	1986
Libyan Arab Jamahiriya (Libya)	(1969) 1977
Liechtenstein	1921
Lithuania	1992
Luxembourg	1868
Macau	1999
Macedonia, Former Yugoslavia	1991
Madagascar	1998
Malawi	1995
Malaysia	1957
Maldives	1968
Mali	1992
Malta	(1964) 1987
Marshall Islands	1979
Mauritania	1991
Mauritius	1968
Mexico	1917
Micronesia	1979
Moldova	1994
Monaco	(1962) 2002
Mongolia	(1960) 1992
Morocco	(1972) 1996
Mozambique	1990
Myanmar	draft
Namibia	1990
Nauru	1968
Nepal	1990
Netherlands	1983
Netherlands Antilles	1959
New Zealand	not written
Nicaragua	(1987) 1995
Niger	(1992) 1999
Nigeria	(1979) 1999
Norway	1814
Oman	1996
Pakistan	2003

Appendix 1.1 *(Continued)*

Name of Country	Year of Current (and Recent) Constitutions
Palau	1981
Panama	(1972, 1983) 1992
Papua New Guinea	1975
Paraguay	1992
Peru	1993
Philippines	1987
Poland	1997
Portugal	(1976, 1982, 1989) 1997
Qatar	(1970) 1972
Romania	(1991) 2003
Russia	1993
Rwanda	2003
Saint Kitts and Nevis	1983
Saint Lucia	1979
Saint Vincent and the Grenadines	1979
Samoa	1962
San Marino	(1600, 1926) 1974
Sao Tome and Principe	(1975, 1900) 2003
Saudi Arabia	1992
Senegal	(1963) 2001
Serbia and Montenegro	1992
Seychelles	1993
Sierra Leone	1991
Singapore	(1959) 1991
Slovakia	1992
Slovenia	1991
Solomon Islands	1978
Somalia	none
South Africa	1997
Spain	1978
Sri Lanka	1978
Sudan	None
Suriname	1987
Swaziland	draft 2004
Sweden	1975
Switzerland	(1848) 2000

(continued)

Appendix 1.1 (*Continued*)

Name of Country	Year of Current (and Recent) Constitutions
Syrian Arab Republic	1973
Taiwan	(1946) 2000
Tajikistan	1994
Tanzania	1982
Thailand	1997
Tibet	1991
Timor-Leste	2002
Togo	1992
Tonga	(1875) 1970
Trinidad and Tobago	1976
Tunisia	(1959, 1991) 2002
Turkey	1982
Turkmenistan	1992
Tuvalu	1978
Uganda	1995
Ukraine	1996
United Arab Emirates	1971
United Kingdom of Great Britain	unwritten
United States of America	1787
Uruguay	(1830) 1967
Uzbekistan	1992
Vanuatu	1980
Venezuela	1999
Vietnam	1992
Yemen	1991
Zambia	(1991) 1996
Zimbabwe	1979

SOURCES: U.S. Department of State. www.state.gov/r/pa/ei/bgn/; Constitution Finder, School of Law, University of Richmond. confinder.richmond.edu/
NOTE: Not all early constitutions listed.

Appendix 1.2
Amendments to the U.S. Constitution

Amendment [I] 1791

Congress shall make no law respecting an establishment of religion, or prohibiting the free exercise thereof; or abridging the freedom of speech, or of the press; or the right of the people peaceably to assemble, and to petition the Government for a redress of grievances.

Amendment [II] 1791

A well regulated Militia, being necessary to the security of a free State, the right of the people to keep and bear Arms, shall not be infringed.

Amendment [III] 1791

No Soldier shall, in time of peace be quartered in any house, without the consent of the Owner, nor in time of war, but in a manner to be prescribed by law.

Amendment [IV] 1791

The right of the people to be secure in their persons, houses, papers, and effects, against unreasonable searches and seizures, shall not be violated, and no Warrants shall issue, but upon probable cause, supported by Oath or affirmation, and particularly describing the place to be searched, and the persons or things to be seized.

Amendment [V] 1791

No person shall be held to answer for a capital, or otherwise infamous crime, unless on a presentment or indictment of a Grand Jury, except in cases arising in the land or naval forces, or in the Militia, when in actual service in time of War or public danger; nor shall any person be subject for the same offence to be twice put in jeopardy of life or limb; nor shall be compelled in any criminal case to be a witness against himself, nor be deprived of life, liberty, or property, without due process of law; nor shall private property be taken for public use, without just compensation.

Amendment [VI] 1791

In all criminal prosecutions, the accused shall enjoy the right to a speedy and public trial, by an impartial jury of the State and district wherein the crime shall have been committed, which district shall have been previously ascertained by law, and to be informed of the nature and cause of the accusation; to be confronted with the witnesses against him; to have compulsory process for obtaining witnesses in his favor, and to have the Assistance of Counsel for his defense.

Amendment [VII] 1791

In Suits at common law, where the value in controversy shall exceed twenty dollars, the right of trial by jury shall be preserved, and no fact tried by a jury, shall be otherwise re-examined in any Court of the United States, than according to the rules of the common law.

Amendment [VIII] 1791

Excessive bail shall not be required, nor excessive fines imposed, nor cruel and unusual punishments inflicted.

Amendment [IX] 1791

The enumeration in the Constitution, of certain rights, shall not be construed to deny or disparage others retained by the people.

Amendment [X] 1791

The powers not delegated to the United States by the Constitution, nor prohibited by it to the States, are reserved to the States respectively, or to the people.

Amendment [XI] [judicial jurisdiction; 1795]

Amendment [XII] [Electoral College; 1804]

Amendment [XIII] 1865

Neither slavery nor involuntary servitude, except as a punishment for crime whereof the party shall have been duly convicted, shall exist within the United States, or any place subject to their jurisdiction.

Amendment [XIV] 1868

Section 1. All persons born or naturalized in the United States, and subject to the jurisdiction thereof, are citizens of the United States and of the State wherein they reside. No State shall make or enforce any law which shall abridge the privileges or immunities of citizens of the United States; nor shall any State deprive any person of life, liberty, or property, without due process of law; nor deny to any person within its jurisdiction the equal protection of the laws.

Section 2. [Population apportionment for number of representatives]

Section 3. [Any engaged in engaged in insurrection or rebellion may not hold major political office]

Section 4. [public debt]

Amendment [XV] 1870

The right of citizens of the United States to vote shall not be denied or abridged by the United States or by any State on account of race, color, or previous condition of servitude.

Amendment [XVI] [Income tax, 1913]

Amendment [XVII] [Vacancies in Senate, 1913]

Amendment [XVIII] [Prohibition of liquor, 1919]

Amendment [XIX] 1920

The right of citizens of the United States to vote shall not be denied or abridged by the United States or by any State on account of sex.

Amendment [XX] [Terms of president, vice president and members of Congress, 1933]

Amendment [XXI] [Repeal of eighteenth article of amendment (prohibition) 1934]

Amendment [XXII] [Term limits for president, 1951]

Amendment [XXIII] [District of Columbia, 1961]

Amendment [XXIV] 1964

The right of citizens of the United States to vote in any primary or other election for President or Vice President, for electors for President or Vice President, or for Senator or Representative in Congress, shall not be denied or abridged by the United States or any state by reason of failure to pay any poll tax or other tax.

Amendment [XXV] [Provisions for filling vacancies of elected officials, 1967]

Amendment [XXVI] [voting age set to eighteen and older, 1971]

Amendment [XXVII] [salaries of congressional representatives, 1992]

SOURCE: www.whitehouse.gov/constitution/constitution.html

NOTE: Ratification history and notes deleted; clauses with congressional enforcement power deleted. Omitted amendments in brackets.

Appendix 1.3
Vienna Declaration and Programme of Action, as Adopted by the World Conference on Human Rights on June 25, 1993, Part I, Extracts

————Recognizing and affirming that all human rights derive from the dignity and worth inherent in the human person, and that the human person is the central subject of human rights and fundamental freedoms, and consequently should be the principal beneficiary and should participate actively in the realization of these rights and freedoms,————

————promoting and encouraging respect for human rights and fundamental freedoms for all and respect for the principle of equal rights and self-determination of peoples, peace, democracy, justice, equality, rule of law, pluralism, development, better standards of living and solidarity,————

1. [R]eaffirms the solemn commitment of all States to fulfill their obligations to promote universal respect for, and observance and protection of, all human rights and fundamental freedoms for all. . . . The universal nature of these rights and freedoms is beyond question.————Human rights and fundamental freedoms are the birthright of all human beings; their protection and promotion is the first responsibility of Governments.

2. All peoples have the right of self-determination. By virtue of that right they freely determine their political status, and freely pursue their economic, social and cultural development.————

5. All human rights are universal, indivisible and interdependent and interrelated. The international community must treat human rights globally in a fair and equal manner, on the same footing, and with the same emphasis. While

the significance of national and regional particularities and various historical, cultural and religious backgrounds must be borne in mind, it is the duty of States, regardless of their political, economic and cultural systems, to promote and protect all human rights and fundamental freedoms.———

8. Democracy, development and respect for human rights and fundamental freedoms are interdependent and mutually reinforcing. Democracy is based on the freely expressed will of the people to determine their own political, economic, social and cultural systems. . . .———

10. [R]eaffirms the right to development . . . as a universal and inalienable right———The human person is the central subject of development.———

15. ———The speedy and comprehensive elimination of all forms of racism and racial discrimination, xenophobia and related intolerance———

18. The full and equal participation of women in political, civil, economic, social and cultural life, at the national, regional and international levels,———

19. ——— The persons belonging to minorities have the right to enjoy their own culture, to profess and practise their own religion and to use their own language———

23. The World Conference on Human Rights reaffirms that everyone, without distinction of any kind, is entitled to the right to seek and to enjoy in other countries asylum from persecution, as well as the right to return to one's own country

25. [A]ffirms that extreme poverty and social exclusion constitute a violation of human dignity———

28. The World Conference on Human Rights expresses its dismay at massive violations of human rights especially in the form of genocide, "ethnic cleansing" and systematic rape of women in war situations, creating mass exodus of refugees and displaced persons. While strongly condemning such abhorrent practices it reiterates the call that perpetrators of such crimes be punished and such practices immediately stopped.

36. The World Conference on Human Rights reaffirms the important and constructive role played by national institutions for the promotion and protection of human rights, in particular in their advisory capacity to the competent authorities, their role in remedying human rights violations, in the dissemination of human rights information, and education in human rights.———

SOURCE: Office of the United Nations High Commissioner for Human Rights, Geneva, Switzerland.

Appendix 1.4
Indicators of Economic Decline and Inequality in the United States

Between 1992 and 2001, the net wealth of low-income U.S. households increased by only 7 percent—from $6,261 to $6,720. By comparison, the net wealth of all U.S. households increased by 42 percent—from $60,695 to $86,100.

In 2001 the net wealth of the typical poor household was $6,720, compared to $86,100 for the typical U.S. household, a wealth gap of thirteen to one.

Chief Executive Officers (CEOs) and Workers; Corporate Profits and Taxes
- While the average worker earned $517 per week in 2003, the average CEO for a large company earned $155,769 a week.
- Those in the middle of the earnings scale and below (at or below the fiftieth percentile) are losing ground—their weekly earnings were lower, after adjusting for inflation, at the end of 2003 than one year earlier.
- Since 2001, corporate profits have expanded by 57.5 percent, while private wage and salary income has contracted by 1.7 percent; 60 percent of U.S. corporations pay no taxes.

The Uninsured
- Almost forty-four million people—15.2 percent of the total U.S. population—were uninsured in 2002, up from 14.6 percent in the previous year. The percentage of the non-elderly population that is uninsured is 17.3.

Minimum Wage

- From its peak in 1968, the purchasing power of the minimum wage has declined over 36 percent.
- During most of the 1960s and 1970s, working at the minimum wage kept a family of three out of poverty. Today such a family is 24 percent below the poverty level.

Racial Inequalities

- The average black man is paid $16,876 less than the average white man.
- The mean weekly wage for Hispanics was $235 dollars less than the mean for Whites.
- On average, blacks get three-quarters of the health care that whites receive.
- Nearly one-third of Latino adults report lacking health insurance.
- Two-thirds of Latinos who report being uninsured are employed.

Childhood Poverty

- One of every six children (16.7 percent) is poor. A child in America is more likely to live in poverty than a child in any of the other industrialized nations.

Housing and Homelessness

- Families comprise 41 percent of the urban homeless; nationally children make up approximately 39 percent of the homeless population.

Overtime Changes

- In 1967, the lowest fifth of households had 4 percent of aggregate income, the middle fifth had 17.3 percent, and the top fifth had 43.8 percent. In 2001, the lowest fifth had 3.5 percent, the middle fifth had 14.6 percent, and the top fifth had 50.1 percent. The top 5 percent of households had 17.5 percent of the income in 1967 and 22.4 percent in 2001.

SOURCES: Center for American Progress, Economic Policy Institute, Drum Major Institute, Cover the Uninsured Week, Fiscal Policy Institute, Center for American Progress, Inequality.org, Children's Defense Fund, National Homeless Coalition.

The Social Foundations
of Human Rights

Imagine that a man slaps a woman in rural KwaZulu-Natal, South Africa. At the same time, another man slaps a woman in a popular neighborhood in Tehran, and yet a third does the same in a café in Madrid. All three women protest: the woman in Madrid that her rights have been violated, the woman in Tehran that her dignity has been violated, and the woman in KwaZulu-Natal that custom has been violated. Every victim protests.[1]

Mahmood Mamdani's account, above, highlights an especially important feature of human rights, and implies a profound dilemma about them as well. First, no matter how they are embedded in each individual society—as rights, as dignity, or as custom—they are universally comprehensible and agreed to. Slapping a woman is a violation of rights (or dignity, or custom) no matter where it occurs. Second, the dilemma is that few take notice elsewhere that rights have been violated.

The challenge in the world today is to universalize our empathy and convert that universalized empathy into international norms, not only about the treatment of women, but also about access to clean water, employment, and decent housing; rights to a fair trial; access to communications; the rights of children to an education; and so forth. Why? We might consider economic globalization as possibly bringing opportunities to everyone on the planet, but so far economic behemoths have trampled down societies and people, enriching the already rich and impoverishing those already poor. We have shared stakes in human rights.

Another important feature of this challenge, which Americans and their government have not recognized, is that while rights are universal, they are uniquely embedded in each society. It is important that women everywhere have all the rights that men do, yet women capture and express their rights differently depending on whether their societies are traditionally patrilocal, matrilocal, or neolocal; predominately Islamic, Catholic, or another religion; agricultural or urban. Women's rights in trade unions are especially important in European countries and Latin America, while securing property inheritance is important in predominately agricultural societies. Respecting universal rights is respecting the rights to difference. We can be relativists in some respects, absolutists in others.

To elaborate, like America and Europe until quite recently, and still in some societies, custom dictates separate spheres—male dominance in worldly matters, female dominance in domestic matters. But regardless, gender asymmetrics have always everywhere been condoned. The transition to a new world order whereby men and women share the same spheres of equality has still not been achieved worldwide (and not completely in any society), but progress in that direction has been remarkable.[2] Within even decades, and certainly over a century, women have made great strides in many Western countries in achieving greater equity in the spheres of the economy and politics. A few state constitutions require approximate gender parity in their parliaments,[3] and international agreements advocate equality of women in work and public life.[4]

We must not forget how recent this has been. In 1915, the liberated American woman threw away her corsets, bobbed her hair, and smoked cigarettes, whereas halfway round the world, a liberated Chinese woman may have refused to bind the feet of her infant girl. Nor must we underestimate the importance of volition. To an American woman today, female circumcision is a vicious practice that degrades women, and to the shock of Westerners, female circumcision is widely practiced, with rates of over 80 percent in Egypt, Ethiopia, Djibouti, Sierra Leone, and Somalia.[5] But to illustrate how rapidly things can change, Djibouti has organized a six-country coalition in support of the Maputo Protocol, which makes the practice of female genitalia mutilation illegal.[6] In contrast, the United States has not codified the rights of women to equal wages with men.

Gender roles are deeply interwoven in the very warp and woof of the social fabric, and so therefore are peoples' conceptions of human rights in connection with gender equality. Americans must not consider that they lead the world in the advance of women's rights. Women make up 50 percent of the commissioners of the African Union (AU), and in Rwanda, women succeeded in winning 49 percent of seats in parliament, ranking the country among the highest in the world in terms of women's shares of seats in parliament,[7] while the United States lags behind European countries in the percentage of women at the top levels of government.[8] As we will later see, a main reason why American women lag behind their counterparts elsewhere is because the United States is virtually unique in not having constitutional provisions that affirm gender equality. However, generally, women around the world have made great strides in the past decades, as noted by the United Nations Development Fund for Women (UNIFEM) while stressing that "much remains to be done."[9] This conclusion is supported by national-level data compiled over time by the United Nations on indicators such as the percentages of girls attending school and the share of women in nonagricultural employment.[10]

Of all the United Nations' Millennium Development Goals, the goal to achieve gender equality has made the most progress. A main reason is that in the great wave of constitutional revisions, beginning in the late 1980s, women fought hard to include women's rights in new constitutions, and their efforts largely paid off.[11] Another reason has to do with the global economy. Whereas domesticity was the prevailing pattern in many developed economies through much of the twentieth century, most women now must work, even if they prefer to stay at home and raise their families. Among highly industrialized nations (the Organisation for Economic Co-operation and Development [OECD] countries), women's time devoted to household responsibilities is about twice that of men.[12] Thus, it is evident that in the West, women are heavy contributors to both market and nonmarket activities. Also noteworthy is that both men and women in these advanced industrialized countries are employed outside the home for nearly the same hours in an average week, sixty-nine for men and fifty-two for women. Are the economic returns commensurate with their effort? Has the quality of work improved with globalization? Economist Robert Pollin makes a powerful case that neither economic returns nor the quality of work has improved worldwide or in the West alone. In fact, he argues that peoples' economic uncertainty has increased substantially.[13]

The Cake of Custom

Human dignity is the right of every human, but so are identity and the rights to their social memberships. Collectively we can agree that economic exploitation is wrong, and we are justified in intervening when others are exploited. There are other rights violations that people themselves fix of their own accord. If being slapped is a violation of rights no matter where and when, can the same thing be said—no matter where or when—of forbidding women to eat with men, polygamy, or discriminatory inheritance practices? Diane Bell, writing about the subjugation of women among Australian aboriginals, describes the cultural context of marriage that "binds kin in a web of reciprocal obligations, rights, and responsibilities that have implications for land ownership and ceremonial duties" and while the roles that women play were, from a Westerner's perspective, humiliatingly inferior, they are "part and parcel of the survival of the culture."[14] Westerners need be careful about intervening.

Australian aboriginals would be shocked at the extent to which Americans disregard others in their unrelenting pursuit of self-interest, their overindulgence of children, selfishness, and wastefulness. Most of the world's state constitutions allow for direct democracy; the United States is one of the exceptional few (thirteen) that sidesteps direct democracy in favor of indirect democracy and its system of the Electoral College.[15] The point here is that both democracy and human rights are rapidly advancing around the world, and no single country can stake the claim that it is superior to others.

The Betrayal

The coming together of the world's population on matters of human rights—universal freedom, the rights to individual dignity, the right to develop, and the wherewithal to live lives of capacity and meaning—is truly remarkable. Something new has happened in the world for this to occur. As United Nations Secretary-General Kofi Annan recently declared: "State sovereignty, in its most basic sense, is being redefined. . . . States are now widely understood to be instruments at the service of their peoples, and not vice versa . . . [while] individual sovereignty—by which I mean the fundamental freedom of each individual . . . has been enhanced by a renewed and spreading consciousness of individual rights."[16]

The closer integration of the world around human rights, we believe, is a response to an immense and devastating betrayal of the world's people by financiers and multinationals. They have ruthlessly exploited workers, devastated societies, and afflicted great harm on the world's ecosystem. We have experienced together a collective *slap*, but worse, we are the victims of a hoax—a betrayal—because we—the world's peoples and governments —were told that rising tides would lift all boats. Instead, these tides have lifted only the yachts, while many boats have sunk.

Global capitalist actors, aided by the Bretton Woods institutions (the World Bank, the International Monetary Fund, and the World Trade Organization) have greatly increased poverty in many parts of the world by undercutting local economies; destroying infrastructures through water, soil, and air pollution; dismantling social and educational programs; and privatizing collective enterprises.[17] After displacing local economies, multinationals have extracted huge concessions wherever they go. Because they have the option of exit, they can find cheaper labor elsewhere. The West has not experienced the *betrayal* with the full force that peoples of the Third World have, but they too have experienced the ripple effects: namely, the decline of social and economic security. We will later see how governments have responded formally in revising their constitutions.

Rights in America as Social and Economic Processes

In chapter 1 we presented the constitutional provisions for Americans' rights. Formally, they are all the rights that Americans have, and they are quite limited by international standards. Americans can (by and large) speak their conscience, expect a fair trial, vote, and hold office. But the Constitution rests on some unstated assumptions that are deeply buried in American society and public life. These are: first, libertarianism—a commitment to fair processes rather than to substantive justice (which is why African Americans and indigenous Americans have difficulty overcoming histories of disadvantage and oppression); second, utilitarianism —a commitment to maximizing future returns (rather than equity and justice); and, third, liberalism—a commitment to individual autonomy and voluntarism.

The consequences of these American biases, as evident in institutions as well as in American culture, are that the individual is elevated above what is potentially shared and collective, and individuals do not have a sense of duty or responsibility to society. While it can be argued that Americans' charitable contributions (which are considerable) belie our observation, we instead believe that acts and contributions of charity reinforce and express the attitudes of the privileged in ways reaffirming inequality. Harsh, perhaps, but consistent with a long line of social science research that highlights the unusually important role that individual striving, achievement, and autonomy play in America at great cost to solidarity, society, and equality. Of the many commentators on American individualism, it is useful to quote Henry Steele Commager because he early noted the connection between individualism and patriotism:

> [Americans] believed passionately in themselves and their destiny, and their deep sense of gratitude to Providence did not preclude pride in what they had themselves accomplished. Born of geography, nourished by history, confirmed by philosophy, self-reliance was elevated to a philosophical creed, and in time individualism became synonymous with Americanism. As the rich and spacious continent had dazzled but not confounded their imagination, so their speedy conquest of it induced a sense of limitless power.[18]

Elevating individuals above their societal responsibilities poses difficulties enough for their ability to understand the human rights of others, but patriotism makes such understanding all that more difficult. Patriotism, like nationalism, impedes the comprehension of the human rights we all share. Many American philosophers, such as John Rawls and Robert Nozick, have grappled with the problem as to how liberalism and libertarianism can be consistent with equitable outcomes and tolerance. Yet it is indicative of the problem that individualism poses that philosophers feel they need to make such arguments. As social scientists, we do not believe the grafting of tolerance onto individualism will take, nor do we believe that people can be equitable when their self-interests within the capitalist economy work against it.

The Specificity and Universality of Human Rights

The nomenclature of human rights is confusing. They can be *doctrine, practices, attitudes,* and *laws.* Because our focus is the formalization of prescribed practices—in constitutions—we are mostly dealing with human rights as they are embodied in formal statements. International human rights statements have different origins and statuses. Some are statements of agreed-upon principles, without enforcement mechanisms. The Universal Declaration of Human Rights (UDHR) is such a statement, and owing to its sheer scope it lays the foundations for all subsequent development of international human rights agreements. This declaration sets forth the human rights and fundamental freedoms to which all peoples, everywhere in the world, are entitled. Besides the UDHR, there are many more international human rights declarations that have moral, but not legal force. The United Nations refers to all formal statements about human rights, including the

UDHR, as *instruments* and those having enforcement and complaint mechanisms as *treaties* or *covenants*. On the ground, all of the international human rights doctrine and laws are constantly being drawn upon to implement and change local practices. By the same token, international nongovernmental organizations (INGOs), nongovernmental organizations (NGOs), and states propose, and sometimes locally implement, new human rights provisions, such as the Maputo Protocol against female genitalia mutilation, and a declaration against housing evictions, which is evolving under the leadership of the Center on Housing Rights and Evictions, collaboratively with other NGOs around the world.[19]

Constitutions and Human Rights

The main purpose of any constitution is to provide the basic framework for government and to state the principles of how laws and policies will be made, and how continuity can be ensured irrespective of who is in power.[20] An equally important purpose is to clarify the social contract between the people and the state: that is, the responsibilities of the state to its citizens and the peoples' rights that the state will protect. From early on, state constitutions included provisions for peoples' rights. The U.S. Constitution of 1789 includes the Bill of Rights that specifies citizens' civil and political rights. The French Constitution of 1791 incorporated the key provisions of the 1789 Declaration of the Rights of Man and of the Citizen, including those for equality before the law, representative government, and free speech. Britain does not have a constitution, but rather something like, as one scholar put it, a "tapestry," an interweaving of common law with laws of governance, and this tapestry builds on a foundation of individual rights, including the Magna Carta (1215), the Petition of Right (1628), the Habeas Corpus Act (1679), and the Bill of Rights (1689).[21]

The elements of this early stream of traditions having to do with legally guaranteed protections and rights of individuals are now embraced by all party states of the United Nations. Additionally, these protections and rights have been incorporated into all state constitutions. They are considered the foundation of human rights, albeit based on the Western historical experience. Moreover, they are straightforward, that is, they map easily onto to a set of laws that are empirically objectifiable. (That is, in contrast to such human rights as dignity and having a decent standard of living, individual civil rights, such as having the right to a trial or to peacefully assemble, are objectifiable.) These early Western rights were specified as rights vis-à-vis the state, whereas contemporary human rights relate as much to society as to the state.

The importance of embedding human rights in society as a whole emerged forcefully after the German genocides, and did so interestingly to shore up the fundamental human rights—of human equality, of human dignity, the right to a personality, and so forth—as well as to shore up international law dealing with crimes against humanity. At the root of contemporary human rights thinking is the idea that if fundamental human rights were universally recognized, there would be no wars, no genocide, and no crimes against humanity. These concerns after the end of World War II led to the crafting of the UDHR, which was approved in 1948, and, then the 1966 International Covenant on Economic, Social, and Cultural Rights (ICESCR) and the 1966 International Covenant on Civil and Political Rights (ICCPR), both of which entered into force in January 1976.

The 1966 (1976) ICCPR draws extensively from principles of Western rights. The 1966 (1976) ICESCR deals with what we have been describing as human rights (as distinct from individual political rights) and states, for example, the "right of everyone to the enjoyment of just and favorable conditions of work," with "equal pay for equal work," "a decent living," "safe and healthy working conditions," "equal opportunity to be promoted," "reasonable working hours," "remuneration for public holidays," and the right to "join the trade union of choice." It includes provisions for social security, education, the well-being of minority populations, cultural rights, nondiscrimination, and the right to an adequate standard of living, as well as stating that people have responsibilities to their community and society. Its focus is on the full development of the human personality and the development of society.

The implications of the ICCPR are not so profound for Americans, the English, Canadians, and Europeans, who pioneered these rights in the early stages of nation-state formation. However, the implications of the ICESCR are particularly complicated for Americans, who have had a tradition of highly independent and self-absorbed individuals, combined with a relatively weak society, as Henry Steele Commager and others observe. The ICESCR has a vision of democracy, even if mostly implicit, through its emphasis on inclusion, participation, openness, and accountability.[22] The U.S. constitutional Framers never could have imagined such a participatory, society-based democracy; they distrusted the citizenry and put virtually all power in the hands of the government. It is useful to point out here that Eleanor Roosevelt was one of the framers of the UDHR, and

Franklin Delano Roosevelt, as we will later show, attempted to implement some of the provisions of the ICESCR in America, and totally failed.

American Isolation in the International Human Rights Community

Opposing human rights treaties, refusing to sign international agreements, withholding funds from the United Nations (UN), arming dictatorial states, supporting states with abominable human rights records, the United States has politicized human rights and undermined their advance.[23] The United States has been a rogue state in the advance and implementation of human rights. At the beginning of the UN, the United States played a leading role, supporting its charter for peaceful coexistence, signing and ratifying the UN Declaration of Human Rights, and ratifying the 1966 ICCPR. But since then America has largely been contemptuous of the UN, while arrogantly pursuing programs, such as development of nuclear and biological weapons, which the UN opposes. Just as conspicuously, the United States abstains from supporting human rights provisions.

Kenneth Roth, director of Human Rights Watch, calls U.S. ratification of International Rights Treaties "a charade."[24] He writes, "on the few occasions when the US government has ratified a human rights treaty, it has done so in a way to preclude the treaty from having any domestic effect." Roth elaborates that whenever a new treaty has a requirement that might be more protective of U.S. citizens' rights than a preexisting law, Justice Department lawyers negate that part of the treaty and send it to the Senate. After this exercise of stripping human rights treaties, the U.S. government declares that the treaty in question is "not self-executing." In summarizing these legal charades and the hypocritical arrogance of the United States, Roth states:

> The refusal to apply international human rights law to itself renders US ratification of human rights treaties a purely cosmetic gesture. It allows the US government to pretend to be part of the international human rights system, but it does nothing to enhance the rights of US citizens.[25]

Even with such elaborate mechanisms to ensure that those treaties it does sign have little or no legal standing, the United States has ratified only a few international human rights treaties. There are a total of twelve, five of which the United States has ratified. The United States has signed three, but because being a signatory on a treaty carries no legal implications beyond recognizing the existence of a treaty, the United States is not a party to seven. America has ratified the following: the ICCPR, the Convention on the Elimination of All Forms of Racial Discrimination, the Convention against Torture, the Optional Protocol to the Convention on the Rights of the Child on Involvement in Armed Conflict, and the Optional Protocol to the Convention on the Rights of the Child on the Sale of Children, Child Prostitution, and Child Pornography.

The United States is not a ratifying party to the following human rights treaties: the ICESCR; both Optional Protocols to the ICCPR; the Convention on the Elimination of All Forms of Discrimination against Women and its Optional Protocol; the Convention on the Rights of the Child; and the Convention on the Protection of the Rights of All Migrant Workers and Members of Their Families.

Very few states have ratified as few human rights treaties as the United States has. The United States is the only government, except for Somalia, that has never ratified the Convention on the Rights of the Child, and the reason the United States has not is because the Convention's provisions are at odds with U.S. policies regarding the application of the death penalty against juvenile offenders.[26] It has not ratified the ICESCR because it maintains these are not inalienable rights, and it has not signed the Convention on Discrimination against Women, presumably to avoid enforcing equal pay provisions. Because the United States uses the death penalty it has neither signed nor ratified the Second Protocol to the ICCPR.

To document such roguish behavior is important because Americans' tend to feel that the United States is leading the world in the advance of human rights, whereas quite the contrary is the case. The United States refused to ratify the Kyoto Protocol on the UN Framework Convention on Climate Control ("unsigning" Clinton's initial agreement) because the State Department contends that reducing carbon emissions would harm the U.S. economy. America withdrew from the Anti–Ballistic Missile Treaty in June 2002, never ratified the Comprehensive Test Ban Treaty because it wants to reserve the right to use nuclear weapons, and refuses to sign the Mine Ban Treaty because it claims that land mines protect American soldiers. It included reservations when it ratified the Chemical Weapons Convention that prohibits certain sites to be inspected on the grounds of national security. The United States did not sign the Rome Statute that provides for the International Criminal Court,[27] because it wants to protect those who, like Henry Kissinger, have helped to perpetrate crimes against humanity, in Cambodia and Chile. Any state that uses reasons of national security to obstruct international efforts obviously reduces the security for everyone else, and gross human rights violations committed by the United States against detainees after 9/11 ups the ante for terrorists and degrades the international standards of human rights.[28]

There is another reason why the United States is an obstructionist regarding human rights. Consistent with its political liberal tradition, it is loathe to interfere with capitalists on behalf of society to, say, promote, sustainable development and preserve environmental resources, or on behalf of workers and their families. Of course, this is not the case in any absolute sense, but it is relative to other countries, particularly if the comparison is with other OECD countries, or advanced industrialized countries.

The United States gives two reasons for not cooperating with the international community. The first has to do with national security, although paradoxically, asserting sovereignty claims undermines global security. Refusing to stop development of nuclear bombs, and stockpile biological and toxin weapons only intensifies their development elsewhere. The second main reason the United States gives for not complying with international weapons treaties and human rights treaties is economic. The Kyoto Protocol would harm U.S. industries, it is argued, but instead it now is evident that when nations sign the protocol it stimulates innovation among their industries to develop alternative energy sources, such as wind power, and new recycling technologies.

To anticipate a later discussion, the Cold War had irrevocable negative consequences on the progressive adoption of human rights agreements. After unanimous affirmation of the Universal Declaration, the United States insisted that only those provisions for civil and political rights could be considered as human rights, and opposing not only the Soviet Union, but also Europe and the newly independent nations, refused to sign the ICESCR. It went into force, without U.S. participation, in 1976. As earlier noted, among its important provisions are nondiscrimination; equal rights for men and women; the right to work, fair wages, and a decent living; equal promotion opportunities; the right to rest and paid holidays; the right to join a union; and the right to strike. The International Covenant on Civil and Political Rights (ICCPR) also went into force in 1976. It embodies the long English, French, and U.S. traditions of political liberties, legal securities, and individual freedoms of speech, worship, and conscience. However, the short- and long-term consequences of America's rejecting the "human rights standing" of the ICESCR have been considerable.

The decision further aggravated the split between the Soviets and the United States, while alienating much of Europe from the latter; reified the difference between political and other rights; and greatly diminished the importance of economic and social security in world affairs.[29] It is hard to distinguish here America's political goals from its economic interests, but regardless of which played the dominant role, the price was paid by ordinary citizens whose economic and social security are fragile without any national commitment to their well-being. Additionally, the United States sets the tone in international affairs. When poorer countries reject upholding human rights standards, they refer to the United States, and justify their rejection on ideological grounds.[30] Likewise, redistribution of wealth either nationally or internationally, according to the liberal ideology, is counter to the logic of capitalism. The consequences continue to play out on the world stage. As Sara Steinmetz writes, "The issue of human rights abroad has frequently been relegated to a secondary place on the foreign policy agenda; it has proven useful insofar as it has complemented pursuit of the national interest, or at least, did not interfere with it."[31]

We are not at all making an argument that political and civil rights are trivial. Far from it. In fact, the United States could be better using its economic resources and investment strategies to leverage countries to comply with national and international standards of political and civil rights. China and Bangladesh are countries in which U.S. companies have major production operations and with which the United States trades. Both have abysmal records when it comes to the abuse of prisoners and unwarranted detentions. Freedom House, which ranks countries on political rights and civil liberties, gives both countries low scores, with China receiving a somewhat lower score (6.5) than Bangladesh (4.0) on its 1 to 7 Freedom Scale.[32] Likewise, Amnesty International criticizes both governments for illegal detentions and especially singles out China for its abuse of prisoners and use of the death sentence.[33]

Democracy and Rights

Distinctions between political and civil rights, on the one hand, and, economic, social, and cultural rights are helpful for comparative purposes and in conceptualizing how rights policies can be improved and implemented. Political and civil rights hint at an antagonism between citizens and the state, aggravated in the United States by "the war against terrorism," which has encroached on rights through surveillance and false arrests. Even at its best, liberal democracy is not participatory democracy, but, instead, a mixture of representative democracy and indirect democracy for the highest offices in the land. Federal and state statutes prevent third parties from playing more than a token role in national and state elections.

To place any emphasis at all on economic, social, and cultural rights is to make a claim for authentic democracy, in which citizens are happy to participate because their interests are at stake. Partisanship in America always veers toward the center, and, in any case, the two major parties support big business, are beholden to lobbyists, and play to powerful and rich constituents. We exaggerate, but not by much. Under these conditions, people do not feel that they have stakes in their society.

Society in the generic sense is a large population of people who do not know one another, but nevertheless have an affinity with one another owing to their understandings of what they share—their economy, standard of living, retirement plans, schooling, ecological resources, their environment, and so forth. As they can discover, the advance of their individual rights can be indistinguishable from the advance of their collective rights. Unlike a competitive, individualistic society where the gains of some are at the cost of others, a society organized around universal rights to housing, a job, health care, education, and social and economic security entails greater rights and freedoms for all. Such societal arrangements quite inevitably accompany democratic participation.

In a recent General Social Survey, administered by a University of Chicago research center, Americans were asked about whether or not they carried out any political activities, such as helping political parties, engaging in political movements, or working in election campaigns; only 29 percent said they did.[34] This compares with 50 percent who report they participate in church activities. U.S. voter turnout is among the lowest in the world. In its ten-year comparisons, which includes Western European nations and those in North and South America, the Center for Voting and Democracy finds that the U.S. average is practically the lowest, 45 percent, with the lowest being Colombia (32 percent) and Guatemala (24 percent).[35] In a longer time series, compiled by the International Institute for Democracy and Electoral Assistance, over all years from 1945 to 2003, the United States has an average turnout of 48.3, ranking 139th out of 172 countries.[36]

Such indications of voter apathy might suggest underlying voter cynicism, but we lay the blame on the U.S. government. Most countries have direct elections to fill top positions, such as prime minister or president, and most have multiple parties.[37] Both of these electoral arrangements increase citizen interests, and a multiparty system requires local politics, which in turn, raises the level of political participation. This usually requires power-sharing arrangements at the top level, which, at least in principle, ensures that there are coalitions that continue to represent a diverse cross section of the citizenry, while giving citizens whose parties lose a national election hopes of gaining in the future or at the local level.

We cannot stress enough that the conception of democracy has changed over the last two centuries, and now countries are experimenting with ways of ensuring direct democracy and participation of citizens in making substantive decisions, made extremely easy with the Internet. Again, it is important to highlight the contrast between liberal politics and substantive politics. Liberal politics evolved in a place and time when the educated and wealthy minority was deeply suspicious of the majority—the masses—and devised ways of limiting the latter's involvement in direct democracy. But then central problems of the nation-state centered on nation building and, in the view of political leaders, nurturing capitalist institutions. But things have changed; now that mature capitalism holds the state hostage, the contemporary nation-state needs to ensure the well-being and protection of its population.

Summary

It is useful to summarize the foundations of human rights to suggest the ways they differ from those of liberal rights.

First, human rights are themselves organically related, and enhancing one enhances the others. They all follow from the same premise, namely that all humans have dignity and are entitled to security of personhood.

Second, a human rights regime and a liberal regime differ in that the former advances equalities and solidarities, whereas the latter highlights the divisibility of resources and peoples' rights to compete over resources. Human rights are above all reciprocal,[38] whereas liberal rights are individual.

Third, while a human rights regime emphasizes the inherent moral equality of humans, a liberal regime ignores the relevance of the human dimension in favor of the person-as-citizen within the context of laws and the nation-state.

Fourth, the human rights regime accompanies responsibilities, a neglected idea in capitalist societies, but one that did enter American and French political thinking in the eighteenth century by way of Thomas Paine's writings and pamphleteering. He wrote in *The Rights of Man* (1791–1792): "A Declaration of Rights is, by reciprocity, a Declaration of Duties also. Whatever is my right as a man is also the right of another; and it becomes my duty to guarantee as well as to possess."[39] The idea of solidarities and the pursuit of collective goals, and of privileging and advancing the others' rights, withered on the vine as capitalism took hold. But

Thomas Paine, Eric Foner points out, was the most radical voice and among the most utopian of writers in the Age of Revolution in either America or France.[40] It takes only a moment to reflect on why his ideas about solidarity and duty did not survive capitalism's onslaught. Not only does capitalism rip through societal solidarities, it also erodes societal norms about the importance of reciprocity and duties regarding the other. Here we should also note the difference between charity and reciprocity. The former is based on inequalities that are hard to undo owing to the initial presumed asymmetry of the relation, and the latter reinforces equality. When we discuss the duties associated with human rights, we are describing egalitarian-enhancing relations.

Fifth, although abstract ideas, such as democracy, equality, freedom, and opportunities, all lie behind human rights thinking, human rights are themselves not all that abstract. As the list above indicates, human rights are practically grounded in the matters affecting the human condition, such as peoples' needs for water, food, and housing, and recognize the special needs of members of particular groups who are vulnerable or who have been historically oppressed. These practical rights are concrete and specific while they refer to the most general of all human conditions and the universal needs of humanity.

Sixth, it should be understood, however, that central to the idea of human rights is the premise that every single human being is unique, with their own personality and identity that draws from their family, community, race, culture, and ethnicity. Consistent with that truism, cultural diversity is recognized as a universal good, and therefore people have rights to their identities, and identities are configured in societies as tribes, languages, ethnicities, races, religion, clans, and families. Recognizing the importance of such diversities also entails affirming the rights of individuals to their identities and the rights of groups to nurture their own distinctive cultures.

Finally, owing to the integrity of each and every person, human rights are *entangled*. Freedom to develop, in Amartya Sen's felicitous phrasing, is the freedom to develop as a full human being, and therefore social rights, political rights, economic rights, and cultural rights are, at some profound level, inseparably entangled. This implies an ethic of recognition of the human dignity of each and every person. Recognizing the uniqueness and dignity of others becomes, under the sovereignty of human rights, fully premised on the human capacity for reciprocity. The *slap* is the archetypical example of much that we have discussed in this chapter. There is universal agreement that the *slap* is an affront to personal dignity, that the *slap* is an abuse of power differences, and that it violates the very basic princi-ple that humans are in solidarity both because they are equal human beings and because they are different from one another.

Notes

1. Mahmood Mamdani, "Introduction," in *Beyond Rights Talk and Culture Talk*, ed. Mahmood Mamdani, 1 (Cape Town, South Africa: David Philip Publishers, 2000). We have changed the place names that Mamdani uses, but otherwise it is a direct quotation.

2. UNIFEM, *Progress of the World's Women: Gender Equality and the Millennium Development Goals* (New York: UNIFEM, 2002).

3. Some states mandate that women have 50 percent representation in elected bodies, such as parliament.

4. There are six major international charters and treaties pertaining to women's rights: Convention on the Elimination of All Forms of Discrimina-tion against Women; Optional Protocol to the Convention on the Elimination of Discrimination against Women; Declaration on the Elimination of All Forms of Discrimination against Women; Declaration on the Elimination of Violence against Women; Convention on the Political Rights of Women; Declaration on the Protection of Women and Children in Emergency and Armed Conflict. The first two are treaties (with legal standing), and have been ratified respectively by 177 and 60 state parties as of June 2004 (Source: Office of the United Nations High Commissioner for Human Rights, Status of Rat-ifications of the Principal International Human Rights Treaties: www.unhchr .ch/html/intlinst.htm).

5. World Health Organization, "Female Genital Fact Sheet": www.who .int/docstore/frh-whd/ FGM/infopack/English/fgm_infopack.htm

6. UN Office for the Coordination of Humanitarian Affairs (IRIN), Febru-ary 21, 2005: www.irinnews.org/report.asp?ReportID=45684&SelectRegion= Horn_of_Africa&SelectCountry=DJIBOUTI

7. "The Power of Women's Voices," statement by Noeleen Heyzer, executive director, UNIFEM, International Women's Day 2004: www.unifem.undp.org/

8. United Nations Development Programme, *Human Development Report 2003* (New York: United Nations and Oxford University Press, 2003), table 25, 327–30.

9. UNIFEM, *Progress of the World's Women*.

10. Trend data for individual states can be found at: millenniumindicators.un .org/unsd/mi/mi_goals.asp

11. Alexandra Dobrowolsky and Vivien Hart, *Women Making Constitutions* (New York: Palgrave, 2003).

12. United Nations Development Programme, *Human Development Report 2003*, table 26, 326.

13. See Robert Pollin, *Contours of Descent* (London: Verso, 2003).

14. Diane Bell, "Considering Gender: Are Human Rights for Women Too?" in *Human Rights in Cross-Cultural Consensus*, ed. Abdullahi Ahmed An-Na'im, 339–62 (Philadelphia: University of Pennsylvania Press, 1992), 345.

15. UN Ace Project: www.aceproject.org/

16. Kofi Annan, "Two Concepts of Sovereignty," *The Economist*, September 18, 1999; quoted in *The Globalization of Human Rights*, ed. Jean-Marc Coicaus, Michael W. Doyle, and Anne-Marie Gardner, 1–19 (Tokyo: United Nations University Press, 2003), 1.

17. Gøsta Esping-Anderson, *The Three Worlds of Welfare Capitalism* (Cambridge: Polity Press, 1990).

18. Henry Steele Commager, *The American Mind* (New Haven, Conn.: Yale University Press, 1950), 29.

19. Center on Housing and Rights from Evictions: www.cohre.org/feframe.htm

20. Nils Karlson, Niclas Berggren, and Joakim Nergelius, *Why Constitutions Matter* (New Brunswick, N.J.: Transaction, 2002).

21. Robert L. Maddex, *Constitutions of the World* (Washington, D.C.: Congressional Quarterly, 1995), 295.

22. Richard Burchill, "The Role of Democracy in the Protection of Human Rights," in *Human Rights and Diversity*, ed. David P. Forsythe and Patrice C. McMahon, 37–58 (Lincoln: University of Nebraska Press, 2003).

23. Stephen Zunes, "US Arrogance on Display in UN Human Rights Commission Flap," Foreign Policy in Focus (May 2001): www.globalpolicy.org/

24. Kenneth Roth, "The Charade of US Ratification of International Human Rights Treaties," Chicago Journal of International Law (Fall 2000): www.globalpolicy.org/

25. Roth, "The Charade of US Ratification of International Human Rights Treaties."

26. Global Policy Forum, "US Position on International Treaties," July 2003: www.globalpolicy.org/

27. Source: Global Policy Forum, "US Position on International Treaties."

28. The American academic and scientific community has strongly condemned U.S. foreign policies and human rights abuses. For reports and statements, see: Economists Allied for Arms Reduction (www.ECAAR.org); Federation of American Scientists (www.fas.org/); Center for Nonproliferation Studies of the Monterey Institute of International Studies: cns.miis.edu/. A summary report of the Center for Economic, Social, and Cultural Rights (*Beyond Torture: US Violation of Occupations Law in Iraq*, June 2004) states: "The Bush Administration is committing war crimes and other serious violations of international law in Iraq as a matter of routine policy. Beyond the now-infamous examples of torture, rape, and murder at Abu Ghraib prison, the United States has ignored international law governing military occupation and violated the full range of Iraqis' national and human rights—economic, social, civil and political rights." www.cesr.org/

29. Coicaud, Doyle, and Gardner, *The Globalization of Human Rights*; David P. Forsythe, "US Foreign Policy and Human Rights," in *Human Rights and Comparative Foreign Policy*, 21–48 (Tokyo: United Nations University Press, 2000).

30. Abdullahi A. An-Na'im, "Introduction: 'Area Expressions' and the Universality of Human Rights," in *Human Rights and Diversity: Area Studies Revisited*, ed. David P. Forsythe and Patrice C. McMahon, 1–24 (Lincoln: University of Nebraska Press, 2003).

31. Sara Steinmetz, *Democratic Transition and Human Rights: Perspectives on U.S. Foreign Policy* (Albany: State University of New York Press, 1994), 18.

32. Freedom House. *Freedom in the World 2004* (Lanham, Md.: Rowman & Littlefield, 2004): www.freedomhouse.org/

33. Amnesty International, *Annual Report Statistics* 2004: www.amnesty.org/

34. From the 1998 General Social Survey: The questions were: 1. "Have you done any voluntary activity in the past 12 months in any of the following areas? Voluntary activity is unpaid work, not just belonging to an organization or group. It should be of service or benefit to other people or the community and not only to one's family or personal friends." 2. "During the last 12 months did you do volunteer work in any of the following areas [list]": webapp.icpsr.umich.edu/GSS/

35. Center for Voting and Democracy: www.fairvote.org/turnout/intturnout .htm

36. International Institute for Democracy and Electoral Assistance, "Voter Turnout from 1945 to Date": www.idea.int/vt/survey/voter_turnout_pop2.cfm

37. See Ace Project: www.aceproject.org/main/english/es/esy_ar

38. Stephen Eric Bronner, *Reclaiming the Enlightenment* (New York: Columbia University Press, 2004), 134.

39. Thomas Paine, *The Rights of Man*, ed. Gregory Claeys (Indianapolis, Ind.: Hackett, [1791–1792] 1992), 82.

40. Eric Foner, *Tom Paine and Revolutionary America* (London: Oxford University Press, 1976).

Constitutions: Overview and Comparisons

C itizens feel that their nation-state is healthy and thriving when there is little contention and conflict, peoples' needs are met, and there is hopefulness about the future. When there is trust. At the core of a healthy and thriving state are legal institutions that are fair, equitable, and transparent. The framework for all these legal institutions—courts, laws, statutes, codes, and regulations—is, of course, the state's constitution. The Constitution of the United States, designed and written by eighteenth-century visionaries, no longer meets the needs of its citizens in the twenty-first century. Peoples' trust in one another has painfully eroded.

We have already indicated what some of these difficulties are. The U.S. Constitution fails to take into account the security needs of the population by exclusively dealing with the political rights they have vis-à-vis the state. Society, community, solidarities, and human rights have no place in the Constitution. Additionally, the privileging of corporate personhood rights derails the rights of individuals and often undermines collective, or public goods, such as the environment, but also transparent governance. The U.S. Constitution cannot stop corporate interests from hijacking federal government agencies to promote their interests, whether it be the privatization of wetlands, setting the agenda of scientific research, or rolling back federal programs to advance the interests of the private investment sector.

A leading indicator that the Constitution is not fulfilling its intended purposes is that Americans, far more than any other people, have to litigate to fight for their rights. Without a normative framework for human rights, the constitutional protection of contract law, as well as the balancing of corporate rights with individual rights, Americans depend on lawyers and lawsuits to seek redress. The United States has more than half of the world's lawyers.[1]

An objective of this chapter is to juxtapose eighteenth-century federalism with emerging forms of federalisms. American federalism was based on premises about countervailing forces, or checks and balances. The first was that there ought to be checks and balances between the national and state levels. The second was that there ought to be checks and balances involving the executive, judicial, and congressional branches. That is, American federalism grew out of three distinct fears—first, that a despot could seize power; second, that the common people, with the giddiness of revolution just fading, could themselves seize power; and third, that one branch of government would usurp power. Checks and balances in both directions—horizontal and vertical—presumed tensions and potential conflict.

There still may be fears among twenty-first century constitutional framers about coups and popular uprisings, but there has been collective learning since state formation at the end of the eighteenth century, and most states that adopt a federalist structure these days have sought to strengthen the incipient bonds of shared interests within their countries rather than to emphasize competing interests. The reason is quite simple; global challenges are too great to split and aggravate competing tensions. We will contrast eighteenth-century U.S. federalism with twenty-first-century federalism, using the European Union (EU) as the comparison.

The important major difference is that the EU evolved by creating increasingly larger inclusive structures to coordinate national interests in the interest of promoting a stronger union that could discipline or humanize capitalism, whereas the United States emerged full-blown as an operating model virtually within a decade. Of course individual states were later added, but they replicated the original model. To clarify the context, the EU at the beginning of the twenty-first century is trying to harness turbulent markets and protect societies and states, whereas the United States was nurturing incipient capitalism and to do so provided a governance structure that we might say was self-preoccupied and would not impede this goal. Even while we put this a bit too simply, recent historical scholarship supports this interpretation.[2] It is important to stress, however, that neither the United States nor any of the states that comprise the EU initially intended to promote full-scale democracy. As the EU enlarges, it does so under the subsidiarity principle, which vaguely encourages local democracy and harmonization across the various units of governance. The United States remains stuck with its original institutions, notably, the Elec-

toral College and electoral districts, both of which are plagued with problems. These problems occupy center stage, preempting any public discussion about genuine democracy.

The Exceptionalist Argument

American leaders have always drawn on the exceptionalist argument,
which is rooted in the idea that America has a unique mission to inspire
and transform the world, or as Bush recently put it, "America has an obligation to unleash freedom in the world."[3] It is a rhetorical proposition that
is used opportunistically and simplistically to justify both good causes—
early space exploration—and ferociously mean-spirited ones—wars fought
in the pursuit of power and resources. While it is often summoned up on
the international stage to justify American intervention, it runs deeper and
draws on Americans' conceptions of themselves and their nation. In his
classic study, Seymour Martin Lipset describes American culture as one derived from exceptionalist claims as being rooted in individualistic and anti-
statist values, which draw from Protestant morality.[4] His especially useful
observation for the purposes of our argument is that individual morality is
completely inflexible, making patriotism, when roused, unconditional and
stubborn.[5]

It is not too cynical to say that what gives lonely, alienated Americans
a unique sense of solidarity is war. In the aftermath of September 11, 2001,
consistent with Lipset's interpretations, Americans have interwoven patriotism with something of a salvationist fundamentalism, allowing the Bush
administration, as Andrew Arato puts it, to cross the line from emergency
government to a constitutional dictatorship.[6] We would need two hands to
count on our fingers the number of national and international laws that the
United States has violated since 9/11: American civil and political freedoms (the Patriot Act); the UN Charter (the doctrine of "preemptive attack"); the International Covenant on Civil and Political Rights
(sovereignty rights); treaties governing the treatment of civilians, including
the 1907 Hague Convention; the 1949 Geneva Convention and its supplemental Protocols for the treatment of prisoners; the Convention on the
Rights of the Child and its optional protocols; the Paris Convention governing cultural and natural heritage (by allowing Iraqi museums to be
sacked and destroyed); and, as cases are now evolving, the Rome Statute
that authorizes the International Criminal Court.

To the extent that American exceptionalism is at its core all about
political freedoms, never before in the country's history have political

freedoms become so entangled in economic (and religious) freedoms, and never before have demands for individual freedoms been so incessantly cast in contentious terms. The very fabric of society is being shredded by these demands for individual freedoms, made worse by the government's wrapping the flag of nationalism around them, thereby legitimating them.

How Is the American Constitution Doing These Days?

We believe that the U.S. Constitution is in deep trouble, and one main reason is that little can be inferred from the concept of freedom—or everything can, depending on your point of view. We return to this argument at the conclusion of this chapter. Constitutions matter generally because they allocate authority to officeholders, set rules for voting and clarify the relationships between citizens and the state,[7] and most important for us, constitutions matter because they lay out the rights of citizens. What is relatively unique about the U.S. Constitution is the way it defines rights, namely, as S. E. Finer puts it, draws "a ring-fence around the individual against invasion by the public authorities."[8] And we would add that the fence is drawn as well to protect the corporation against invasion by public authority.

A main feature of the U.S. Constitution is that it explicitly divides governance along two axes. The first is the division between the federal level—with its own constitution—and each of the states, with their own constitutions. We have already described the extent to which that creates logjams and often leads to endless litigation. The second axis is the division into branches at the federal level of government—Congress, the judicial branch, and the executive branch. The purpose of this was to curtail the power of each of the branches, but the Framers did not anticipate that when a single political party was in power it could lessen the independence of each of the branches. The consequence currently is a thoroughgoing politicization of the three branches as well as the federal agencies, and attendant paralysis at times.

One anachronism is the Electoral College, which was a partial attempt to buffer high office from a popular, mass plebiscite (reinforced in early times by another buffer, namely, the provision that only white, male property holders could vote), which revealed itself as fully anachronistic in the presidential election of 2000. In contrast, virtually every modern constitution stipulates direct elections and outcomes depend on popular support.[9] Another anachronism of the U.S. Constitution is the close relationship of the courts to elected politicians who appoint them. Regardless of their differences, notable constitutional scholars such as Richard Epstein,[10] Owen Fiss,[11] Ronald Dworkin,[12] and Bruce Ackerman[13] all hold that the close relationship between the judiciary and the executive branch undermines democracy.

The past few years have revealed the flaws of this close relationship between the chief justices and the ideological grounds of their appointment. Within the 2003–2004 session, the Supreme Court failed to uphold cases involving separation of church and state, contradicting the principles of the First Amendment;[14] has not challenged the legality of the administration's extensive secret classification;[15] upheld all cases it heard on the death penalty;[16] and ruled against the environment in the case allowing trucks without standard emission compliance to travel throughout the United States.[17] In only one notable case did the high court rule against the Republican administration; specifically, it ruled in a 6–3 vote that American courts do have jurisdiction to consider the claims of U.S. citizens who have been held as "enemy combatants" in violation of their rights.[18]

In its 2001–2002 term, the Court ruled in favor of state laws that violated federal law, deprived privacy rights to students, upheld a school voucher plan that gravely disadvantages public schools, and only narrowly confirmed protections for patients' rights and the environment.[19] In 2000, it will be recalled that the Supreme Court disallowed a recount of the Florida votes; Scalia noted "the recount would threaten irreparable harm to petitioner (Bush) . . . by casting a cloud upon what he claims to be the legitimacy of his election."[20]

The Conflict between the State and Federal Levels

Namely, a general problem with the American legal system is that states have their own constitutions and laws, which are sometimes in conflict with federal law. States have their own laws about sentencing, death penalties, abortion, gay marriage, and the minimum wage. Sixteen states and the District of Columbia have never repealed restrictive laws ruled unconstitutional by *Roe v. Wade*.[21] Again, for purposes of illustration, the state of Utah provides little protection against search and seizure, whereas Vermont allows police little authority for search and seizure if the person opposes it.[22]

Criminal culpability is set at different ages in different states. In some states it is virtually impossible to get an abortion, and in other states easier. In a few states, same-sex civil unions and marriages are possible, while illegal in most states. States vary greatly in their gun control laws. One Web guide designed for migrants in the United States candidly states: "there are laws for each separate U.S. state, as passed by the state legislature and signed into law by the state governor. It exists in parallel, and sometimes in conflict with, U.S. federal law. *These disputes are often resolved by the courts.*"[23] That is, court appeals privilege the interpretation of the law, and therefore the resources to litigate, over the uniform application of justice.

In principle, this gives individual citizens more leeway in appealing their case from lower to higher courts. In practice, this means that constitutional law has become a methodological nightmare, with little clarity for citizens and logjams throughout the court system. Rich citizens, who can afford private attorneys, are the only ones who can tackle appeals, taking advantage of the contradictory laws.[24] Contemporary constitutions, by and large, are instead promulgated around a unified jurisprudence, with a lesser emphasis on distinguishing jurisdictions and a greater emphasis on coherence around citizens' rights.[25]

According to conservative legal scholar Forrest McDonald, the U.S. judiciary, is superior in protecting the rights of citizens owing to its fluid structure.[26] However, *fluid* is a misleading term, and increasingly so. Recently, state systems have become increasingly powerful over the federal judiciary, creating more contradictory decisions and more logjams. The administrations of Ronald Reagan, George H. W. Bush, and George W. Bush devoted themselves to promoting a decentralized federalism within the court system, and some Supreme Court judges, notably Antonin Scalia and Clarence Thomas, have pursued the implications of this federalist interpretation, throwing cases back to states rather than making a ruling. This has resulted in opportunistic justice. Because state laws conflict with one another, large corporations especially use these conflicts to their advantage so that they can pursue their cases in different jurisdictions.[27]

While this judicial pattern was intended to create a fluid and creative system, we instead believe that it disempowers people, leaving them at the mercy of attorneys and caught in the middle of complex and confusing contradictions between state and federal laws, unsure of their rights.

We can briefly note that other countries have hierarchical judicial systems. For example, Spain has autonomous regions that operate largely under their own laws for regional governance, but these laws are harmonized with Spain's national constitution.[28] While individual rights are elaborated at both the state and federal levels in the United States, and sometimes conflict with one another, the rights of citizens are guaranteed at the national level in Spain, not at the regional level. The new European Constitution may pose some problems of dualism, just as every regional alliance does, but human rights are protected at the level of the EU, while states may have their own laws about traffic, education, labor, and criminal laws.[29] In other words, European nations distinguish between fundamental human rights, pertaining to rights for minority groups, rights to employment, rights to social security, and so forth, and place these rights at the highest jurisdiction possible, and then allow local jurisdictions to make laws that are more specific to particular contexts.[30]

Likewise, recent constitutions written in the 1990s and later reflect hierarchies of jurisdictions, granting the highest jurisdiction the power to spell out the most general safeguards for human rights and the rights of enterprises and corporations. Such provisions protect individuals and alleviate interregional competition for economic activities and resources. Recent discussions of a global constitution help to clarify how human rights, largely taken from UN declarations, can be codified for the international protections of all the world's peoples, while the laws of sovereign states pertain to their own national jurisdictions and circumstances.[31]

An Institutional Analysis

We have reviewed in chapter 1 the textual basis for property rights and Supreme Court decisions. Anthony Ogus argues that in the constitutional context, the right of individuals to hold property and exploit it for their own purposes has been defended from two perspectives: first, it grants individuals autonomy, and second, property is instrumentally necessary for the economic welfare and efficiency of society.[32] From the first perspective, recognition of property is the first step in the delineation of the private sphere that protects people from coercion. From the second perspective, property is necessary for the economic welfare and efficiency of society, based on the assumption that without property rights, people have little incentive to produce.[33] The U.S. Constitution recognizes individual property rights: Amendment V states that "nor shall [any person] be deprived of life, liberty, or property, without due process of law; nor shall private property be taken for public use, without just compensation." These provisions differ little from other constitutions, and the intent is clear: namely, that individuals, not corporations, have these rights.[34] As we will later see, European countries have instead promoted flexibility in private and public ownership, or what Germany terms *soziale marktwirtschaft* (social market), and have curbed private corporations in the interest of the public.

Compared with other constitutions, the U.S. Constitution is remarkably innocent on matters of property, allowing, as we have argued, the courts to grant personhood rights to corporations. Other states instead treat corporations as part of contract law, allowing them more flexibility to move production of essential goods—such as medicines—into public enterprises, to create joint public–private partnerships, and to curb or regulate advertising, and allows the state more power in establishing child labor laws and protecting workers' rights. In European courts, corporations are a fictional entity without personhood rights.

We will later elaborate on labor laws as they relate to the rights of corporations.

Eighteenth- and Twenty-first-Century Conceptions

In the eighteenth and early nineteenth centuries, the main objectives for any constitution were to establish sovereignty, establish the political rights of citizens, and specify the relationships between the state and its citizens. The Polish State in 1791 stated: [it] "solemnly establish[s]" a constitution "free from the disgraceful shackles of foreign influence; prizing more than life the external independence and internal liberty of the nation; in order to exert our natural rights with zeal and firmness."[35] Another function of these early constitutions was to define the relationships among governance bodies, and the Polish constitution delineates executive, judicial, and legislative functions and bodies. The French and Spanish constitutions of 1791 and 1812, respectively, though different in some respects from the Polish and American constitutions, likewise delineated principles of independence and internal order, and recognize fundamental equality among citizens. Yet another function was to secure the political and civil rights of citizens. For example, Article 4, chapter 1 of Title I of the 1812 Spanish constitution states: "The nation is obliged to preserve and protect by just and wise laws, the civil liberty, the property, and the other legitimate rights of all individuals belonging to it."[36]

These early constitutions were hermetically sealed, to establish statehood and nationhood, and closed to interpretation. They offer no guides, as E. J. Hobsbawm points out, to what the people wanted or were thinking, nor have they been open to evolution.[37] Nations depended on constitutions to define who was in and who was out and to launch imperialist projects from a center defined by the sovereign state.

These early constitutions stressed the homogeneity of the population, partly to unify populations around nationalism, but also to include some while excluding others. What is now considered perilous de-ethnicization was then considered nation-building, and is still reflected in the constitutions of the United States, New Zealand, Australia, France, and the "constitution-like" provisions of British Common Law. Among these older nation-states, others, including Canada, Belgium, and New Zealand, have broken with their earlier liberal constitutions to affirm cultural identities, language rights, and indigenous rights. Contemporary constitutions, as we will show, are far more open-ended, reflecting peoples' awareness about the complexities of their own society and the uncertainties of global processes.[38]

While liberal regimes, such as the United States, Canada, New Zealand, and Australia, in principle grant equal rights to everyone, they nevertheless embody the interests of a dominant ethnic group, as so obviously has the United States. Thus, liberalism, notwithstanding its discursive connections with tolerance, is illiberal when compared with a doctrine of pluralism.[39] Pretenses of color blindness are deceiving.[40]

From the perspective of twentieth-century comparativists, the U.S. Constitution was considered exemplary in the extent to which individual rights were protected, and this was attributed to the diffuse character of the court system in a federated system of state and federal courts and to the independence of the judiciary from the legislative and executive branches. In contrast, in states committed to parliamentary supremacy, the doctrine of constitutional supremacy evolved more slowly, with singular federal courts carving out a sphere of independence. The U.S. Constitution, along with this federated, layered judiciary, is presumed by many American legal scholars to be superior to other systems in its capability to protect the rights of citizens owing to judicial independence and the appeals mechanisms. Its complex and fluid judiciary, according to, for example, Forrest McDonald, has a superior system of protecting the rights of citizens.[41]

To be sure, constitutional supremacy was adopted earlier in the United States than in European countries, owing to the isolation of the judiciary from the executive and legislative bodies, but in practice, European constitutional courts have evolved that handle cases in much the same way and with the same degree of autonomy that the U.S. Supreme Court does. It is a mistake, therefore, to believe that the separation of powers in the United States is distinctive and that Americans' rights are better protected than those of citizens elsewhere. If the U.S. Constitution has not evolved, the question we next address is how constitutions lend themselves to change, specifically how they can be open to international law and human rights.

Evolution of Constitutions

Constitutions are embedded in a variety of other institutions, but hardly in any fixed and unchanging way. There are also different views as to the relationships between constitutions and other institutions. In America, the basic conception is that the Constitution stands independent from elected politicians and plays a foundational role in protecting fundamental rights—which for conservatives like Richard Epstein are property rights;[42] for collectivists like Owen Fiss, the rights of the disadvantaged;[43] and for liberals, like Ronald Dworkin, egalitarian rights.[44] Regardless of these differences, American legal scholars hold a dualist perspective that emphasizes court independence from demands by the political elite. These versions of dualism depend on a certain conception of democracy, the liberal state, and a Lockean conception of individual citizens who aggressively pursue their self-interests regardless of collective interests.

The constitutional court protects interests—those of property holders, the disadvantaged, and the rights of liberal citizens—against political elites—that is, the members of the legislature or the executive branch, political parties. Or does it? While apologists of the U.S. constitutional tradition, such as Bruce Ackerman,[45] contend that the American judiciary has renewed the democratic promise over and over again—especially in New Deal legislation, the *Brown v. Topeka* decision, and its defense of free speech—we are inclined to disagree as the Court has sharply veered in the direction of supporting corporate rights, less the rights of humans.

One fundamental difference involving constitutional law between most countries and the United States today is that constitutional issues are diffused through a complex judiciary in the United States, whereas constitutional issues are handled by a single court in other countries. A second fundamental difference is that because the United States evolved as a federal system, considerable power resides in state courts, which apply state law as well as interpret federal law. In principle, this gives individual citizens more leeway in appealing their cases from lower to higher courts. A third difference is that owing to the government's federated structure, constitutional changes must be ratified at the state level.

It is instructive to examine the proposed European constitution, which has some parallels with the earlier U.S. Constitution: namely, both are based on federated principles, and just as the individual thirteen states had sovereignty, so do the members of the European Federation. The European Federation—the Common Market—evolved around the principles of economic integration just as did the early U.S. republic. The details are important because they provide conceptual comparisons for a similar consti-tution for all Latin American countries, say, or for Mexico, the United States, and Canada. The European constitution shows too that cooperative agreements can evolve to promote trade, but also to handle difficult ques-tions relating to migration, environmental issues, shared scientific research, and so forth. The central difference, as we earlier stressed is that the EU, and the EU Constitution, has evolved from and with existing nation-states, whereas the U.S. federation, the U.S. Constitution, and the constitutions of the individual states emerged as legal entities within a given template.

The European Constitution

Origins, 1930–1950

To start with the European constitution is bold because it has not yet been ratified by the member states, but it is not only important in its own right; it is likely to be the model for future regional constitutions, in Asia, Africa, and Latin America. States need to be buffered against economic forces, and alliances help to build trading partners, and to pool resources. European countries are each relatively advantaged, but they have become more so over the past decades owing to their membership in the EU. A constitution is the next step in binding these relationships. On October 29, 2004, the Heads of State or Government of the twenty-five member states and the three candidate countries (Turkey, Bulgaria, and Romania) signed the treaty es-tablishing a constitution for Europe, which will then need to be ratified by all member states. Summarizing the background briefly is useful.

The first model for the EU, called the "Briand Plan," after Aristide Briand, French foreign minister, was proposed at the League of Nations in May 1930. The Germans were reluctant to jump on board, but the En-glish were hostile.[46] Britain depended heavily on trade with its colonies to bend to pressures from the Continent, especially if that entailed French su-premacy and headed in the direction of a free-trade policy. The League of Nations asked Briand to present a memorandum to them with a concrete project. The French politician presented a "Memorandum on the organi-zation of a system of a Federal European Union" in 1930. It was too late. The outbreak of the Depression had started to sweep away ideas of soli-darity and cooperation in an international sense. Those who continued to promulgate European unity, such as the French politician Edouard Herriot, who published in 1931 "The United States of Europe," became a real minority.

By 1932 Briand had lost his appointment as foreign minister, and the plan died, to be resurrected twenty years later, though modified, in the 1950 Schuman Plan.[47] Yet by 1930, some of the elements of the rationale for European unity were in play: a desire for lasting European peace, economic growth and unity, financial coordination, and shared technological development, but Briand himself was clear: the main objective was to achieve European peace and that end could only be promoted through the other means.

Adolf Hitler's rise to the German Chancellery in 1933 meant the definite end of European harmony and the dramatic ascendancy of nationalism of the worst kind, and Europe had to wait through World War II (1939–1945) to again begin to think about some kind of European integration, and then there were two obstacles: first, the two new superpowers, the United States and the Soviet Union, had economic, political, and military power far superior to the loosely connected European states. Second, there was a widespread conviction that it was necessary to avoid conflict among the European states that would trigger yet another war. After all, the continent had been the killing fields for the first two world wars. Discussions in those early years mainly involved searching for an accommodation between France and Germany that would please the United States. However, Europeans felt the only way to guarantee the peace was through some sort of union, and began to desire the creation of a continent that is freer, fairer, and more prosperous, and one in which international relations develop in a harmonious fashion.

In 1946, British ex-prime minister Winston Churchill delivered a famous speech at the University of Zurich (Switzerland), considered by many as the first step toward integration during the postwar period.

> I want to speak today of the drama of Europe. . . . Amongst the winners, one only hears a Babel of voices. . . . Amongst the losers, we find only silence and desperation. . . . There exists a remedy that, if it is adopted globally and spontaneously for the majority of peoples of the many countries, could, miraculously, completely transform the situation, and make all of Europe, or most of it, as free and happy as Switzerland today. What is the sovereign solution? It consists in reconstituting the European family, or, at least, in so far as we cannot reconstitute it, giving it a structure that permits it to live and grow in peace, in security and liberty. We should create a fortune in the US and Europe.[48]

In response, the Americans abandoned the isolationist position they had adopted after World War I, and instead adopted a somewhat contradictory policy about European unification. On the one hand, the United States was convinced that fettering Germany's free trade after World War I had played a key role leading up to nazification. Therefore, the United States set a condition beginning in 1946 that any European plan ought to be based on free trade policy. On the other hand, the United States wanted to be Europe's benefactor in its opposition to the USSR, and the Truman Doctrine, which had as its goal stopping Soviet expansion, encompassed the Marshall Plan for European countries. This was a way of nurturing the economic development of a destroyed Europe with the political objective of impeding the extension of communism. For these reasons, the North Americans promoted the creation of a centralized European organization that would administer and organize the distribution of the massive economic aid of the Marshall Plan. With this objective, the Organization for Economic Cooperation and Development (OECD) was created (initially called the Organization for Economic Cooperation in Commerce [OECC]). This was one of the first organisms that got the majority of western European countries together. The OECC helped to liberalize commerce between member states, introduced ideas about monetary agreements, and developed, in general, economic cooperation in concrete aspects.

In 1949, after the new North American initiative, the majority of the democratic states of western Europe founded, along with the United States and Canada, the North Atlantic Treaty Organization (NATO), the great Western military alliance against the USSR.[49] Thus, by 1949, the foundations for the EU had been laid, essentially anticommunist politically and capitalist in economic orientation.

Another important step was in the creation of the European Council in 1949. This organism, still in existence today as the EU's main decision-making body, tried to encourage political cooperation between European countries. Its statutes, however, did not take on the objectives of a union, or even a federation of the states, and did not foresee in them any type of granting of sovereignty on the part of the member states. Because its principal function is to reinforce the democratic system and human rights in the member states, we will have more to say about it in a later chapter.

We should note here, however, that the Council has greatly advanced the human rights of all European citizens, through legislation, for example, that ensures gender equity in wages. Furthermore, it has recently enacted policies for the inclusion of migrants as well. In March 2005, the Council's Committee on Social Rights ruled that "legislation or practice that denies entitlement to medical assistance to foreign nationals, within the territory of a State Party, even if they are illegal, is contrary to the [European] Charter." Thus, all migrant workers, with or without documentation, have access to healthcare under this interpretation, which is consistent with the UN Treaty on the rights of migrant workers.[50]

From the Schuman Declaration to the Rome Treaty (1950–1957)

Robert Schuman, French minister of the exterior, took the first step in the creation of the European Community. On May 9, 1950, he proposed a plan, designed by Jean Monnet, to integrate and manage together the French–German production of carbon and steel. This measure of economic integration sought to advance the bringing together of France and Germany, leaving behind once and for good the specter of war in Europe. The initial Treaty of Paris establishing the European Coal and Steel Community (ECSC) was signed on April 18, 1951, and came into force July 25, 1952. Sometimes it is called the Schuman Plan after its principle drafter, and it too was guided by the principle that to ensure peace it is necessary to establish an "organization that will ensure the fusion of markets and the expansion of production."[51] The countries that signed were Germany, Belgium, France, Italy, Luxembourg, and The Netherlands ("The Six"). The community established a sort of parliament that met in September 1952 in Strasbourg for the first time.[52]

The objectives of the ECSC may sound trivial by today's standards, but in 1952 it was ambitious. Article 2 states that it "shall have as its task to contribute, in harmony with the general economy of the Member States and through the establishment of a common market . . . [for] economic expansion, growth of employment and a rising standard of living in the Member States." Article 3 states,

> Ensure that all comparably placed consumers in the common market have equal access to the sources of production; ensure the establishment of the lowest prices; Promote improved working conditions and an improved standard of living for the workers in each of the industries for which it is responsible, so as to make possible their harmonization while the improvement is being maintained; promote the growth of international trade and ensure that equitable limits are observed in export pricing.[53]

In other words, the focus was not only on economic establishments, but on workers and consumers as well.

This same year, the French government proposed the creation of a European Defense Community (EDC), which became the Western European

Union in 1954, which in turn was replaced by NATO. The ministers of foreign affairs of the Six, under the presidency of the Belgian Paul Henri Spaak, met in 1955, in the Messina Conference, and then on March 25, 1957, to establish the Rome Treaty, which created the European Economic Community (EEC) and the European Atomic Energy Community (ERATOM).[54]

The most specific goal of the EEC treaty was a twelve-year plan for a total dismantling of customs, to be achieved by July 1968. Thus the first official common market was exclusively about the free circulation of goods, but the free movement of people, capital, and services was still limited. The other essential element of the Rome Treaty was the adoption of a Policy of Common Agriculture (PAC). Essentially, the PAC established the freedom of circulation of agriculture products inside of the EEC and the adoption of strongly protectionist policies that guaranteed the European farmers a sufficient level of revenue to avoid competition from products from other countries by means of the subsidizing of agricultural prices. The PAC continues to absorb the majority of the community budget and, besides, is objectionable to Third World countries owing to the subsidies it provides to European farmers.[55] The Rome Treaty meant the triumph of what has come to be called the functionalist theory, represented essentially in the legacy of Jean Monnet, one of the founders of the EEC.[56] Faced with the impossibility of agreeing to a political union immediately, the new strategy was to look for a process of integration that would slowly affect diverse sectors of the economy, but in a way that would create supranational institutions in which the states, in various stages, would cede economic, administrative, and finally, political autonomy. In this way, the EEC would have a series of institutions: the Commission, the Council, the European Assembly (later the European Parliament), the Tribunal of Justice, and the Socioeconomic Committee. Thus, the vision was one in which there would be progressive economic integration that would pave the way to the final objective of political union.

The "British Problem" and the Expansion of the EEC in 1973

The principal political problem for the EEC was that the United Kingdom had remained on the margins, and it did so for various reasons: first, the importance of its commercial, political, and even sentimental ties with the members of the Commonwealth; second, its refusal to enter into a customs union; and, third, its resistance to eventual political union with Europe. Following the failure of negotiations for its entry into the EEC, the British government helped to create the European Association for Free Trade (EAFT), which

Sweden, Switzerland, Norway, Denmark, Austria, and Portugal also joined. This association was merely a zone of free commerce, essentially of industrial products, and it did not collect any type of common tariff.

The British quickly realized their error as the EEC was experiencing spectacular economic growth, exceeding the growth of North America, and in August 1961 the British prime minister solicited the initiation of negotiations for the United Kingdom's entry. Nevertheless, after varied negotiating attempts, the French leader, Charles de Gaulle, vetoed its entry, arguing that "Europe of the mother countries" must be independent of the two superpowers, the United States and the USSR—distrustful of the close British involvement in Washington. Again, in 1967, the Labor Party government of Harold Wilson asked for entry into the EEC, and de Gaulle again vetoed the admission of the United Kingdom.

However, despite defending a strong Europe against the United States and the USSR, de Gaulle never believed in a politically unified Europe. For him, French national independence (the country he nevertheless indefatigably tried to keep in the role of power) was a nonnegotiable question. It was not until the resignation of de Gaulle in 1969, following the turbulence of the student uprising, that British admission could be considered, and after overcoming British public opposition to integration, finally the negotiations ended successfully in 1972. In 1973, three new countries entered into the EEC: the United Kingdom, Denmark, and Ireland. The Europe of Nine was born. The Norwegians voted against joining, and their country, against the opinion of its own government, remained on the margins of the Community.

Growth to the Europe of Twelve (1973–1986)

The oil crisis in 1973 put an end to the spectacular economic growth that Europe had experienced for many years. Unemployment, inflation, and the crisis of traditional sectors of the economy plagued the EEC in the second half of the 1970s and the beginning of the 1980s. Although, at some point, journalists coined the terms *euroescepticismo* and *euroesclerosis* to talk about a weakening integration process, the reality is that during these years, important developments took place, as much in the sense of a greater integration, as in the extension of the Community to new members. Let us point out a few key moments.

- In 1975, the European Council was instituted, a periodic meeting of the Chiefs of State and Government, where strategic decisions of the Community were made.

- In 1979, the European Monetary System was created, and termed the ECU (European Currency Unit), the direct antecedent to the Euro. The currency of the member countries remained tied to a tight limit of a 2.5 percent fluctuation of its exchange value. Furthermore, the governments committed themselves to coordinate their monetary policies. This was the first significant step toward a monetary union.
- Also in 1979, the first elections with universal suffrage took place in the European Parliament.
- The fall of the military dictatorships in Greece (1974), Portugal (1974), and Spain (the death of Franco in 1975) brought about the inclusion of these countries: Greece in 1981, and Spain and Portugal in 1986.
- In 1984, a group of European parliaments, directed by Italian Altiero Spinelli, presented to the Parliament a "Project of a European Treaty," which proposed the approval of a new treaty to replace the Rome Treaty and would grant an important step toward European integration. Despite not being approved by the governments, it was valuable because it reinitiated the debate about the future of the Community, anticipating the advances that would take place in the 1990s.
- In 1985, the three countries of the Benelux, France, and Germany signed the so-called Schengen Agreement, which the majority of the Community's countries eventually signed. An ambitious initiative thus began to guarantee the free circulation of people and the gradual suppression of borders between the member states.

In the second half of the 1980s, the integration process would receive an important political impulse, largely through the efforts of Jacques Delors, a French Socialist elected president of the European Commission in 1985. The approval in 1986 of the European Unique Act would eventually lead to the 1992 Maastricht Agreement, which essentially created a large borderless space in which there would be free circulation of merchandise, people, services and capital, and a common currency. In 1994 the first direct election of the European Parliament took place, and by 2004 the EU expanded to include twenty-five countries, on the verge of approving a new constitution. In June of that same year the European Parliament consisted of these twenty-five countries, and the Community was preparing itself to approve its own constitution.

Why a European Constitution?

The obvious progression among Europeans, after successfully achieving market and monetary unification, was to look forward to political unification, the first step being a constitution. Certainly that was the vision of the participants of a convention chaired by Valery Giscard d'Estaing, which started its work in March 2002. Their final document establishes a dynamic between a common power and subsidarities' power[57] that exercises competencies ceded by the member states while this cession presupposes negotiations between each individual state and its constituent communities. The term *subsidarity* though vague, draws attention to both the various local components and the unifying processes, as well as to the importance of the societies that make up the individual states as well as the Union.

One way of considering this constitution is that it reflects cascading relations of delegation and negotiations within a unifying framework of markets, currency, labor protections, and environmental safeguards. Political leaders have been suggesting all along that a constitution would move European countries in the direction of political union, but the next step would require popular democracy, not yet achieved by the constitution.[58] In an interview in *La Vanguardia*, on January 3, 2005, the Spanish president of the European Parliament urged Europeans to vote for it in referenda, proclaiming the constitution, "the beginning of a new chapter in [European] history."

The European constitution, which was approved on June 19, 2004, and has to be ratified by the member states over the course of two years, is a pact that resolves the struggles of power, and in time, establishes a complicated but effective way of maintaining competition. There are competitions proper to the Community, all related to finances, balancing the budget, the customs union, and recently incorporated, the protection of marine biology resources. There are rivalries shared with the states, such as productivity, the common space of justice and liberty, and cohesion.[59] Notable too has been the ratifying process. European governments have been distributing copies of the constitution to their citizens to encourage them to become familiar with it, and to generate discussions.[60] The EU has put a debating forum, "1,000 Debates," online to encourage public discussion of the constitution.[61]

Already there are movements, especially the Federalist European Movement, that are advancing greater political unification within Europe and greater influence in the world, to tackle environmental problems on a global level, to work on humanitarian projects, and to achieve more equitable control over currency transactions and transparent governance.[62] The vision that motivates these programmatic proposals is the distinctive recognition that Europe now surpasses the United States in maintaining peaceful relations with other nations, greatly exceeds the United States in providing humanitarian aid to poor countries, and internally has achieved greater equality among citizens. The short-run obstacle is chiefly establishing mechanisms that give small and medium-sized countries greater voice in the Union so that the big ones, France and Germany, do not dominate. But the constitution would not be more than a treaty between states. European citizens only elect the Parliament, and the people to fill important posts are chosen by the governments.

The ratification process for the constitution requires that all state parties and the three candidate states sign the treaty establishing the constitution, and the process allows ratification through a parliamentary vote or through popular referendum. By June 2005 the following states had ratified the constitution: Austria, Belgium, Cyprus, Germany, Greece, Hungary, Italy, Latvia, Lithuania, Malta, Poland, Slovakia, Slovenia, and Spain. However, the people of France and the Netherlands rejected the text of the constitution in popular referenda held in early summer 2005.

After the French and Dutch referenda, the process was suspended, although not abandoned, while further talks continue. What complicates these ongoing discussions is that there are two sources of opposition. One grows out of traditional nationalism and fears about conceding even more state autonomy to the EU. The other is rooted in opposition to neoliberal capitalism, and concerns that the EU is abandoning its commitment to social welfare, social solidarities, and economic security. In short, what essentially started as a referendum about strengthening a federation has become a referendum about capitalism, the welfare state, and human rights.

Summary

An important point to stress, which is rarely obvious in comparative studies of governance, is that national American politics reinforces other cleavages because it is largely state-based. Americans vote for electoral votes within their states, as well as for senators and representatives. Within states, such as California, there are statewide referenda on substantive issues, but this is rare. Without multiple parties that stand on distinctive platforms (such as the environment, reform, migrants' rights, women's rights, and so forth) in national elections, American politics are centrist, and because they relate to state political machinery, they reinforce provincialism.

We cast our main thesis as follows, summing up the points we made earlier in this chapter. There is a clear articulation among Europeans that common interests must keep the EU together and these center on the shared, albeit vague, goal of humanizing capitalism, while in contrast, individual states in the United States must compete with one another for their shares of capital resources. The differences here are both historical and structural. The U.S. nation-state and individual states emerged nearly simultaneously to check each other. We might say that the federated system in the United States evolved rapidly as insuring a balance of power and was predicated on the idea that neither the individual states nor the nation-state could be fully trusted. In contrast, the EU evolved as an increasingly larger and more complex entity as trust was strengthened, across nation-states, across societies and cultures. Together European states could fight and argue over seemingly trivial issues—whether British chocolate was *really* chocolate; whether condoms should be sized or not—in order to explore and test what should be left to individual countries and what should be shared. These seemingly banal issues helped to clarify shared European values and practices, and what ought to be left up to individual nation-states. There were no such discussions in the United States, and, as a result, individual sovereign states and the larger sovereign federated structure and its Constitution have had less clear relationships. This has bred mistrust, antagonism, and sometimes, fierce jurisdictional battles over slavery, schooling, federally funded programs, taxes, and the death penalty. There are few legal issues in the United States that are not potential grounds for inter-jurisdictional fights.

In a later chapter we will discuss the human rights provisions of the EU, which encompass recognition of the Universal Declaration of Human Rights, the International Covenant on Civil and Political Rights, and the International Covenant on Economic, Social, and Cultural Rights, as well as the European Convention on Human Rights. Here we highlight the relevance of the European constitution for the United States. First, had the United States nurtured its relations in the Western hemisphere as individual European states did, especially after the collapse of the Soviet Union and the unification of Germany, the United States and its neighbors may have had far more beneficial relations now than is currently the case. Second, the United States failed to balance labor provisions and environmental protections with its aggressive backing of corporations, and the consequence now is that there is far more citizen insecurity in America than might have been. Today Europe leads in consumer protections, industrial regulation, and environmental preservation.[63]

Robert A. Dahl pointed out in his 2000 Yale University Castle Lecture that contrary to Americans' idea that the U.S. Constitution has been a model for the rest of the world, all countries, without a single exception, have rejected it.[64] According to Dahl the U.S. Constitution and the governance structure that it allows are fundamentally flawed. He cites these particular reasons: (1) there is enormous inequality in citizens' representation in the Senate owing to the fact that the least populous states have the same number of senators as the most populous states; (2) comprehensive judicial review is granted to a high court whose members are not popularly elected; (3) in presidential elections, small parties have no chance of winning owing to the peculiar character of the Electoral College; (4) there are great inequalities within the Electoral College system; and (5) the American president has unprecedented powers, like a monarch and prime minister rolled into one.[65] We have given additional reasons as well, especially the extent to which political factions and party discipline dominate decision-making among political elites. Dahl's focus is on the implications of the U.S. Constitution for democracy and within the promise of the Declaration of Independence and Americans' conceptions of political rights.

The forces that we have described in this chapter help to explain why, after 9/11, Americans, always vaguely searching for unity and national coherence, seized onto patriotism with unexpected relish, almost like the eager nationalisms observed in newly independent nations. Such patriotism, as Frantz Fanon brilliantly documented,[66] can never be the seedbed of democracy or of national unity. Instead, it is intensely undemocratic and divisive.

Notes

1. Steven Lubet, "'Greedy Lawyers Are Often the Public's Allies,'" *Newsday*, October 4, 2000: www.commondreams.org/views/100400-101.htm

2. See Jeff Madrick, "The Producers," *New York Review of Books* LII (March 10, 2005): 26–29.

3. Michael Massing, "'Bad Apples' or Predictable Fruits of War?" *Los Angeles Times*, May 10, 2004: www.commondreams.org/views04/0510-02.htm

4. Seymour Martin Lipset, *American Exceptionalism* (New York: Norton, 1996), 20, 276, 288.

5. Lipset, *American Exceptionalism*, 20.

6. Andrew Arato, "The Bush Tribunals and the Specter of Dictatorship," *Constellations* 9 (2002): 457–76.

7. Niclas Berggren, Nils Karlson, and Joakim Nergelius, eds., *Why Constitutions Matter* (New Brunswick, N.J.: Transaction, 2002).

8. S. E. Finer, *Five Constitutions* (Brighton, Sussex: Harvester Press, 1979), 23.

9. Arend Lijphart, *Democracies* (New Haven, Conn.: Yale University Press, 1998).

10. Richard Epstein, *Takings: Private Property and the Power of Eminent Domain* (Cambridge, Mass.: Harvard University Press, 1985).

11. Owen Fiss, "Groups and the Equal Protection Clause," *Journal of Philosophy and Public Affairs* 107 (1976): 107–77.

12. Ronald Dworkin, *Taking Rights Seriously* (Cambridge, Mass.: Harvard University Press, 1977).

13. Bruce Ackerman, *We the People: Foundations* (Cambridge, Mass.: Belknap, 1991).

14. Americans United for the Separation of Church and State: www.au .org/site/PageServer

15. American Federation of Scientists, "Project on Government Secrecy": www.fas.org/

16. American Civil Liberties Union: www.aclu.org/

17. Public Citizen, "Supreme Court Ruling in Mexico-Domiciled NAFTA Trucks Case Is a Loss for Communities on Both Sides of U.S.-Mexico Border," July 7, 2004: www.citizen.org/

18. *Hamdi v. Rumsfeld*, *Rasul v. Bush*, and *Al Odah v. United States*. In the case of *Hamdi v. Rumsfeld*, Scalia's dissenting view was based on the premise that the United States had been "invaded" on 9/11, justifying suspension of the writ of habeas corpus. Legal Information Institute, Scalia Dissent, *Hamdi v. Rumsfeld* (03-6696): www.law.cornell.edu/; People for the American Way, "Civil Rights and Civil Liberties in the Supreme Court's 2003-04 Term": www.pfaw.org/pfaw/ dfiles/file_435.pdf

19. People for the American Way, "Courting Disaster Report on the Supreme Court's 2001-02 Term. People for the American Way," www.commondreams .org/news2002/-702-04.htm

20. Howard Garcia, "In Bush vs. Gore Supreme Court Conservatives Bring Disgrace on Their Institution," *Boulder Daily Camera*, December 9, 2001: www .commondreams.org/views01/1209-03.htm

21. These are, in 2004: Alabama, Arizona, Arkansas, California, Colorado, Delaware, D.C., Massachusetts, Michigan, Mississippi, New Hampshire, New Mexico, Oklahoma, Texas, Vermont, West Virginia, Wisconsin.

22. James T. McHugh, *Ex Uno Plura: State Constitutions and Their Political Cultures* (Albany: State University of New York Press, 2003), 171, 208.

23. www.bambooweb.com/articles/s/t/State_law.html; emphasis added.

24. A legal creed that seemingly promotes neutrality, but in fact promotes the status quo, is constitutional literalism. Justice David Brewer described judges' approach in a speech before the New York Bar Association in 1893: "They make no laws, they establish no policy, they never enter into the domain of popular action. They do not govern. Their functions in relation to the State are limited to seeing

that popular action does not trespass upon right and justice as it exists in written constitutions and natural law." New York Bar Association, *Proceedings*, 1893, 46. Cited in Alan Pendleton Grimes, *American Political Thought* (New York: Holt, 1955), 449.

25. Alfred J. Rosenthal, "Afterward," in *Constitutionalism and Rights: The Influence of the United States Constitution Abroad*, ed. Louis Henkin and Albert J. Rosenthal (New York: Columbia University Press, 1990), 397–404.

26. Forrest McDonald, *A Constitutional History of the United States* (New York: Franklin Watts, 1982).

27. McHugh, *Ex Uno Plura*.

28. At issue in Spain is not conflicting laws, but the Basque region's desire for more autonomy.

29. Emilios Christodoulidis, "Constitutional Irresolution: Law and the Framing of Civil Society," *European Law Journal* 9 (2003): 401–32.

30. Romana Bester, "Comparison of Constitutional Minority Protection in the EU Member States," *Razprave in Gradivo—Treaties and Documents* 40 (2002): 40–71. Joseph Marko, "Minority Protection through Jurisprudence in Comparative Perspective," *Journal of European Integration* 25 (2003): 175–88; Janusz Symonides, *Cultural Rights: A Neglected Category of Human Rights*," *International Social Science Journal* 50 (1998): 559–72.

31. Andreas Fischer-Lescano, "A Global Constitution," *Zeitschrift fur Rechtssoziologie* 23 (2002): 217–49.

32. Anthony Ogus, "Property Rights and the Freedom of Economic Activity," in *Constitutionalism and Rights*, ed. Henkin and Rosenthal, 125–50.

33. Ogus, "Property Rights and the Freedom of Economic Activity," 127.

34. The power of governments to expropriate property is universally recognized, along with the due process clause. Taxation is a way of confiscating property, and about that, the U.S. Constitution has plenty to say, including the power of Congress to set and collect taxes, duties, imports, and excises (Article 1, Section 7); to borrow money (Article 1, Section 8); to regulate commerce (Article 1, Section 8); a tax on imported slaves (Article 1, Section 9, subsequently affected by Amendment XVI); the power of taxation (Article XVI); and the right to vote regardless of the citizen's tax status (Article XXIV). Article I, Section 8 also gives Congress the power to regulate the value of money and the power of appropriating money for raising and supporting armies.

35. Albert P. Blaustein and Jay A. Sigler, *Constitutions That Made History* (New York: Paragon House, 1988), 71.

36. Blaustein and Sigler, *Constitutions That Made History*, 117.

37. E. J. Hobsbawm, *Nations and Nationalism since 1780: Programme, Myth, Reality* (Cambridge: Cambridge University Press, 1990), 11–12.

38. Fidelis Edge Kanyongolo, "The Constitution and the Democratization Process in Malawi," in *The State and Constitutionalism in Southern Africa*, ed. Owen Sichone, 1–14 (Harare, Zimbabwe: Sapes Books, 1998); Laszlo Solyom, "The

Role of Constitutional Courts in the Transition to Democracy: With Special Reference to Hungary," *International Sociology* 18 (2003): 133–61; Matthew J. Moore, "Revisiting Constitutional Interpretation," *Studies in Law, Politics and Society* 28 (2003): 3–31.

39. Ilan Peleg, "Ethnic Constitutional Orders and Human Rights," in *Human Rights and Diversity*, ed. David P. Forsythe and Patrice C. McMahon (Lincoln: University of Nebraska Press, 2003): 279–96.

40. In the United States in the 1960s and 1970s the courts took the victim's perspective when they placed limitations on traditional rights—e.g., white businesses excluding customers who were black. But there was a shift from victim to perpetrator in the 1980s, requiring that a perpetrator be identified as an active agent in every unequal outcome. Courts required a cause and effect link to prove a rights violation. This shifted from a deracializing justice to a race-blind justice, thereby biasing the laws in favor of the white perpetrator. See: Kimberle Crenshaw, "Were the Critics Right about Rights?" in *Beyond Rights Talk and Culture Talk*, ed. Mahmood Mamdani, 61–74 (Cape Town, South Africa: David Philip Publishers, 2000).

41. Thomas Fleiner-Gerster, "Federalism, Decentralization and Rights," in *Constitutionalism and Rights*, ed. Henkin and Rosenthal, 19–38.

42. Richard A. Epstein, *Takings: Private Property and the Power of Eminent Domain* (Cambridge, Mass.: Harvard University Press, 1985).

43. Fiss, "Groups and the Equal Protection Clause."

44. Dworkin, *Taking Rights Seriously*.

45. Ackerman, *We the People: Foundations*.

46. Piers Ludlow, "All At Sea: The Meaning of 'Europe' in British Political Discourse," London School of Economics, April 18, 2000: www.iue.it/Personal/Strath/archive/archive_seminars/downloads/ludlow.doc

47. Andrew J. Crozier, "Britain, Germany and the Dishing of the Briand Plan," in *A Constitution for Europe*, ed. Preston King and Andrea Bosco, 213–31 (London: Lothian Foundation Press, 1991).

48. Winston Churchill, speech at Zurich University, 1946: www.europa.eu .int/abc/history/1946

49. Even earlier, Benelux (the Customs Union of Belgium, the Netherlands, and Luxembourg) started up, with the application of a common exterior tariff.

50. Council of the European Union, "Joint Report on Social Protection and Social Exclusion," March 23–24, 2005. See www.picum.org/HOMEPAGE/BreakingNews1.htm; ue.eu.int/ueDocs/cms_Data/docs/pressdata/en/misc/84273 .pdf

51. "The Schumanplan Declaration," EU History: Universiteit Leiden: www.eu-history.leidenuniv.nl/index.php3?m=10&c=29

52. www.spartacus.schoolnet.co.uk/2WWschumanP.htm

53. Treaty of Paris: europa.eu.int/abc/obj/treaties/en/entoc29.htm

54. The treaty that EURATOM instituted is much less important and tried to create "the conditions for the development of a strong nuclear industry." In reality, when we speak of the Rome Treaty, we are referring exclusively, although incorrectly, to that which created the EEC: europa.eu.int/abc/history/1957/index_en .htm

55. Additionally, the Rome Treaty prohibited monopolies and conceded some commercial privileges to the colonial territories of the member states.

56. European Governance: A White Paper, Commission of the European Communities, Brussels, July 25, 2001: europa.eu.int/comm/governance/white_paper/en.pdf

57. Sometimes called a subsidarity, referring roughly to a union in which states are constitutionally protected and operate on the basis of devolved decision-making power. Andrew Adonis, "Subsidiarity: Theory of a New Federalism?" in *A Constitution for Europe*, ed. King and Bosco, 63–75.

58. For example, see Global Policy Forum report: Stephen Castle, "EU Claims Historic Reform of European Agriculture, but Struggling Third World Farmers say Dumping Will Go On," June 27, 2003: www.globalpolicy.org/socecon/ffd/2003/0627claims.htm

59. Beginning a road toward a common policy of security and defense that will translate into the modification of NATO as a structure shared with the United States, but that has been split due to the war in Iraq.

60. euobserver.com/?sid=18&aid=18076

61. europa.eu.int/futurum/1000debates/

62. www.federalunion.org.uk/world/index.shtml;www.europeanmovement.org; www.federalism.ch

63. Mark Schapiro, "New Power for 'Old Europe.'" *The Nation* 279, 22, December 27, 2004: 11–15.

64. Robert A. Dahl, *How Democratic Is the American Constitution?* (New Haven, Conn.: Yale University Press, 2002), 41.

65. Dahl, *How Democratic Is the American Constitution?* 72.

66. Frantz Fanon, *Wretched of the Earth*, translated from the French by Richard Philcox, introductions by Jean-Paul Sartre and Homi K. Bhabha (New York: Grove Press, 2004).

Capitalism and Rights: An Antagonistic Relationship

M ary Wollstonecraft was appalled by mounting poverty in late eighteenth-century London, and outraged that Britain's leading thinker and eminent statesman, Edmund Burke, condoned poverty and growing inequalities. It was Burke's position that because national interests depend on free trade and free competition, economic inequalities were inevitable and inescapable. For Burke, the talented deserved their privileges and their property; the untalented deserved their conditions. It was only a matter of just desserts.

In her letter to the Right Honorable Edmund Burke, with her "blood boiling," she scoffs at his arguments as "factitious," "sophistic," "abominable," and "venomous." She also assails his liberal views about free competition, free trade, and property rights, insisting that economic rights be part of an egalitarian social compact. This was far from a private debate. Burke was a member of Parliament in 1790, a very public figure. Her letter took the form of a public pamphlet, *A Vindication of the Rights of Man*.[1] In it she framed her own political analysis detailing the wrongs of social hierarchies, property rights, economic inequalities, and oppression by the Church and State. For our purposes, her conception of "birthright" is especially important:

> [Economic security] is [t]he *birthright* of man, to give you, Sir, a short definition of this disputed right, is such a degree of liberty, civil and religious, as is compatible with the liberty of every other individual with whom he is united in a social compact, and the continued existence of that compact [emphasis added].[2]

Wollstonecraft may have been the first to defend economic rights as human rights, or as she put it "birthright." Yet she was not the first to have pointed a finger at capitalism as being a particularly devilish cause of unfair and unequal outcomes. Adam Smith recognized its insidious effects and admonished governments to keep capitalism in check, under the domination of society,[3] and John Locke had argued a century earlier that decent societies were equitable ones.[4] Adding to Smith's and Locke's arguments for equity was Wollstonecraft's special insight that capitalism legitimizes the very inequalities that it produces. That has not changed. Inherent in capitalism is the self-justification for the creation of inequalities because these inequalities alone engender the competition that capitalism requires to be dynamic, while holding out the seductive promise of future success to those that fail in today's round of competitive struggle.

She also provides her readers with the pathos of poverty and inequality, and what these imply for the social fabric:

> [Class divisions] are a destructive mildew that blights the fairest virtues; benevolence, friendship, generosity, and all those endearing charities which bind human hearts together, and the pursuits which raise the mind to higher contemplations, all that were not cankered in the bud by the false notions that grew with its growth and strengthened with its strength are crushed by the iron law of property![5]

Of course, there has never been a society without poverty, but under pre-capitalist conditions, inequality within society was never condoned, and there were always homegrown social mechanisms that promoted redistribution.[6] Inequality is, historically, a novelty, because in small-scale societies peoples' fates are intertwined and favorable collective outcomes depend on cooperative strategies. To paraphrase Richard Wollheim and Isaiah Berlin, it is equality, not inequality, that is a natural idea, and it is an idea that is ingrained in human societies.[7] They go on to say that this is because (a) humans are all members of one species, of a single class of objects (i.e., human beings) and (b) all members of a class should be treated uniformly unless there is a good and sufficient reason not to do so.

Granted, inequalities are not unique to capitalist states. After all, Aristotle rallied against inequalities in his *Politics*. Yet Mary Wollstonecraft, like Marx later, maintained that capitalist inequalities are uniquely inhumane and remediable. As she put it, the relations of property create enduring human schisms that fragment and rupture the social order, and estrange and divide humans, thereby blighting " benevolence, friendship, generosity, and all those endearing charities which bind human hearts together." The problem was caused and aggravated by property rights.

Marx incorporated this notion into his theory of value: property owners (whether they produce boots, linen, or any other commodity) stand in the same relation to others and in the same relation to labor, thereby dividing human society.[8] Marx better captured *why* property relations are the structural underpinnings of human estrangement, but it is Wollstonecraft who helps us understand *how* they do. While he is the political economist, she is the ethicist.

It bears repeating that when Americans refer to "rights" they refer to their legal and political rights vis-à-vis the state, not to what Wollstonecraft would term their "birthright" or what is now termed "human rights." Legal and political rights, advocated by Edmund Burke, legitimize and accompany the rights of economic actors to compete, not the rights of people to their economic security. In contrast, human rights rest on a conception that people require economic security and it draws on a social ethic of mutual recognition and regard. Legal and economic rights are inseparable in the liberal polity, and capitalism promotes the liberal state, just as the liberal state promotes capitalism.

Thesis

We will argue in this chapter that capitalism can only survive to the extent that it is protected by the liberal state, and further contend that capitalism cannot withstand globalization. This is counterintuitive, and flies in the face of prevailing interpretation of contemporary global capitalism. The conventional understanding is that global capitalism is inseparable from globalization (and open markets, and transnational global elites). In fact, globalization is defined as being simply the phenomenon of global capitalism.[9] One reason we give for the incompatibility of capitalism with a global economy is that when capitalism is loosened from its secure home base—the liberal polity—it encounters abundant social forms that are hostile to it. Societies are remarkably diverse and heterogeneous, and not all societies find capitalism congenial. A second reason is that the globe cannot withstand the mounting economic inequalities that globalization engenders. As we argue throughout the book, there are emergent social forms that are ascendant now and we can refer to them in the active sense, as social formations. They include antisystemic movements against the West, political and social movements, the activities of nongovernmental organizations (NGOs) and international nongovernmental organizations

(INGOs), and dynamic, emergent community forces. These social formations will pose insurmountable barriers to the advance of global capitalism. To convincingly make this case we need to lay some groundwork.

Basic Considerations

A parable, attributed to Karl Marx, goes like this: sell a man a fish, he eats for a day; but if you teach a man to fish, you ruin a wonderful business opportunity. While capitalist firms are working round the clock and around the globe to sell everything conceivable—including mercury-laced fish—abundant effort is going into teaching people to be their own producers. We might give a few examples of the many counter-capitalist undertakings that have prominently emerged within the last few years: open-source software, organic farm cooperatives, women's cooperatives, expanded cultivation of indigenous crops, self-sustaining energy sources, and domestic production of generic antiviral drugs.

Communities in partnership with NGOs are promoting sustainability over consumerism, and nation-states are beginning to make it difficult for multinationals to exploit local labor and denigrate the environment. Nations are beginning to subject multinationals to upholding labor and environmental rights, although they do so at their peril because multinationals may pull up stakes and leave. Nevertheless, transnational cooperation is just beginning to take shape, particularly within regional blocks, such as the Association of Southeast Asian Nations (ASEAN), the New Partnership for Africa's Development (NEPAD), the Andean Community, Mercado Comun del Cono Sur/Southern Cone Common Market (Mercosur), and the European Union (EU). Although none of these is intent on destroying global capitalism, they are intent on reforming it.

It is important to recognize that economic development in the twenty-first century is very different from economic development in the industrializing period in the West. Industries, factories, production, bureaucratic coordination, and distribution in the classical capitalist period were all organized from the top down. Economic development under contemporary conditions can be achieved at the ground level. The technology is small, and recent developments in nanotechnology, solar energy panels, and polymer construction materials make possible local and flexible use and adoption. The prototypical technology of this century does not depend on centralization and spatial fixity as did the earlier steam engine, assembly line, and steel mills. New technologies lend themselves to local control over production, and, therefore, co-ownership and collectivization. Now we need to backtrack a bit to consider the disjointedness between capitalist forms that were bound to the nation-state, as they were until recently.

From the Mid-Twentieth Century to the Early Twenty-first Century

In the 1950s many progressive Europeans and Americans shared the view that their own older democracies would help launch egalitarian economic programs around the world that would lift people out of poverty everywhere, and not in ways that the Marxian adage has it, by "selling them fish," but instead by "teaching them how to fish." The idea was that this would be achieved through technology transfer and economic development. According to one of Britain's foremost progressive thinkers, R. H. Tawney, nationwide and worldwide sharing of *opportunities* would promote egalitarian outcomes. Specifically, he concluded in the 1964 edition of his 1931 classic, *Equality*, that policies that aim to broadly share opportunities achieve two ends. They "not only subtract from inequality, but add to freedom."[10] Richard M. Titmus points out in his introduction to this second edition that many on both sides of the Atlantic had high hopes for peoples' freedoms and for economic and social equality.[11] They believed that a benevolent capitalism would expand peoples' opportunities for starting their own businesses, jobs, and educations, and would improve agricultural and industrial production around the world.

There were reasons for optimism. By the end of the implementation of the Marshall Plan, industrial production in Europe was up 52 percent over its prewar levels;[12] Japan had adopted a democratic constitution that committed it to renouncing war and the use of force; and both Germany and Italy were democratically governed within frameworks of stable, multiparty systems. Decolonization, which had earlier been achieved in Latin America, accelerated dramatically elsewhere: first in Asia, notably, India and Indonesia, and then in Africa. The signing of the Charter of the United Nations by fifty-one states in June 1945 seemed to many to mark the beginning of a global peaceful order, and while many held out hopes for a socialist-market economy, others assumed it would be capitalist, but with a human face.

Capitalism had its critics even among Western, non-Marxist intellectuals. Max Weber wrote, "The question is: how are freedom and democracy in the long run at all possible under the domination of highly developed capitalism?"[13] Other Western critics denounced the non-freedoms of workers, alienation from production, the poverty that capitalism generated, and the ideological self-deception of the bourgeoisie. However, as Seymour Melman sums up the dominant Western view of that era, capitalism was considered a set of elaborate rules about ownership, property rights, and profits that could not efficiently include workers' rights.[14] We do not disagree with Melman's diagnosis, but we also believe that capitalism, especially American capitalism, depended not only on rules that excluded worker participation, but also on cultural values that were only weakly tied to the institutions of capitalism but helped, nonetheless, to legitimize these institutions. We believe that owners and workers in America shared these values that legitimized capitalism and inequalities. Were it not for this, capitalism would never have survived the shocks that it did, especially the Great Depression. Instead, capitalism thrived, and was broadly legitimate. Indeed, it transformed itself triumphantly, as neoliberalism, beginning around the Reagan administration, and accelerating during Clinton's and George W. Bush's administrations.

Liberal political, cultural, and social ideology in America played a great role in allowing capitalism to triumph as it did. As we have argued, a liberal ideology promotes the view that the economy and individual freedom function best if neither the state nor society intervenes. This view, or rather, ideology, remains pervasive in America. To the extent that this ideology wedded the larger economy with individual freedoms, a wide range of practices were also legitimate: privatization of collective goods, unrestricted movement of capital, accumulation of wealth, as well as poverty and inequalities.

The consequences, we believe, are easy to document for contemporary America. All the countries that went through the long transition of industrialization and urbanization did so more or less at the same time—the United States, all European countries, Canada, New Zealand, Australia—and others followed suit in twentieth century—Eastern European countries, Japan, Korea, India, and most Middle Eastern countries. Of all of these, the United States has the greatest economic inequalities. It also has the highest rate of children living in poverty. These comparisons ought to be humiliating for any American, but they are explicable. Only in America were inequalities condoned to the extent that they were and continue to be. The American ethos is that people have their freedoms to sink or swim, and if they sink, and fall prey to the shark of poverty and destitution, it is their own fault. But, if they make millions, it is to their credit. Sooner or later Americans will wake from this grand delusion—as Marx would say, false consciousness—that poverty is deserved, wealth is earned, and the gap between the homeless and the billionaires reflects "just desserts."

The consequences of global capitalism are the same worldwide as they are in the United States. Yet these consequences are more vicious elsewhere because global capitalist actors have freer reign and fewer encumbrances in Third World countries than they do in the United States or in any of the countries that earlier adopted capitalism. Neoliberalism encounters less initial resistance because national leaders are eager to have employment for their workers and to develop their national economies. During approximately the last twenty-five or thirty years, poor countries have not had a choice but to go along with privatization and they have opened up their borders to multinationals and financiers. Without resistance and without setting limits, this has created havoc.

Simply to illustrate, we can describe a deal that the United States imposed on Mexico whereby the United States would export its subsidized genetically modified (GM) corn to Mexico, which would "encourage" *campesinos* to leave their villages and go to work in the U.S.-owned factories. It did not work out that way. U.S.-owned factories have been rapidly leaving Mexico, pursuing cheaper labor in China. However, the price of tortillas, the staple food, increased five-fold as the imported corn was expensive. Without cash, the living standards of rural Mexicans plummeted, compounded by joblessness at the border where firms were closing. Additionally, evidence of GM maize contamination appeared in Mexico 2001, threatening the native varieties. However, *campesinos* that remained in their rural villages are forced to buy seeds if they used any that were GM, because these varieties do not yield seeds.[15]

The cumulative effects of U.S. policies in Mexico were devastating: unemployment, higher food costs, and dependence on high-priced seeds. Additionally, having created economic havoc in Mexico, the United States increasingly implements a schizophrenic migration policy—both encouraging migration and militarizing the border with Mexico. More generally, it is becoming increasingly evident that the worldwide liberalizing economy is creating massive social upheavals and economic destitution. To survive the onslaught, many children and women have no choice but to become virtual slaves in the sex trade, the healthiest of poor families must migrate, and many turn to terrorism against the West as ways of defending their own societies against the massive social and cultural destruction that is caused by the marketization of entire societies and social relations within them.

By marketization of societies and social relations, we refer to the destruction of social institutions and social norms of cooperation and trust. Pierre Bourdieu described neoliberalism in these terms: "in the name of a narrow and strict conception of rationality as individual rationality, it brackets the economic and social conditions of rational orientations and the economic and social structures that are the condition of their application." It is, he says, "A program for destroying collective structures."[16] Perhaps with somewhat more accuracy, we could say it has become *a pogrom of destruction*, not simply a program. Yet we wish to stress that what has helped to legitimize neoliberal economic policies is American liberalism. It is so deeply entrenched in American society that Americans fail to see its implications for inequality and its adverse effects on social relations, communities, and human habitats.

The American Case

Affluence

There is no question that the United States is the richest country in the entire world. Its workers and families have historically done well because the nation had vast territory that could be exploited for its resources, such as minerals, timber, oil, and abundant fertile lands. Through much of American history, the valve that controlled immigration was easily switched on and off, making it possible to fine-tune the labor supply to protect Americans' jobs or to make sure that Americans have the best jobs. Native workers, and more specifically, native white workers have historically done very well.

But like their counterparts in industrializing Europe, which is the apt comparison here, white American workers struggled to achieve their rights, and capitalist employers only begrudgingly granted rights. These were collective struggles, and through the long period of industrialization, workers fought for and often achieved their rights in solidarity with one another, in strikes, walkouts, protests, but always collectively. Labor historian Herbert G. Gutman describes the working class solidarity that sustained workers and their families over generations and even over centuries.[17] Yet in America, as he also describes, this culture of solidarity was often undermined by other formidable beliefs, namely those of individualism, but also racism and xenophobia. Additionally, worker solidarity became suspect in the United States during the Cold War, just as socialism did.

During the middle decades of the twentieth century, and following the devastation of World War II, many European states were adopting pro-worker policies and many revised their constitutions to grant workers certain rights and in keeping with the provisions of their welfare states. However, the U.S. Congress was hostile to all such reform. The United States had too much at stake in its ideological battle with the Soviet Union to grant workers formal rights.[18] At the end of the twentieth century and into the twenty-first century, the economic rights of Americans declined owing to the rapid restructuring of American businesses. While plants close and move offshore, hire overseas workers, eliminate pension and benefit plans, and retrofit operations to eliminate employees, most Americans experience growing uncertainties, decline in the quality of their lives and health, and often, joblessness.[19]

Capitalism

Poverty and joblessness in America are differently experienced than elsewhere. In the United States, poverty and joblessness are considered individual problems, as personal failings. Elsewhere poverty and joblessness are considered to be collective problems requiring collective solutions. Additionally, in much of the Third World, joblessness is defined as a problem created by capitalism. This makes perfect sense. A drought can bring as much misery as factory layoffs do, but only the gods can be blamed for the drought and all workers know full well that capitalists, not gods, are responsible when a factory closes its doors. The success of capitalism in the West has rested on the conception that risks and gains are individuated. This is the core of Max Weber's brilliant thesis about the origins of capitalism.[20] But Weber's thesis was about the legitimization of capitalism within society, and we can see, with hindsight, that capitalists could in turn act on that presumption and abdicate responsibility for the harms that capitalism causes.

By individuating risk and abdicating responsibilities, capitalism generates poverty just as it generates wealth, and it does so at uneven rates accompanying cycles of over- and underproduction (often termed Kondratieff cycles, after the Russian statistician[21]). It was Britain that first responded to capitalism's cyclical production of poverty, introducing paupers' laws in the nineteenth century and welfare programs in the early twentieth century. It was only after the Great Depression that the United States implemented welfare programs, in particular for the aged and unemployed. However, from their very beginnings, American welfare programs were comparatively ungenerous.

These programs were also racist, as Jill Quadagno shows.[22] In the original Social Security Act, blacks were largely excluded by virtue of the occupations they were in, and in the postwar Housing and Urban Development program, they were excluded by virtue of the neighborhoods they lived in. The Aid to Families and Dependent Children (AFDC) program explicitly provided disincentives for women to marry. Welfare programs carried out, albeit more subtly, the segregationist antiblack strategies of the South.

Additionally, while some welfare programs, notably AFDC, targeted poor minorities, a myriad of opportunity programs—including educational loan programs and low-interest mortgage loans—were designed for the white middle class. In contrast, the classic European model was designed for all social classes, crossing the lines of the rich and poor, with subsidized education, child care, health care, and public transportation while taxing the rich higher in order to pay for them. What this accomplishes is the expansion of the availability and quality of collective, in contrast to private, goods. Indirectly, it keeps the public sphere vibrant and diverse, because all have stakes in maintaining the collective welfare. The European model also increases resilience within the population because of the safeguards against, among other things, homelessness and poverty. In contrast, in America, where the rich pay relatively low taxes and where many basic amenities are privatized, the gap between the poor and rich is wide and getting wider. Additionally, the rich retreat from civil society, reducing further their commitment to the collective welfare.

Legislation in Congress these days has the stamp of corporate interests, from bills for the military budget (which benefit the producers of war paraphernalia, such as Boeing, and contractors, such as Halliburton) to bills for reforming Social Security (which would be a bonanza to the financial sector). This is because corporations are the major contributors to political campaigns, and Congress is an enthusiastic supporter of American corporations. To simply illustrate, credit card companies, led by MENA, gave generously to the campaigns of members of Congress in return for their voting against a bill that would reform the bankruptcy laws and benefit the country's very lowest wage earners. MENA was the biggest corporate donor to the Bush campaign.[23] MENA got its way. It is important to put current practices in their historical context to understand that they are not an aberration. The Republicans during the George W. Bush era have simply used the tools that were already available to them. We earlier described the centrality of corporate personhood rights in interpretations of the Constitution. Additionally, U.S. corporations benefit from government largesse, in the form of tax reductions, tax write-offs, local and state development grants, and subsidized training and legal services.

American political and social culture has naturalized the rights of capital while denaturalizing the rights of workers, but this has been a process and did not happen overnight. Yet the process is comprehensible within the overarching frame of liberalism, which considers inequalities of outcome as just desserts of variation in individuals' "inputs" (education, effort, perseverance), a corollary of the premise that opportunities are ubiquitous. In this liberal milieu there is no stopping capitalism. Anticipating the conclusion of this chapter, capitalism has triumphed over society, if what we mean by society are varied practices, social connectedness, and public spheres and spaces protected from commodification and marketization, and so long as we refer only to the United States. Few nation-states have societies that are as compatible with capitalism as the United States is because few started out with a comparable emphasis on liberalism. Great Britain, Australia, and Canada come the closest.

Workers' Rights

In 1943 Franklin Delano Roosevelt proposed to Congress a piece of legislation titled "The Economic Bill of Rights." This truly remarkable document probably had a ghost of a chance only at this precise time in American history. We will describe this bill below, but it essentially outlined key rights that were later enshrined in the Universal Declaration of Human Rights and the International Covenant on Economic, Social, and Cultural Rights. The reasons we suspect that it could conceivably have had a chance are probably identical to those Roosevelt had for proposing it when he did.

The nation had survived a crippling depression, and there had been great loss of human life in Pacific and European battles. Still in the midst of war, both with Germany and Japan, the country was united as it had never been before, and Roosevelt may have hoped that such unity would find expression in a desire for creating conditions for greater equality. His hopes were no doubt strengthened by the success of his earlier legislation that greatly helped lift people out of poverty that followed in the wake of the Great Depression: relief for farmers, land purchasing program for tenants, the National Industrial Recovery Act (which guaranteed the rights to collective bargaining), the Works Project Administration and the Federal Writers' Project (both of which provided employment), and the Federal Emergency Relief Administration (for public projects).

In a recent book, Cass R. Sunstein describes the efforts that Roosevelt made in 1943 to enact legislation, the "Economic Bill of Rights," that would include fundamental rights, especially for labor.[24] A hint of this proposed legislation came nearly two years earlier in his State of the Union address on January 6, 1941. In it, Roosevelt advanced four essential human freedoms, two of which draw from the U.S. Bill of Rights: specifically, freedom of speech and expression, and freedom to worship. A third would be freedom from fear, and it would be achieved by the worldwide reduction of armaments. The fourth was "freedom from want," which he translated into world terms as economic understandings to promote a healthy peacetime life for every nation's inhabitants.[25] He argued, "essential to peace is a decent standard of living for all individual men and women and children in all nations. Freedom from fear is eternally linked with freedom from want."[26]

Later that year, he asked the National Resources Planning Board (NRPB) to develop a set of proposals—a "Second Bill of Rights"—somewhat along the lines of his "four freedoms" talk, adding in his instructions to the NRPB that this new bill of rights would apply without discrimination, irrespective of race, creed, or color. This Second Bill of Rights was sent to Congress in March 1943, and is summarized in appendix 4.1.[27]

Its provisions anticipate the 1948 Universal Declaration of Human Rights and many of the constitutional provisions of other states. It includes the right to work (item 1); the right to fair play (item 2); the right to adequate food, clothing, housing rights, and medical care (item 3); the right to security, with freedom from fear of old age, want, dependency, illness, unemployment, and accident (item 4); right to education for many purposes, including work, citizenship, personal growth, and happiness (item 8); and the right to rest, recreation, and adventure, to enjoy life and take part in advancing civilization (item 9). It also restates some of the provisions that are either implied or stated in the U.S. Constitution's Bill of Rights, including free enterprise (item 5), freedom of movement (item 6), and equality before the law (item 7).

Again we want to emphasize that this document anticipates the range of protections that became known as "socioeconomic rights" that are included in the Universal Declaration and the International Covenant on Economic, Social, and Cultural Rights, such as the rights to a decent job, medical care, and security through old age. The bill never made it out of Congress, and the NRPB itself was abolished several months later. Although the Second Bill of Rights was not at all popular with Congress, Roosevelt's thinking played an important role in subsequent discussions at the United Nations, and Eleanor Roosevelt served on the committee to draft the Universal Declaration, which started its work in 1947. Her role, according to Sunstein, in drafting the Four Freedoms speech and the Second Bill of Rights will never be known, but regardless, the bill was unique in American history for envisioning that economic and social security ought to be the responsibility of the nation.[28]

America and the Cold War

As we have implied, America's economy bustled along through the decades of the Cold War, and Americans thumbed their noses at the Soviets ("commies") and tooted at the Europeans for "putting people on the dole." Though the United States signed the Universal Declaration, which affirms all persons' socioeconomic rights, this declaration is not a treaty, but an affirmation of desired goals, and the United States refused to sign any treaty that embodied social and economic rights. (Treaties have mechanisms to advance implementation and compliance.)

Thus, if anything, the liberal ideology became more sharply defined, even polarized, during the Cold War because it was politically manipulated and strengthened as being at odds with collectivism, socialism, and communism. There was not just one subtext, but many, as is so often the case in ideological struggles. One went something like this: "Capitalism is for rugged, macho, Protestant types, whereas Socialism is for sissy, lazy types." Another was: "Having economic rights only coddles people." These various Cold War subtexts drew on religious differences, entrepreneurial qualities, patriotism, and imagery about American economic freedoms as being related to political freedoms. The Cold War was not only political; it was also about the defense of capitalism.

Materialism also played a crucial role in mobilizing the U.S. population around capitalism. John Kenneth Galbraith was probably the first to recognize the importance of commodities and commodification during the Cold War years.[29] In *The Affluent Society*, he argued that the capitalist economy was self-legitimizing through the abundance of cheap commodities that artificially induce wants—that is, the wants for oversized automobiles, clothing fashion, gadgets, novel household appliances, and abundant other paraphernalia. The connections between materialism, capitalism, and patriotism were never so crudely made as they were by George W. Bush. Within days after 9/11 he told the national audience that the best thing they could do was go to the malls and shop.

American foreign policy during the Cold War was explicitly fine-tuned to protect capitalist expansion. The battle with communism raged for over several decades, fueled for a while by McCarthy's dramatic attempts to "hunt down communists," but also by accounts by leading academics of how capitalism would bring riches to the entire world, after triumphing over evil. In 1960, the prominent economist Walt Whitman Rostow published *The Stages of Economic Growth: A Non-Communist Manifesto*.[30] In it Rostow laid out the great virtues of capitalism at home, advocated for worldwide capitalism, and raged against communism, collectivism, and socialism. Capitalism throughout most of the twentieth century drew for legitimacy on several simple assumptions: opportunities were abundant for any that availed themselves of them; economic freedom was sufficient for well-being; material acquisition was a sign of economic achievement, while "going on welfare" was a sign of personal failing.

Again, in the early twenty-first century, economic inequalities approach what they were before the Great Depression and exceed what they were in the years between the two world wars.[31] Yet, the federal and state programs that formerly provided a modicum of support to those in dire circumstances are rapidly shrinking and sometimes disappearing. Just as Mary Wollstonecraft described, when free markets command the economy, they advantage the rich and disadvantage the poor, and aggravate existing inequalities. This occurs anyway under free-market conditions, but is particularly devastating when the rich are already initially advantaged (through, for example, relatively low taxes) and the poor are already initially disadvantaged (through for example, wages that lag behind increases in the cost of living).

The Promise of Globalization

In the early years of globalization, there was great optimism. Globalization promised to bring great benefits to the world's population by integrating poor nations into global markets, creating new trading partnerships, providing employment for workers, and helping to stabilize local economies. However, disillusionment has set in and even those economists who were optimistic in the 1970s and 1980s that poor nations could harness foreign investments and production to meet the needs of their populations are now pessimistic.[32]

Little did the optimists realize through the 1970s and 1980s that the rules of global capitalism were changing. A brief account of the differences is useful. Capitalism has always faced crisis of accumulation, or overexpansion in production and excesses of inventory, but it met these crises by stimulating demand (sales) through production (with high employment) and running down inventories (with layoffs and unemployment).

These cycles have persisted nearly from the beginning of capitalism, but there has also been a secular trend adversely affecting labor. As firms invested in new technologies, they could get by with fewer workers. These rules held so long as capitalist producers depended on local labor, but fell apart when production became, through global commodity chains, international. To illustrate this, no car today is made within a given country; rather its parts are outsourced to firms around the world and then assembled quickly at a given location.[33] These economic cycles that affect production are beyond the reach of nation-states to regulate or buffer their effects on populations, and capital itself is global, which likewise weakens the capabilities of the nation-state to regulate its own economy. The cycles can now be manipulated by large multinationals so that they are local, not global, which makes it possible for large multinationals to avoid them. They simply move locations to take advantage of over- and underemployment, over- and underinventories, and over- and underproduction.

Has Globalization Broken Capitalism?

According to some economists, we cannot evaluate these current trends as being continuous with capitalist expansion.[34] We wish to push their argument a bit further by contending that the global economy of today is very different from the capitalism that preceded it up until around the 1970s, with the introduction of global production, deregulation of international currency exchange rates, just-in-time assembly, and computerization of production. Today Wal-Mart coordinates production, sales, and distribution by satellite![35] This is a very different kind of capitalism than that under which industrialization occurred.

To highlight our premise, we will argue that capitalism "broke" in the 1970s and its contemporary, globalized version, neoliberalism, is quite different in terms of the rules under which it operates. Most simply, the connections involving owners, managers, workers, transporters, and consumers are so attenuated that the process has been completely depersonalized, so that satellites track these relationships, and computer programmers are in charge of production, distribution, and sales. Another way of looking at this is that neoliberalism has become detached from humans, communities, and societies. It is hard to see that neoliberalism, being detached from abundant, myriad societies, can possibly survive what it has created. The sheer diversity among and within societies challenges the cold logic of neoliberalism, which can only apply to markets. People will not tolerate the stresses to which they are subjected.

Of course, we rely greatly on Karl Marx's thesis that capitalism will self-destruct owing to its own internal contradictions, but our thesis is somewhat different in that we see these contradictions as involving societal complexities as well as capitalist logic. When Marx considered worldwide capitalism, it was not the sort that penetrated deeply into virtually every community. In the nineteenth century, when he wrote, capitalism did especially penetrate into leading liberal nation-states—Britain and the United States—and somewhat into European countries, but mainly affected urban elites in Asia, Latin America, and elsewhere. The penetration of neoliberalism into every nook and cranny so threatens societies that it will begin to experience great opposition. Indeed it already has, as is evident in the many formations that oppose it, including the World Social Forum, some governments, NGOs, labor unions, and many political and social movements.

Lessons from History and a Closer Look at Neoliberalism

It was not inevitable that the transition from capitalism to global capitalism would involve neoliberalism, or the sovereignty of pure market principles and the subordination of society to markets. In this regard it is useful to briefly sketch the accounts of economists that help to explain the transition from industrial capitalism to global capitalism. Industrial capitalism was not what Edmund Burke had hoped it would become; at the end of the nineteenth century it was already evident that populations needed protecting, and this is what the Keynesian reforms did in Britain and Roosevelt's reforms did in the United States. Indeed, it has been argued that Keynes and Roosevelt together saved capitalism, for if they had not provided populations with some security, people would have revolted.

Most of the twentieth century was, therefore, an easy truce between capitalism and the welfare state. The structural dynamics changed in the 1970s with deindustrialization in the United States, which was simply one expression of globalization. Bennett Harrison and Barry Bluestone were among the first economists to capture the full significance of the structural dynamics underlying the shift to the global economy in their 1986 book *The Great U-Turn*.[36] They described how deindustrialization—the exit of manufacturing to other countries—along with the privatization of the public sector—"zapped labor," and the vast new worldwide speculation in currency, stocks, and land, which resulted from the abandonment of the Bretton Woods agreements in the early 1970s.

The next shift involved a move away from what we could call a "supervised global economy" to something called "the New Economy" (under the first Reagan and Thatcher administrations) which was a movement toward further liberalization, and then, soon after, to neoliberalism, a further radical move to free up markets even more and to push governments into reforms that would accommodate these markets. Doug Henwood believes that the term *New Economy* was used first in a speech that Ronald Reagan gave at Moscow State University in 1988, bestowing it with religious mysticism:

> In the new economy, human invention increasingly makes physical resources obsolete. We're breaking through the material condition of existence to a world where man creates his own destiny. Even as we explore the most advanced reaches of science, we're returning to the age-old wisdom of our culture, a wisdom contained in the Genesis in the Bible. In the beginning was the spirit, and it was from this spirit that the material abundance of creation issued forth.[37]

Later, the term *New Economy* became *Neoliberalism* to describe the further radicalizing of economic policies, namely, an endorsement of market freedoms for commodities regardless of the consequences and a cynical protectionist approach to financial markets. In the United States, and elsewhere, this has led to a dramatic increase in economic inequalities, job loss, and the dismantlement of welfare programs.[38]

Similarly, inequalities rose dramatically in Latin America, Europe, some African countries, Russia, Iran, Turkey, and Korea. James K. Galbraith and Jiaqing Lu conclude that inequality was rising everywhere, the only major exceptions being China and India. They write, "In a liberalized and globalized world economy, only a general compression of earnings structures can create an environment where equalization prevails on the global development scene."[39] The liberalization of financial markets, severing the dollar's link to gold, destabilized developing countries as "hot money" zoomed in and out of countries to maximize returns in very short periods of time,[40] severely destabilizing countries' economies, contributing, for example, to the Asian crisis, and huge distortions in trade and outflows in currency.

The end result, according to Doug Henwood, led to an extreme concentration of wealth, cycles of boom and bust in poor countries, and a stock-centered world dominated by banks, multinationals, and big investors. He notes that basically it is a system designed to drive down costs and maximize the flow of profits to shareholders.[41] The World Bank, which, after all, helped to spearhead globalization, along with the International Monetary Fund,[42] now concludes that (neoliberal) globalization has led not only to an unacceptable level of worldwide inequalities, but that it also "has led to a decline in global world growth."[43]

A Reassessment of the Thesis

As Vandana Shiva states, "Globalization is a break from all earlier stages of human relationships with the earth and her resources."[44] As she implies, global capitalism is very different from world capitalism, and we must understand it *sui generis* not so much as a continuous development but as the evolution of an economic system that began with the expansion of trade and commerce in the sixteenth century. Nevertheless, there is nothing inevitable about globalization. We have posed two distinct but related contradictions that undermine the logic of global capitalism.

First, free markets are designed to work impersonally, subject only to financial constraints and driven by efficiency, and while this may be compatible with Western, and perhaps, Asian economic culture, we do not believe it is elsewhere. Computers control complex commodity chains, production, distribution, and sales. A sale of a Barbie doll in Ghana triggers a switch in a computer on a satellite to adjust the production of a Barbie doll and the restocking of the store in Ghana. The production itself takes place in a global network—say, body parts in Sri Lanka, clothes in the Philippines, and assembly in Puerto Rico. Promoting demand in a particular place works by the same principle. iPods are shipped to various outlets around the globe, advertised, and when sold, restocked in the same way that the Barbie doll was restocked. One might conclude that such hegemonic commodifcation will dominate the world. But we don't believe it for a moment. People come to realize it is manipulative and destructive of local practices, tastes, and sensibilities. Besides, these production and consumption chains circumvent social relations, locales, and community. It is inconceivable that people the world over will fall into line.

The legitimization of capitalist markets, impersonal exchanges, and mass markets is rooted in long-standing Western values dealing with the sovereignty of individual choice, materialism, efficiency, and status consciousness. Much of the rest of the world, hardly implicated in the West's long history with consumer capitalism and little enamored with Western commodities, will be taken in by the glitter and glitz of what capitalists have to sell. Of course, that is not entirely true. Anything that has to do with communications—cell phones, computers, the Internet—is widely embraced, especially in Third World countries. The evidence is not all in, but accounts suggest that communications products are being used in poor countries to build robust social networks and for community empowerment. The processes that we have described dealing with impersonal markets and lack of legitimacy for Western goods and the way they are produced suggest that capitalism itself will become entangled in its own contradictions. The central point is free markets have evolved to the point where they are hermetically sealed from the populations they need to reach for capitalism to survive.

Second, capitalism has always needed to expand, but its expansion historically has been industrial, agricultural, cars and appliances, extractive commodities (such as oil and minerals), and only to a limited extent in consumer products such as clothes, toys, housewares, games, and household gadgets. To reach mass markets, which it must to be efficient and profitable, the capitalist enterprise needs to reach every corner of the globe with its Barbies, its household garlic presses, dress designs, T-shirts, baby bibs, dog toys, and barbeque gadgets. This is doomed to failure because of the infinite variety of societies, all of which have many tastes, cultures, traditions, religious codes, and social practices.

These are contradictions in the logic of global capitalism, similar to those that Marx identified in the logic of classical capitalism. Yet, we see now that these contradictions loom larger because they not only involve capitalism itself, but the relations between capitalism, on the one hand, with a myriad of societies on the other. By its very nature, capitalism abhors particularities, local variation, diversity, and heterogeneity. We cannot think that capitalism can withstand the onslaught of societies. One indication of the power of these contradictions is that Western consumers are uniting in solidarity with workers elsewhere to promote fair trade over free trade, sustainable communities, fair wages, environmental preservation, and indigenous crops. This counter-capitalist movement cannot be underestimated.

Summary

Harry Braverman wrote the following assessment of capitalism in 1974: "the capitalist mode of production takes over the totality of individual, family, and social needs and, in subordinating them to the market, also reshapes them to serve the needs of capital."[45] About two decades later, Pierre Bourdieu provided a similar critical assessment of neoliberal, global capitalism, yet with more optimism, concluded: "[A new social order] that will not have as its only law the pursuit of egoistic interests and the individual passion for profit and that will make room for collectives oriented toward *the rational pursuit of ends collectively arrived at and collectively ratified.*"[46]

Far more now than when Braverman wrote, there is hope that collectivities will be ascendant and will prevail over raw, ruthless capitalism. We believe that global capitalism has more contradictions than did its earlier versions, and furthermore, national governments are aligning themselves with their citizens and in opposition to their economic elites. We will be clarifying this in subsequent chapters in which we present materials from state constitutions. However, these struggles do not take place solely within nations. These struggles are internationalized in partnerships by large-scale social and political movements (such as those that are spawned by the World Social Forum), INGOs, and in regional alliances, such as NEPAD for African countries, and Mercosur and the Andean Community for Latin American countries. Moreover, there are formal international frameworks for advancing labor rights. There are two stories to tell here. One is the obstructionist role played by the United States, while the second is the continuing significance of international frameworks that advance the rights of people to their security and dignity.

Our main thesis, however, is that global capitalism is facing two crises of its own making. The first is that the concentration of wealth is draining the world of its resources, and the second is that neoliberalism cannot face the abundant diversity of human societies. Besides, counter-capitalist movements are everywhere evident.

Notes

1. Mary Wollstonecraft, *A Vindication of the Rights of Men with a Vindication of the Rights of Woman and Hints* (Cambridge: Cambridge University Press, [1790] 1995).

2. Wollstonecraft, *A Vindication*, 7.

3. Adam Smith, *The Wealth of Nations* (New York: Random House, [1789] 1937), 51, 55, 118–20, 134–35, 142–43.

4. John Locke, *Second Treatise of Government* (Indianapolis, Ind.: Hackett Publishing, [1690] 1980), 23.

5. Wollstonecraft, *A Vindication*, 23.

6. James C. Scott, *The Moral Economy of the Peasant* (New Haven, Conn.: Yale University Press, 1976).

7. Richard Wollheim and Isaiah Berlin, "Equality: Parts 1-2," *Aristotelian Society for the Systematic Study of Philosophy* (London) 56 (1955–1956): 281–326.

8. Karl Marx, *Capital, Vol. 1* (Moscow: Progress Publishers, [1887] 1954), 82.

9. Globalization is far beyond the control of nation-states. Perhaps most clearly summarized by William I. Robinson, globalization is transnational, as the very process annihilates space and time barriers, creating far-flung production and distribution chains, with power and wealth concentrated in a transnational capitalist class. William I. Robinson, *A Theory of Global Capitalism* (Baltimore, Md.: Johns Hopkins University Press, 2004).

10. R. H. Tawney, *Equality* (London: Unwin Books, 1964), 235.

11. Richard M. Titmus, "Introduction," in Tawney, *Equality*.

12. Jan Palmowski, *Oxford Dictionary of Contemporary World History* (Oxford: Oxford University Press, 2003), 414.

13. Max Weber, *From Max Weber*, trans. and ed. H. H. Gerth and C. Wright Mills (London: Routledge, 1948), 71.

14. Seymour Melman, *After Capitalism* (New York: Knopf, 2001).

15. Laura Carlsen, "The People of the Corn," *New Internationalist* 374 (2004): 12–13.

16. Pierre Bourdieu, "Utopia of Endless Exploitation: The Essence of Neoliberalism," *Le Monde Diplomatique,* December 1998: mondediplo.com/1998/12/08bourdieu

17. Herbert G. Gutman, *Work, Culture, and Society in Industrializing America* (New York: Random House, 1976).

18. Youcef Bouandel, *Human Rights and Comparative Politics* (Aldershot, U.K.: Dartmouth Publishing, 1997), 16–18.

19. Edmund F. Byrne, *Work, Inc.* (Philadelphia: Temple University Press, 1990).

20. Max Weber, *The Protestant Ethic and the Spirit of Capitalism* (New York: Scribner, [1904–1905] 1930).

21. Nathan H. Mager, *Kondratieff Waves* (New York: Praeger, 1987).

22. Jill Quadagno, "Creating a Capital Investment State," *American Sociological Review* 64 (1999): 1–11; also see Herbert J. Gans, *The War against the Poor* (New York: Basic, 1995), 74–102.

23. Philip Shenon, "It's Pay Back Time: Lobbying Campaign Led by Credit Card Companies and Banks Nears Bankruptcy Bill Goal," *New York Times,* March 13, 2001: http://www.commondreams.org/headlines01/0313-02.htm

24. Cass R. Sunstein, *The Second Bill of Rights: FDR's Unfinished Revolution and Why We Need It More Than Ever* (New York: Basic, 2004).

25. Sunstein, *The Second Bill of Rights*, 81.

26. Sunstein, *The Second Bill of Rights*, 11.

27. H.R. 1040, "A Living Wage, Jobs for All Act" was introduced in February 2003. Sponsored by Barbara Lee of California, along with twenty-five cosponsors, it states:

REAFFIRMING BASIC rights—To reaffirm public discourse on the human rights proclaimed by President Roosevelt more than half a century earlier, express them in terms that have been developed in more recent years and, as part of the bridges to the twenty-first century, affirm basic rights regarding dignity, personal security, collective bargaining, the environment, information, and voting. Declares that the Congress affirms the basic economic rights and responsibilities under the 1944 "Economic Bill of Rights," while updating and extending it to include: (1) certain rights to decent jobs, income security for individuals unable to work for pay, a decent living for farm families, freedom from monopolies, decent housing, adequate health services, social security in old age, sickness, accidental injury, and unemployment, and education and work training; and (2) certain other rights relating to collective bargaining, a safe working environment, information on trends in pollution sources and products and processes that affect the well-being of workers throughout the world, voting and campaigning, and personal security (see: www.house.gov/lee/votes.htm).

28. The United States had never been a country hospitable to the redistribution of wealth, to unions, or to workers. Roosevelt may have been a popular president for bringing the Depression to an end and as a war president, but his popularity could not override about 150 years of pro-business and anti-worker sentiment. For example, the 1890 Sherman Anti-Trust Act was ironically used to break up unions, not monopolies. Morison, Commanger, and Leuchtenburg write: "In case after case the courts emasculated or nullified the act. . . . The legislature failed to amend the act; the executive failed to enforce it. . . . Only when the law was applied to labor unions . . . did the government win a series of victories." See: Samuel Eliot Morison, Henry Steele Commager, and William E. Leuchtenburg, *A Concise History of the American Republic* (New York: Oxford University Press, 1983), 371.

29. John Kenneth Galbraith, *The Affluent Society* (Boston: Houghton Mifflin, 1958). Also see: Harry K. Girvetz, "Welfare State," in *International Encylopedia of the Social Sciences, Vol. 16*, ed. David L. Sills, 512–21 (New York: Macmillan, 1968).

30. W. W. Rostow, *The Stages of Economic Growth: A Non-Communist Manifesto* (New York: Cambridge University Press, 1960).

31. James K. Galbraith and Vidal Garza Cantú, "Inequality in American Manufacturing Wages, 1920–1998: A Revised Estimate," in *Inequality & Industrial Change: A Global View*, ed. James K. Galbraith and Maureen Berner, 79–91 (Cambridge: Cambridge University Press, 2001).

32. See Joseph E. Stiglitz, *Globalization and Its Discontents* (New York: Norton, 2002). See also Jeffrey Sachs, Dean Baker, Gerald Epstein, and Robert Pollin, *Globalization and Progressive Economic Policy* (Cambridge: Cambridge University Press, 1998).

33. Kate Bronfenbrenner, *Uneasy Terrain: The Impact of Capital Mobility on Workers, Wages, and Union Organizing* (Ithaca: New York State School of Industrial and Labor Relations, Cornell University, 2000).

34. For example, see William A. Taub, *Unequal Partners* (New York: New Press, 2002); David Harvey, *The Limits to Capital* (Chicago: University of Chicago Press, 1982); Bennett Harrison, *Lean and Mean: The Changing Landscape of Corporate Power in the Age of Flexibility* (New York: Basic, 1994).

35. Simon Head, "Inside the Leviathan," *New York Review of Books,* December 16, 2004: 80-89.

36. Bennett Harrison and Barry Bluestone, *The Great U-Turn: Corporate Restructuring and the Polarizing of America* (New York: Basic, 1986).

37. Quoted in Doug Henwood, *After the New Economy* (New York: New Press, 2003), 8–9.

38. Henwood, *After the New Economy*, 225; also see: Paul Krugman, *The Great Unraveling: Losing Our Way in the New Century* (New York: Norton, 2003) and Robert Pollin, *Contours of Descent* (London: Verso, 2003).

39. James K. Galbraith and Jiaqing Lu, "Measuring the Evolution of Inequality in the Global Economy," in *Inequality and Industrial Change: A Global View*, 161–85 (Cambridge: Cambridge University Press, 2001), 179.

40. James Tobin, "A Proposal for International Monetary Reform," *Eastern Economic Journal* (1978): 153–59; "Financial Globalization," *Proceedings of the American Philosophical Society* 143 (1999): 161–67.

41. Henwood, *After the New Economy*, 145–74.

42. Suzanne Bergeron, "Challenging the World Bank's Narrative of Inclusion," in *World Bank Literature*, ed. Amitava Kumar, 157–71 (Minneapolis: University of Minnesota Press, 2003).

43. World Bank, "Inequality, Poverty, and Socio-economic Indicators": www.worldbank.org/poverty/inequal/index.htm. Many of the leading early defenders of global capitalism and free markets have become critical. They include Joseph Stiglitz (former chief economist, World Bank), Jeffrey Sachs (architect of the "shock therapy programs" applied to Latin American countries), and Paul Krugman (Princeton economist).

44. Vandana Shiva, "Earth Democracy," in *New Socialisms: Futures beyond Globalization*, ed. Robert Albritton and Richard Westra, 3–70 (London: Routledge, 2004), 53.

45. Harry Braverman, *Labor and Monopoly Capital* (London: Monthly Review Press, 1974), 271.

46. Pierre Bourdieu, "The Essence of Neoliberalism," *Le Monde diplomatique* December 1998: mondediplo.com/1998/12/08bourdeiu/ [emphasis added].

Appendix 4.1
Roosevelt's Second Bill of Rights, Proposed by the U.S. National Public Resources Board, March 1943

1. The right to work, usefully and creatively through the productive years;
2. The right to fair play, adequate to command the necessities and amenities of life in exchange for work, ideas, thrift, and other socially valuable service;
3. The right to adequate food, clothing, shelter, and medical care;
4. The right to security, with freedom from fear of old age, want, dependency, sickness, unemployment, and accident;
5. The right to live in a system of free enterprise, free from compulsory labor, irresponsible state power, arbitrary public authority, and unregulated monopolies;
6. The right to come and go, to speak or to be silent, free from the spyings of secret political police;
7. The right to equality before the law, with equal access to justice in fact;
8. The right to education, for work, for citizenship, and for personal growth and happiness; and
9. The right to rest, recreation, and adventure, the opportunity to enjoy life and take part in advancing civilization.

SOURCE: Reproduced from Cass Sunstein, *The Second Bill of Rights: FDR's Unfinished Revolution and Why We Need It More Than Ever* (New York: Basic, 2004), 86–87.

Growing Inequalities

5

M ary Wollstonecraft's argument brings us closer to the differences between thinking about economic security as a human right ("birthright") and economic competition in the marketplace. As one economist, P. H. Wicksteed, informed his readers in his 1910 textbook, investment choices are like deciding how high a cliff one would dive off to save one's mother-in-law.[1] For many in America the cliff is high indeed; they make employment choices: between, say, being a Wal-Mart "associate," a prison guard, or a grocery clerk. These jobs pay about minimum wage and do not come with health benefits, and virtually none have retirement plans. Not much choice here. The waters are shark infested, and the rocks below are jagged.

The wealthy do have abundant choices about, say, investments, stock options, and which properties to buy. They really do not take risks. On holiday, the mother-in-law is no doubt snorkeling safely in the shallow waters off Bermuda while her son-in-law and daughter are tanning themselves on the beach. No high cliffs here. They are not the risk takers; it's the poor who bear the risks. Wollstonecraft would insist that humans must be universally secure, and that the poor not carry the burden of risks for all the others. The investment brokers may describe the risks that their wealthy clients must endure. These are two different worlds of understanding, experience, and knowledge. How do we convince the wealthy that they are anomalous in a world of shrinking resources and growing interdependencies, and that they share an imperiled planet with so many that are poor or impoverished?

Both the glorification of wealth and the rags-to-riches story are central narratives in capitalist America. The narratives are driven into Americans' consciousness from childhood and they are embellished by accounts of American entrepreneurs and by the retelling of Horatio Alger stories. Even the least likely of American presidents, Abraham Lincoln, celebrated the capitalist rags-to-riches story: "The prudent, penniless beginner in the world, labors for wages awhile, saves a surplus with which to buy tools or land, for himself; then labors on his own account another while. . . . This . . . is free labor—the just and generous, and prosperous system, which opens the way for all."[2] So powerful is this myth, we believe, that it poses the single biggest obstacle in the United States for the advance of human rights, economic equity, and equality. The enormity of the gap between rich and poor needs to be underscored, because this economic gap reinforces the psychosocial isolation of the rich from the poor and therefore further deludes the rich that what they possess they have by entitlement.

In Wollstonecraft's quaint manner, these inequalities are like a "destructive mildew that blights the fairest virtues; benevolence, friendship, generosity, and all those endearing charities which bind human hearts together and the pursuits that raise the mind to human contemplation."[3] In this chapter we will briefly review the extent of inequalities in America, then provide some comparisons using the member states of the Organization for Economic Cooperation and Development (OECD), and in chapter 6 provide examples of provisions for economic rights in a sample of state constitutions.

Inequalities in the United States

A few Americans are so wealthy that their wealth exceeds that of entire nation-states. There is also a larger number of very wealthy Americans who exert disproportionate influence in setting policies for large corporations and thereby have economic power that influences political policies. The top 1 percent of the American wealth owners control an estimated 70 percent of the total business assets in the United States, 53 percent of all stock,[4] and 47 percent of the nation's total financial wealth.[5] Because taxes are regressive, capital gains taxes have declined precipitously, and inheritance laws can be easily manipulated to avoid capital gains tax and benefit heirs, the economic power of a small elite is predicted to only increase.[6]

While rich Americans are experiencing increases in their incomes, poor Americans are experiencing declines in theirs. The Center on Budget and Policy Priorities, using the latest U.S. Census Bureau data, released a report in December 1997 showing that during the last two decades "incomes of the richest fifth increased by 30 percent or nearly $27,000 after adjusting for inflation." The average income of the top 20 percent was $117,500, or

almost thirteen times larger than the $9,250 average income of the poor-
est 20 percent.[7] According to their report, the real income of 90 percent
of American families barely grew at all—1.6 percent over a decade. By
contrast, the richest 1 percent of families saw their income rise by 89 percent in that same time period. Such comparisons as these help to explain
why increasing numbers of poor families are living in shelters because they
cannot afford housing.[8] They also explain rises in food insecurity. According to a 2003 report of the Center for Hunger and Poverty at Brandeis
University, 12.5 percent of Americans live in households that experience
food insecurity, a rise of 22 percent in three years.[9] Additionally, an estimated thirty-five million Americans are food insecure, with food insecurity and the necessity of food stamps being experienced by at least four in
ten Americans between the ages of twenty and sixty-five.[10]

U.S. corporations pay a fourth in taxes of what individuals now pay,
with enormous tax breaks, of $53.3 billion in 2003. Additionally, they re-
ceived $51 billion in 2003 in direct subsidies. This $104.3 billion giveaway
to businesses contrasts with the $75.1 billion total cost of all federal wel-
fare programs for individuals, including help for the blind and deaf, drug
and alcohol treatment, assistance to the handicapped and elderly, care for
the mentally retarded, children's vaccination and immunization programs,
and food stamps (50 percent of which go to children).[11]

The U.S. military has been the main gravy train for corporate contracts.
The Pentagon's "Big Three" contractors—Lockheed Martin, Boeing, and
Northrop Grumman—alone split over $50 billion in prime contracts
among them in fiscal year 2003. To put this in some perspective, Lockheed
Martin's Pentagon awards, at $21.9 billion, are greater than one large fed-
eral program, TANF, Temporary Assistance for Needy Families.[12]

International Comparisons

But did we not say that America was the richest country in the world?
There is no question about it. Its Gross Domestic Product (GDP) is about
10,000 billion dollars, two and half times that of Japan, and five times that
of Germany, the next two richest countries.[13] However, in many respects
the United States does not do as well as many of the less rich countries. Its
public health expenditures per capita, 6.2 percent, is on the low end of industrialized countries, while its private health expenditures, 7.7 percent, is
the highest in the world, after Cambodia.[14] Among the OECD countries,
the United States ranks second on percentage living below 50 percent
of the country's median income,[15] and fourth on the percent below the

poverty line.[16] It ranks second to last on an indicator of national social assistance,[17] and second on the percent of child poverty, or more specifically, the percent of children living in households with incomes below 50 percent of the national median.[18]

Among the OECD countries it has a low life expectancy, 77.1.[19] On a per capita basis, it ranks right along with the Middle Eastern countries—Israel, Kuwait, the United Arab Emirates, Saudi Arabia, and Jordan—as being the leaders of military spending.[20] Its unemployment rate, contrary to popular opinion, is about equal to that of European countries. The reason U.S. unemployment appears relatively low is due in large part to differences in the ways that unemployment is conceptualized and measured.[21] For example, so-called passive jobseekers—persons who conduct their search only by reading ads—are included among the unemployed in Canada but not in the United States. Those waiting to start a job are counted as unemployed in European Union countries, but not in the United States.

Sanderson and Alderson conclude, using data from the World Bank (WB), that richer countries are more equalitarian than poorer countries.[22] However, the United States is the least egalitarian of the OECD countries. The poorest 10 percent share less than 2 percent of the total income, whereas the richest 10 percent have nearly 30 percent (29.9) of the total income. This disparity exceeds that of other affluent OECD countries, and is closer to the disparity indicator for Ecuador or Turkey. A more concise comparison is obtained with the Gini coefficient. The values for the United States, Ecuador, and Turkey are, respectively, 40.8, 40, and 43.7. And while the Gini coefficient of inequality is 40.8 for the United States, the values of this coefficient for European countries are all smaller, in the range of 25 to 35.[23]

The World Bank has compiled a useful database on poverty for all countries in the world.[24] It is less precise than the comparisons presented for the OECD countries, but the WB series is superior because of its wide coverage. Termed the "Millennium Indicator of Poverty," it is the poorest quintile's share in the total national income. In other words, it is a summary of how much or how little of the total national wealth the bottom one-fifth receives. Country variation is quite systematic. For the most part, European countries have comparatively high values, on the order of 7 percent to 10 percent. For example, the value for Finland is 10.1 percent, for Denmark 10.3 percent, with somewhat lower percentages for countries without much in the way of welfare programs, such as Switzerland, for which the value is 6.9 percent.

The poor tend to be relatively better off in countries in the former Soviet bloc, such as Hungary (10.0 percent). Interestingly, poor Asian countries also have relatively high values: 9.0 percent for Bangladesh, 8.1 percent for India, 7.6 percent for Nepal, with China being the exception, with a low value of 5.9 percent. The value for the United States is more like China's, as well as that of many Third World countries. In the United States, the poorest one-fifth share only 5.2 percent of the total income. This is comparable to that for China, as well as that of other poor countries: Burundi (5.1 percent), Ghana (5.6 percent), Kenya (5.6 percent), and Trinidad and Tobago (5.5 percent). While it is true that the income pie is bigger in the United States than in Burundi, Ghana, and these other countries, these comparisons reveal the extent to which poor Americans are relatively deprived. It is also true that the cost-of-living pie is bigger in the United States than in these poor countries.

Worldwide Poverty and Inequality

The demands around the world for economic fairness and justice are loud and growing. It is important to understand the context of these demands. As a benchmark for poverty, international organizations have decided that using $1 a day as an estimate of extreme poverty makes sense, at least as a quick snapshot when measuring poverty is so important and other estimations require much greater time and expense to compile. Besides, most of the world's population is more or less integrated into global wage and commodity markets. The percentage of people living on less than $1 per day is about one in three worldwide, and about one in two in Sub-Saharan Africa.[25] Moreover, wealth is highly concentrated. The world's richest 1 percent receive at least as much income as the poorest 57 percent.[26] According to one estimate, the world's 358 richest people own an aggregate fortune that is greater than the combined incomes of 2.3 billion people, or nearly 40 percent of the world's population![27]

Thus, we can conclude that worldwide poverty is extensive and there is an extreme concentration of wealth. What about disparities? Inequalities in earnings and wealth have increased within Western industrialized nations since 1972,[28] particularly in the United States,[29] and these inequalities have increased within the world since 1950.[30] In the period between 1970 and 1990, there was more inequality in the world than anytime before that, and after 1990, inequality has increased.[31] Analysis over time shows that global macro-economic processes *produce* income inequalities.[32]

The details, however, are important. The proportion of the world's people living in extreme poverty fell from 29 percent in 1990 to 23 percent in 1999, due to the decline in extreme poverty in East Asia and the Pacific, while during the same period the number of people in extreme poverty in Sub-Saharan Africa rose from 242 million to 300 million.[33] Poverty has not only increased in Sub-Saharan Africa, but it also has increased dramatically in the many nations that made up the former Soviet Union.[34] The annual growth rate for the world between 1975 and 2000, and for the shorter time series between 1990 and 2000, was flat. The GDP of high-income nations and low-income nations is smaller in the 1990–2000 period than it was in the 1975–2000 period, and the overall flat rate of growth was due solely to the fact that China's growth rate overcame the overall trend.[35] China, of course, with its 1.3 billion population counts heavily in any global comparison.

The UNDP *Human Development Report 2003* sums up gloomy news: "More than 50 nations [out of 189] grew poorer over the past decade."[36] Poverty is not simply a self-contained problem; it leads to vulnerabilities that create epidemic disease, and a wider range of civil disorder.[37]

The UNDP presented data in its 2001 *Human Development Report* that were alarming: in 1999 the richest 20 percent of all people received 85 percent of the world's wealth, while the remaining 80 percent had access to 15 percent and the poorest 20 percent received only 1.0.[38] These gaps are new—they are due to the accelerating economic inequalities of the past few decades. "This is the new *global social apartheid*," according to William I. Robinson.[39]

But multinationals move about. To give an example, the wages of the workers in the *maquiladoras* had not risen from $4.20 an hour—not enough to support a family with two children. Factories began leaving in droves beginning in about 2000 since they could pay workers in China less than $1 a day. Close to half a million Mexicans lost their jobs as multinationals moved to China and elsewhere. Property holders can move their property, as they take advantage of tax breaks, trade laws, gradients in land costs, and most of all, gradients in wages. As the International Confederation of Free Trade Unions reports, "multinationals are completely in the driver's seat."[40]

In contemporary constitutions, European states have formal protections for workers, whereas the U.S. Constitution has none. The Spanish constitution, for example, protects collective bargaining, promotes an equitable distribution of incomes within the nation, and has provisions for the length of the workday, worker safety, vacations. The Netherlands and Germany have similar protections. Norway asserts the rights of employees in unions, specifying in stronger language than most constitutions that these are rights of "codetermination," thereby stressing labor power; allows for the expropriation of private property; and restricts the inheritability of privileges granted to trade and industry.[41] Eastern European countries have even stronger language protecting workers' rights; for example, Poland's constitution guarantees freedoms to unions, occupational organizations, farmers' societies, but, also interestingly, "freedoms for citizens' movements." Similarly, Latin American countries generally have pro-union and pro-labor constitutional guarantees.

A further indication, although indirect, of the extent to which the state protects the public and the public interest lies in the realm of state provisions to confiscate property, an area of constitutional law that has largely been neglected.[42] While such rights can be used oppressively, they are written into constitutions to explicitly advance the public good. European countries such as Spain, the Netherlands, and Germany explicitly allow the state the right to expropriate private property under the condition that there are important public needs that must be met (subject to other laws and on assurance of compensation). Former Socialist countries, such as Poland, discipline the private sector more than European states, and much more than the United States. Article 20 of Poland's constitution states the principles of public–private sector relations: "A social market economy, based on the freedom of economic activity, private ownership, and solidarity, dialogue and cooperation between social partners, shall be the basis of the economic system of the Republic of Poland."[43]

In sum, private–public–state relations vary considerably, but the conflict between property rights and social rights is evident in constitutions. As Gaston V. Rimlinger argues, the historical strengthening of property rights in the West, and most especially in the United States, has led to a corresponding weakening of labor rights.[44] After the Great Depression and World War II, Western states expanded welfare programs, and then throughout the world, late twentieth-century constitutions incorporated more specific provisions for labor. This was a reaction, no doubt, to the growing economic inequalities that neoliberal capitalism brought about. European states adopted new language, such as "social democracy" and "social market economies," to signal both their commitment to the welfare state and to curbing the excesses of capital.

Thus, the strictly legal reasons why capitalist enterprises have had so much power and workers relatively little in the United States is because its constitution enunciates no principles about workers' rights and courts have interpreted enterprises as being persons. But these legal provisions rely on

American liberal values that embrace autonomy, individualism, and competition and are antithetical to broadening opportunities for the disadvantaged, but important institutions such as a constitution interact with and reinforce widely held values, and it would be impossible to say which plays the more important role.

The economic well-being of the population depends on many things, of course, but especially employment availability, low unemployment, decent wages, safe working conditions, and interesting jobs that provide workers dignity. Unions have traditionally served the interests of workers in fighting for jobs, job security, better wages, and quality jobs. Yet unions are not well organized for service-sector employment, which is growing many times faster than industrial employment. Besides, employers outsource jobs, making organizing extremely difficult. For these reasons, the state has become more important in ensuring that people have job security, health care, safe working conditions, and social security.

Every society wants to do away with jobs that are dangerous or exceedingly boring—such as ones in coal mining, poultry factories, and textile mills. Every society wants to promote work that is a source of dignity and meaningfulness. Here it is important to make the analytical distinction between the state and society, because the state may not have the same goals as its people do. Increasingly this is a problem with globalization because of the state's vulnerability in the larger world order and because some states want to maintain their dominance in that order. Besides, interstate trade and financial exchanges play a bigger and bigger role in the global economy. The state may very well want to please its multinationals whose CEOs contribute to the party's campaign contributions, or that work in tandem with military operations as contractors, or that make aircraft and other war paraphernalia. In other words, with globalization, there is the mounting danger of a growing gap between what the population wants and what a government wants.

In this chapter we have presented a great deal of empirical data that lends credibility to our several claims. First, that the United States, despite its great affluence, has severe problems with poverty and that the gaps between the rich and poor are comparable to those in poor countries, not rich countries. Second, that worldwide poverty is a staggering problem that must be addressed. What remains to be shown is what international organizations have done to advance people's economic security, and what individual countries are doing to advance their own people's economic security. Our focus is not the actual practices, but what has been internationally agreed to and what countries are trying to achieve.

Notes

1. Cited in Kenneth E. Boulding, *Economic Analysis, 3rd ed.* (New York: Harper & Brothers, 1941), 888.

2. Matthew Warshauer, "Who Wants to Be a Millionaire," American Studies Today Online: www.americansc.org.uk/Online/American_Dream.htm

3. Mary Wollstonecraft, *A Vindication of the Rights of Men with a Vindication of the Rights of Woman and Hints* (Cambridge: Cambridge University Press, [1790] 1995), 5.

4. Lisa A. Keister, *Wealth in America* (Cambridge: Cambridge University Press, 2000), 93–94.

5. G. William Domhoff, "Which Side Are We On? Redefining Who's Us and Who's Them," *In These Times,* March 14, 2003: www.commondreams.org/views03/0520-07.htm

6. Center on Budget and Policy Priorities: www.cbpp.org/; Samuel Bowles, Herbert Gintis, and Melissa Osborne, "The Determinants of Earnings," *Journal of Economic Literature* 39 (2001): 1137–76; Jenny B. Wahl, "From Riches to Riches: Intergenerational Transfers and the Evidence from Estate Tax Returns," *Social Science Quarterly* 84 (2003): 278–96.

7. Michael Parenti, "The Super Rich Are Out of Sight," Friday, December 27, 2002: www.commondreams.org/views02/1227-06.htm

8. Bruce Bradbury and Jantti Markus, "Child Poverty across Industrialized Nations," Florence: UNICEF Innocenti Occasional Papers, Economic Policy Series, 71 (92 pp.). www.unicef-icdc.org/cgi-bin/unicef/aut_down.sql?AuthorID=4685

9. Center for Hunger and Poverty, November 2003: www.centeronhunger.org/

10. Anuradha Mittal, "Hunger in America," *Oakland Institute*, December 2004: www.oaklandinstitute.org/

11. www.corporations.org/welfare/

12. World Policy Institute, "Is What's Good for Boeing and Halliburton Good for America? Contractors Are Cashing in on the War on Terror," February 24, 2004: www.commondreams.org/cgi-bin/newsprint.cgi?file=/news2004/0224-04.htm

13. World Bank, *World Development Indicators* (Washington, D.C.: WB, 2003).

14. UNDP, *Human Development Report 2004* (New York: Oxford University Press, 2004), table 6, 157–59.

15. IMD International Business School, Geneva, Switzerland: www.nationmaster.com/red/graph-T/eco_pop_bel_med_inc&id=OECD&int=300

16. Luxembourg has the highest GDP. See: *CIA World Factbook, December 2003*: www.nationmaster.com/

17. OECD, *Benefits and Wages,* table 2.9: "Maximum Social Assistance Monthly Amounts" (Paris-Cedex, OECD, 2002): www1.oecd.org/publications/e-book/8102091E.PDF

18. United Nations Children's Fund (UNICEF): www.nationmaster.com/red/graph-T/eco_chi_pov&id=OECD&int=300

19. UNDP, *Human Development Report, 2004*, table 9, 168–71.

20. UNDP, *Human Development Report, 2004*, table 10, 202–5.

21. Constance Sorrentino, "International Unemployment Rates: How Comparable Are They?" *Monthly Labor Review* 123 (2000): 1–20.

22. Stephen K. Sanderson and Arthur S. Alderson, *World Societies* (Boston: Pearson, 2005), 188. Another indicator of economic inequality is the Gini index, which is calculated from the Lorenz curve. Of all the OECD countries, the United States ranks third highest, with the high values reflecting high inequality. Mexico and Turkey have higher values than the United States: *CIA World Factbook, December 2003*: wwwnationmaster.com/graph-T/eco_dis_of_fam_inc_fin_ind&id=OECD.

23. UNDP, *Human Development Report, 2003*, table 13, 282–85.

24. United Nations, Statistics Division, "Millennium Indicators": unstats.un .org/unsd/mi/mi_goals.asp. Years vary, but the great advantage of this series is that it has coverage for virtually all countries.

25. Stephen Devereux and Simon Maxwell, "Introduction," in *Food Security in Sub-Saharan Africa* (Pietermaritzburg, South Africa: University of Natal Press, 2001), 1–12.

26. Branko Milanovic, "True World Income Distributions: 1998 and 1993," Development Research Group, World Bank, October 1999: www.worldbank.org/

27. His Royal Highness Prince El Hassan bin Talal, "A New World Order without Ideologies," Presidential Address, Swiss Federal Institute of Technology, Zurich, Switzerland, February 4, 2003: www.alumni.ethz.ch/veranstaltungen/vorlesung/hassan_bin_talal.pdf

28. See University of Texas Inequality Project: utip.gov.utexas.edu/

29. James Crotty, "Trading State-Led Prosperity for Market Led Stagnation: From the Golden Age to Global Neoliberalism" (Amherst, Mass.: Political Economy Research Institute, 2000): www.umass.edu/peri/

30. World Bank, "Inequality, Poverty, and Socio-economic Indicators": www.worldbank.org/poverty/inequal/index.htm

31. UNDP, *Human Development Report 2002* (New York: Oxford University Press, 2002), 19

32. See James K. Galbraith and Maureen Berner, *Inequality & Industrial Change: A Global View* (Cambridge: Cambridge University Press, 2001).

33. UNDP, *Human Development Report 2002*.

34. Devereux and Maxwell, "Introduction."

35. UNDP, *Human Development Report 2002*.

36. UNDP, *Human Development Report 2003* (New York: Oxford University Press, 2003), v.

37. Moses Shayo, "Poverty, Militarism, and Civil War," 2004: Economists for Peace and Security: www.epsusa.org/

38. UNDP, *Human Development Report, 2002*.

39. William I. Robinson, *A Theory of Global Capitalism: Production, Class and State in a Transnational World* (Baltimore, Md.: Johns Hopkins University Press, 2004), 153 [emphasis added].

40. International Confederation of Free Trade Unions: www.icftu.org/

41. www.oefre.unibe.ch/law/icl/no00000_.html#A110_

42. Richard Cothren, "A Model of Plunder and Economic Growth," *Journal of Macroeconomics* 22 (2000): 385–407; James D. Gwartney and Richard E. Wagner, *Public Choice and Constitutional Economics* (Greenwich, Conn.: JAI Press, 1988).

43. www.oefre.unibe.ch/law/icl/pl00000_.html

44. Gaston V. Rimlinger, "Capitalism and Human Rights," *Daedalus* 122 (1983): 51–79.

The Global Struggle for Economic Security

On December 10, 1948, the General Assembly adopted the Universal Declaration of Human Rights (UDHR). We might, quoting L. S. Stavrianos, say that this was one of those rare moments in human history when it looked as if we were finally "growing up as a species."[1] The extraordinary vision that the signers shared grew out of a commitment to make certain that their populations had the sorts of security that never again would there be the massive barbaric slaughter of a minority population that the Germans committed. The understanding emerged that when a majority population experiences deprivation, as had Germans after World War I, they are not likely to look for scapegoats. In today's world, there is a renewed understanding that the fates of all humans are connected.

That understanding bound the framers of the Universal Declaration together in a shared commitment to world peace and stability, but also in a shared commitment to enhance the security of the world's population. The declaration sets forth the human rights and the fundamental freedoms to which all men and women, everywhere in the world, are entitled to without any discrimination.[2] Article 3 is the key article for civil and political rights: it introduces Articles 4 to 21, which set out specified rights, including freedom from slavery, torture, and inhuman or degrading punishment; the recognition everywhere as a person before the law; the right to a fair trial; the right to be presumed innocent until proven guilty; the right of asylum; and other rights. The second key set of provisions is Article 22, which introduces Articles 23 to 27, in which economic, social, and cultural rights are set out as rights to which everyone is entitled "as a member of society."

As early as 1946, when the United Nations formed a drafting committee to prepare an "international bill of rights," the stated intention was, as the General Assembly later stated to clarify, "the enjoyment of civic and political freedoms and of economic, social and cultural rights are interconnected and interdependent."[3] However, in the treaty drafting stage, the United States made it clear that it would not sign a treaty that included economic, social, and cultural rights. In the context of late 1940s geopolitics, the United States' position was that endorsing such rights would only lend credence to communism. Retrospectively, we could say that this was as much a "party line," as was the Soviets' about the dictatorship of the proletariat. In America, politicians told the people that in a free society (aka, the capitalist state), employment and jobs would be created by the forces of the market, and there would be no need for "handouts," "welfare," and "free lunches."

Therefore, the United States signed the Universal Declaration, which has no enforcement mechanism, and ratified the treaty related to political and civil rights that is derived from particular articles of the UDHR (Articles 3–21), namely the International Covenant on Civil and Political Rights (ICCPR), but refused to sign the International Covenant on Economic, Social, and Cultural Rights (ICESCR), derived from Articles 22–27 of the UDHR. There are now 157 state parties to the ICCPR, and 150 state parties to the ICESCR.[4]

International treaties such as the ICCPR and the ICESCR are, of course, difficult to enforce, but there is a formal complaint procedure and United Nations committees monitor state progress on compliance. However, they have far-reaching important consequences, because they become part of public discourse, and often public policy, and international nongovernmental organizations (INGOs) and nongovernmental organizations (NGOs) become treaty advocates, working with local communities and governments. Most importantly, treaty provisions become incorporated into formal provisions of regional bodies, such as the European Union's Convention and Constitution, and into state constitutions.

Since the ICESCR went into effect in 1976, other important UN treaties have been ratified. These include: International Convention on the Elimination of All Forms of Racial Discrimination (1969), Convention on the Elimination of All Forms of Discrimination against Women (1981), Convention on the Rights of the Child (1990), and International Convention on the Protection of the Rights of All Migrant Workers and Members of Their Families (2003). The United States has ratified only one of these, specifically, the one dealing with racial discrimination. There are approximately eighty additional declarations, which do not have treaty status, but are statements of principles and provide guidelines for concrete action.[5]

Economic Rights

What specifically in the UDHR and in the ICESCR irritated the Americans so much? The objectionable provisions centered on economic rights; specifically, in the UDHR:

Article 23 states:

(1) Everyone has the right to work, to free choice of employment, to just and favorable conditions of work and to protection against unemployment.
(2) Everyone, without any discrimination, has the right to equal pay for equal work.
(3) Everyone who works has the right to just and favorable remuneration ensuring for himself and his family an existence worthy of human dignity, and supplemented, if necessary, by other means of social protection.
(4) Everyone has the right to form and to join trade unions for the protection of his interests.[6]

When the General Assembly found that the only way to move forward was to have two treaties, it stipulated two conditions: first, that the two covenants have as many similar provisions as possible and, second, that they both include a phrase about peoples' rights to self-determination,[7] which became Article 1 of both: "All peoples have the right of self-determination. By virtue of that right they freely determine their political status and freely pursue their economic, social and cultural development." In 1954 the General Assembly asked member states to publicize and circulate both covenants for discussion and comment, and, after discussion within the Assembly, both were adopted by resolution in December 1966 and opened for state signatures and ratification.[8] The ICESCR went into force January 1976, and today, the United States is among five nations that have not either signed or ratified it, the others being Botswana, Haiti, Mozambique, and South Africa. It is not as if the ICESCR is rigidly demanding. Articles 29 and 30 refer to the flexibilities that states have in implementing the covenant.

The ICESCR is reproduced in appendix 6.1. Among its provisions are: the rights of all workers to have jobs with fair wages that provide a decent living, the rights of all workers to join unions and to strike, the rights of women to have leave before and after childbirth, and the right to an education (e.g., equally accessible higher education). As we have shown, Congress had no use for Roosevelt's 1943 proposed legislation, and it had no use for the ICESCR, either between 1966, when the ICESCR was sent to states for signing and ratification, and 1976, when the ICESCR went into force, or in any subsequent year in which the ICESCR was introduced into Congress.

The conception that underlies the ICESCR is that the raison d'être of the nation-state is to promote the well-being of its citizens. A comparison of Roosevelt's Economic Bill of Rights in appendix 4.1 with the ICESCR in appendix 6.1 is useful. They match up fairly closely in terms of their provisions, with the ICESCR being more detailed and expansive. Both advance workers' rights and the socioeconomic rights of citizens. Both were spurned by the U.S. Congress, and in the case of the ICESCR, many times over, as congressional representatives have repeatedly proposed adopting it.

Thus, the United States, by refusing to endorse the ICESCR, is out of compliance with a multinational agreement that recognizes the rights to work, to enjoy just and favorable conditions of work, to form and join trade unions, to social security and social insurance, to the widest possible protections and assistance for the family, to an adequate standard of living, to the highest possible attainable standard of physical and mental health, to education, and to take part in cultural life.[9]

The geopolitical context was so very different from what it is now. India had just achieved its independence in 1947 (and Myanmar and Sri Lanka did in 1948), but virtually all of Africa (except for Ethiopia) and the Caribbean, Indonesia, Laos, the Philippines, Vietnam, and what are now Pakistan and Bangladesh were colonies of Western powers. The UDHR played a major, but immeasurable, role not only in the many struggles for freedom from colonial domination, but in providing the language that authorized these struggles on behalf of citizens' well-being. Political freedoms that are achieved by states and by citizens are, according to the vision of the UDHR, inseparable from economic and social rights. The U.S. constitutional tradition, instead, advances political freedoms and has no provision for the economic and social rights of citizens.

International Labor

The ICESCR is not exclusively about labor rights, although it stresses them, but there are other very specific multinational agreements on labor standards, which fall under the jurisdiction of the International Labour Organization (ILO), a body of 178 national members and an affiliate of the UN. Because the ILO was initially part of the League of Nations, its earliest multinational agreements predate the UN. The ILO sets standards for labor and to advance labor interests and works with state and local govern-ments, employers, communities, labor unions, and workers on issues deal-ing with employment policy, industrial relations, working conditions, social security, and workplace health and safety. A complaint may be filed under Article 26 of its constitution by another country that has ratified the same convention, or filed by a delegate to the International Labour Con-ference or by the governing body of the ILO.[10]

The ILO works on an ongoing basis with states, employers, and work-ers to raise standards for the latter, and its nearly 180 conventions deal with all aspects of work, such as safety, gender equity, and wages, and with the needs of workers in specific occupations, such as fishing, mining, and agri-culture. Yet there are eight conventions that are most fundamental: they deal with freedom of association, forced labor, discrimination, and child la-bor. These are described in appendix 6.2.

When states ratify an ILO convention, they are bound by Article 22 of the ILO constitution to submit regular reports on their law and practice, which are examined by the Committee of Experts on the Application of Conventions and Recommendations, made up of independent experts in law and social policy. States are also obliged to send copies of their reports to employers' and workers' organizations, and they have the right to com-ment on them.

The United States has ratified few ILO conventions, and of the eight fundamental conventions, it has ratified only two. As appendix 6.2 shows, the United States has not ratified the following: Freedom of Association and Protection of the Right to Organize Convention (No. 87); Right to Organize and Collective Bargaining Convention (No. 98); Forced Labor Convention (No. 29); Discrimination (Employment and Occupation) Convention (No. 111); Equal Remuneration Convention (No. 100); and Minimum Age Convention (No. 138). Of the eight, it has only ratified two: Abolition of Forced Labor Convention (No. 105), and The Worst Forms of Child Labour Convention (No. 182). Only four states in the world have signed fewer. Except for Lao People's Democratic Republic, these are tiny countries: the Democratic Republic of Timor-Leste (popu-lation, 780,000; achieved independence in 2002), Vanuatu (a string of is-lands near Australia, population, 212,000); and the Solomon Islands (volcanic islands with a population of 447,000, south of Papua New Guinea).

Failure of the United States to ratify the ICESCR and the ILO stan-dards hurts American workers, and increasingly, under the conditions of globalization, multinationals that are U.S.-based plead immunity from labor standards, intensifying labor abuse worldwide, and obstructing monitoring and imperiling workers' conditions.[11] Whereas many human rights treaties are difficult to enforce, including those pertaining to health and discrimination, labor standards are relatively easy to enforce. Besides, upholding labor rights greatly enhances family and community well-being and security, and contributes to a nation's economic stability. Many new state constitutions, as we will see, include provisions for worker rights, and the new European constitution has a full complement of provisions for labor.[12]

It is important to stress that economic rights have far-reaching implications —for peoples' autonomy, their capability of making choices, and their well-being in many, many respects. As Youcef Bouandel describes, the right to work is linked with core social values that have to do with societal cohesion as well as individual dignity.[13] The people living in countries that have ratified the ICESCR and International Labour Standards rank higher on health indicators than people living elsewhere.[14]

Constitutional Provisions for Workers

Constitutions are crafted to establish and legitimate governance structures and citizens' rights. All constitutions spell out the rights of citizens and all have provisions for political and civil rights. These may not be realized, but constitutions are not designed to clarify what has been achieved, but rather what the country is trying to achieve. The majority of constitutions are relatively new, written or substantially revised within the past decade or so. States are responding to the uncertainties of global interdependencies and responding in ways that will allow them to maximally protect their citizens against the onslaught of global economic forces and environmental decline.

Our aim is to clarify how constitutions enunciate labor rights and provisions for the economic security of their populations. We also feel it is important to capture the language and legal frameworks used in constitutions, and the only way we can do this is to reproduce sections of constitutions. We cannot possibly do this for a large number of constitutions, and our solution was to simply select, virtually at random, state constitutions from various regions of the world. In appendix 6.3 we reproduce these provisions.

We have selected three state constitutions from each of the four major regions of the world (Asia, Middle East, Africa, Europe, and the Americas). Our criterion for selecting countries was simply to provide as much diversity as possible. We present in appendix 6.3 their key provisions for economic rights.

In anticipation of one conclusion, predominately Catholic countries stress the economic securities of their populations more than do Protestant ones, as we might expect based on Weber's analysis,[15] and Islamic countries couch economic rights within a social ethic of egalitarianism.[16] The United States is excluded from consideration because its constitution has no provisions for workers or economic security. We think this exercise is important because while many have stressed the importance of international standards for labor rights and economic security, to the extent that nation-states stress these rights, we can expect dramatic transformations in the near future.

It is important to show how individual states are incorporating provisions for human rights that relate to their citizens' economic security into their constitutions. Many contemporary analyses of human rights cast them in nonspecific universal contexts,[17] and we aim to show that in spite of great variation, current constitutions specify such rights and in very specific ways that are consistent with their traditions, history, and demographic patterns. In all of the cases we will be looking at, aspirations are ahead of reality, but this was also the case with the United States when it crafted its constitution.

Asia

To illustrate the range of Asian countries, we have selected ones that are integrated in various ways in the world economy: Bangladesh, the People's Republic of China, and Japan. Bangladesh is extremely poor, with an estimated 35 percent of the total population undernourished[18] and 83 percent living on $2 a day or less.[19] China, officially a communist state, but in practice, more a mixed economy, is rapidly becoming one of the world's strongest market economies. Compared to the population of Bangladesh, the peoples of China are relatively well off. An estimated 9 percent of the total population is undernourished,[20] with less than half (47.3 percent) living on $2 a day or less.[21] If development were considered to be linear over time, Bangladesh is roughly four decades behind China.[22] Japan is one of the wealthiest countries in the world and has trivial percentages that are undernourished or that live on less than $2 a day.

These countries have had varied positions in the world system. Bangladesh was a British colony until 1947 as East Pakistan, and with India's help, became independent of West Pakistan in 1970. With the highest population density in the world, most of its landmass at sea level, and reoccurring monsoons, Bangladesh's poverty is confounded by chronic environmental disasters. Divisions between secularists and fundamentalists pose difficulties in governance, but Bangladesh, like India, has embraced eclectic development strategies—formal and informal, socialist and capitalist. Bangladesh actively pursues foreign investors, largely through opportunities in the Export Processing Zones, which are billed on the government's webpage as being a "bonanza for foreign investors," with tax exemptions and accelerated depreciation on equipment. So important are jobs to an impoverished country like Bangladesh that the prime minister's main function is to attract foreign investors.[23]

Japan is a capitalist, not a socialist state, but it has strong socialist traditions, with a coalitional Socialist Party the main opposition party between 1955 and 1993, when the country launched ambitious plans to ensure that workers had continuous job security. Its companies have long been regarded as superior to those in Europe and the United States in providing continuous employment after schooling.[24] Slowly the Japanese government is absorbing more of these welfare functions with the lessening welfare support of corporations.[25] The Japanese constitution expresses indigenous conceptions of interpersonal responsibilities, as well as the human rights conceptions of the UDHR, but it was powerfully influenced by American constitutionalism as well. The draft constitution was prepared with considerable input from an American military committee appointed by General MacArthur, while Japan was still under U.S. occupation.[26]

Labor Provisions

In their constitutions, Bangladesh and China each affirm socialist principles, while they both support capitalist practices. China states in its constitution (Article 42.3) that the "State promotes socialist labor emulation,"[27] while the Bangladeshi constitution states in Article 13, "people shall own or control the instruments and means of production and distribution, and with this end in view ownership shall assume the following forms:" "state," "cooperative," and "private ownership." In Article 20, it draws from Marx: "From each according to his abilities to each according to his work."

Leaving aside the commitment to socialist principles, the three Asian constitutions are similar in that they all affirm that "work is a right" and "work is a duty" or "obligation." Both China and Bangladesh embellish the meaning of work, with China's stating that work is a "glorious duty" and further encouraging citizens to "take part in voluntary labor." Both, in spite of socialist principles, recognize that inequality of effort is joined with inequality of return, but Bangladesh, perhaps owing to its Islamic traditions, condemns unearned incomes (usury). Yet work in both these constitutions is treated as a matter of human fulfillment, self-expression, and human enrichment.

In contrast, work in the Japanese constitution is treated in more matter-of-fact terms, more in line with market economies than either the Chinese or Bangladeshi constitution.[28] Elsewhere in the Japanese constitution, provisions for social security and socioeconomic rights are stressed, making it more similar to European constitutions than to other Asian ones or the U.S. Constitution. It is useful to note that the 1889 Meiji constitution that the 1947 constitution replaced was also strikingly Western in its emphasis on property rights, social security, and political freedoms. There has been, therefore, more continuity than often implied by Westerners in their descriptions of Japan's 1947 constitution.[29]

Middle East

In our Middle Eastern comparisons, we include Egypt, Jordan, and Turkey. As before, we use percent of undernourished people as an indicator of poverty. Only 4 percent and 6 percent of the Egyptian and Jordanian populations, respectively, are undernourished, and only an insignificant percent in Turkey can be detected in epidemiological surveys.[30] Using another indicator of poverty, the percentage that live on less than $2 a day, we have a somewhat different picture. In Jordan and Turkey, it is relatively low compared with that of countries with similar gross national products, specifically, 10.3 percent for Jordan, and 7.4 percent for Turkey. In contrast, 43.9 percent of the Egyptian population lives on less than $2 a day.

All three countries are predominately Muslim, and while all stress the importance of societal responsibilities, a distinguishing feature of Islam, none of these constitutions reflects the orthodoxy of Shari'ah law. Like the Bangladeshi constitution, those of Jordan and Egypt stress social progress and justice, consistent with their Islamic traditions, but draw from Western jurisprudence, which has been greatly influenced by English common law and the U.S. Constitution.[31] Turkey has maintained a strong secular tradition, in spite of the fact that its population is predominately Sunni.

In spite of their proximity to one another, their structural relations to one another and to the West have varied considerably. Under the rule of Ataturk, in 1923, Turkey emerged as a pro-Western regime, whose goals were to advance an aggressive assimilation of national minorities, adopt Western state reforms, and free the state and society of religion. In spite of gradual accommodation with ethnic minorities, which European Union countries have approved, Turkey's negotiations over entry into the European Union remain stalled over issues of democratic stability and human rights, notably the death penalty, press censorship, and the establishment of political and cultural rights for minorities.

Egypt, earlier part of Turkey's Ottoman Empire, became a British protectorate in 1914 and a constitutional monarchy in 1923, and became independent in 1936. While President Nasser advanced socialist reforms with land redistribution and nationalization, his successor Sadat reversed those policies by liberalizing the economy and breaking ties with the USSR, but as the constitution makes clear, Egypt remains committed to socialist principles. Jordan, too, was part of the Ottoman Empire, and came under British control as part of the League of Nations Mandate covering Palestine, Iraq, and Jordan. Burdened by over a million Palestinian refugees, and destabilized by the Palestine Liberation Organization (PLO), it expelled the PLO through a fierce civil war in 1970–1971. Jordan, under King Hussein and King Abdullah II, has strived to stabilize the region, with something of a nonaligned policy, assuaging the United States, while trying, like Egypt, to play a peacekeeping role in the Arab states.

Only Egypt is a self-proclaimed socialist country. Its constitution's preamble reads in part: "We, the people, who in addition to shouldering the trust of history, carry the responsibility of great present and future objectives whose seeds are embedded in the long and arduous struggle, and which hosted the flags of freedom, socialism and unity along the path of the great march of the Arab nation." In contrast, in its preamble, Jordan's constitution instead stresses Western liberal rights and political freedoms. In Article II of its constitution, Turkey states: "The Republic of Turkey is a democratic, secular and social state governed by the rule of law; bearing in mind the concepts of public peace, national solidarity and justice; respecting human rights; loyal to the nationalism of Atatürk."

Labor Provisions

Even though Egypt is the only one of the three Middle Eastern countries that describes itself as socialist, in the relevant sections on work that relate to ILO standards (described in appendix 6.2), all three states make provisions for the protection of workers and make explicit or implicit connections involving economic equity, private enterprise, and workers' welfare (see appendix 6.3). Egypt's constitution states in Article 13: "work is a right, a duty, and an honor." Egypt's constitution makes a commitment to reducing income inequality while protecting earnings. Article 4 of Egypt's constitution is a clear example of how Islamic principles of justice are brought into line with the realities of a market economy.

Of these three constitutions, Jordan's is the most matter-of-fact, with an outline of labor policies about wages, wage differentials, special provisions for older workers, women, juveniles, worker health, and trade unions. In two respects, it is distinctive. First, an organic connection is drawn between individual work and the national economy (Article 23.1). Second, workers with dependent family members are provided with additional compensation (Article 23ii c).

Turkey, which early aligned itself with secular, materialist traditions, emphasizes economic freedoms and private enterprise (Article 48), but also commits itself to promoting the conditions of labor, and the standard of living of workers, and protecting the unemployed. In these respects, Turkey's constitution is more in line with most modern constitutions and very different from that of the United States.

Africa

We have chosen three African countries that vary in their colonial histories and ethnic diversity, but vary little in their national wealth. These are Cameroon, Ethiopia, and Malawi. For the sake of comparison with the other countries on indicators of poverty, we again use percent of the population that is undernourished and the percent of the population living on $2 a day or less. The percentages undernourished are: Cameroon, 25 percent; Ethiopia, 44 percent; and Malawi, 33 percent. The percentages of the population living on $2 a day or less are: Cameroon, 58 percent; Ethiopia, 82 percent; and Malawi, 76 percent. For the sake of comparison, Algeria, which benefits from oil and gas reserves, provides better economic opportunities for its population: 15 percent live on $2 a day or less. All three countries are dependent on their agricultural exports, which in the world market have been chaotic, owing to the decline in the dollar, the high rate of subsidies paid to U.S. agriculturalists.[32] Besides, all have incurred soaring debts through World Trade Organization and International Monetary Fund (IMF) policies.[33]

The modern state of Cameroon was formed in 1961 as a union between British and French colonies, having earlier been a German colony. It is one of the most heterogeneous countries in Africa, with around two hundred ethnic groups, but also with very high literacy rates. A war with its neighbor, Nigeria, over oil reserves has imperiled economic development, but nevertheless, as we again remind readers, state constitutions establish the fundamental principles for the state and its peoples. When a state veers into war, corruption, absolutism, or any other political or economic catastrophe, the constitution is expected to provide the principles that will steer the state back again on the course that the framers envisioned.

Ethiopia was the first free nation in Africa, securing its independence from Italy in 1941 after short-lived colonial status. It is, like many other African nations, multi-tribal and multilingual. It has four major languages: Amharic, Oromo, Tigrinya, and Somali. Its strategic location in the Horn of Africa makes Ethiopia attractive to the United States as a gateway for arms shipments, in violation of a current international ban on such shipments, but with UN peacekeepers on the border between Ethiopia and Eritrea, the UN Security Council has upheld the ban against the United States.[34] Nevertheless, Ethiopia and the United States have had scrappy relations, starting in 1984 when Ethiopia became a communist regime and promulgated a Soviet-style constitution, and continuing into the 1980s when the United States failed to provide food aid to Ethiopia during one of its worst famines.

Malawi achieved its independence from Britain in 1964, becoming a republic in 1966, and losing foreign aid in the 1990s; it rapidly declined to become one of the poorest countries in the African continent. Producing primarily tobacco, tea, sugar, and cotton, Malawi, like other African countries dependent on agricultural products for export, is rapidly losing ground in trade, which has been greatly accelerated by IMF pressures to relinquish social and economic programs that otherwise buffer Malawians against famine and illness. The independent organization ActionAid has particularly criticized the IMF for its imposition of structural adjustment programs precisely when Malawi has been under such severe food distress.[35] Beset by corruption, refugee flows from Mozambique, failed harvests in the 1990s, and high rates of population growth, and disadvantaged by being landlocked, with reoccurring droughts, Malawi is one of the poorest countries in Africa.

What we therefore wish to highlight is the vulnerabilities of the African countries under consideration, and the enormous toll on their populations that has been extracted by colonists, and then when colonists left, by capitalists. This certainly is the way that the recent generations of Cameroonians, Ethiopians, and Malawians have experienced it.[36]

Labor Provisions

The provisions for work in Cameroon's constitution are best described in its preamble, which we reproduce in appendix 6.3. It states that work is a right and obligation, but places it in the context of international agreements, specifically the UDHR, the Charter of the United Nations, and the African Charter on Human and People's Rights. It also captures contemporary thinking about promoting conditions necessary for development, linking individual development with national development. Cameroon's 1996 constitution exemplifies how poor countries are linking human rights with development and progress.

Ethiopia's current constitution was promulgated in 1994, replacing its early communist one, but still reflecting egalitarian principles and its commitment to economic fairness. Article 40 codifies the practices established after 1975 during the period of social reforms aiming to improve the lot of peasants by providing them with free land, thereby helping to curb urban unemployment that results from rural to urban migration. Article 41.8 further provides agriculturalists with assurances for their compensation and a commitment that they will benefit in the country's economic and social development. Article 41.1–7 likewise links individuals' rights to work with the responsibilities of the state to provide social services, to ensure health and education, and to increase opportunities in the public sector. Ethiopia's constitution thoroughly entangles economic freedoms and rights with the state's responsibilities to its citizens.

Malawi's constitution, like Cameroon's, relies on contemporary conceptions of development by making clear that the right to work is also the right to develop, and that individual development is inseparable from the development of the state and its peoples generally. The constitution of Malawi also provides for fair and safe labor practices in Article 31 (1) and the freedom to join or not join labor unions (2), and makes explicit its antidiscriminatory policies (3).

All African constitutions have been recently revised, as shown in appendix 1.1. The ones we have selected embrace the principles of the ICESCR by stressing the state's responsibilities to citizens and labor rights. Such provisions are common in all African constitutions that have been revised in the postcolonial period.[37] Notwithstanding soaring unemployment and poverty, corrupt governments, and ethnic conflict, African constitutions reveal not only confidence in economic growth but a commitment to their citizens' economic well-being.

Europe

We selected the Netherlands, the Russian Federation, and Spain for their constitutional provisions on work. None have the poverty we have described for Asian, Middle Eastern, and African countries, but the Russian Federation has slipped dramatically within the last few years. Although relatively little data are available for Russia, in 2004 it ranked about the same as Brazil and Venezuela on the Human Development Index (HDI). In the period since the breakup of the Soviet Union in 1991, there has been economic turmoil. The transition to a market economy has gone very badly, in part owing to the policies of the World Bank, the IMF, and wealthy nations.[38] Between 1991 and 1993, inflation soared to 930 percent, while the gross domestic product (GDP) declined at about 10 percent per year. State insolvency, government restructuring, and deeply entrenched government corruption accompanying privatization has created deep resentment among the population. The war in Chechnya has further drained the coffers, and as former Bloc members Georgia and the Ukraine have elected Western-oriented leaders, Russian politics remain deeply in disarray. Otherwise, we will not provide the details for these countries that we did for the others owing to readers' greater familiarity with them.

Labor Provisions in the Netherlands

The Netherlands' constitutional provisions for work, reproduced in appendix 6.3, reflect the high priority it places on employment security, coupled with provisions for workplace democracy ("co-determination"), support for the unemployed (worker participation in decision making and representation on boards), and a statement about the government authorities' responsibility to secure the means of subsistence and to better distribute wealth. In other words, its constitution provides for population security within a market and capitalist economy. The Netherlands also has its Declaration of the Rights of Man and of the Citizen, which was adopted in 1795 after the French Declaration in 1789. Like its French counterpart, it stresses political liberties and the sovereignty of the people.

Labor Provisions in the Russian Federation

The conventional interpretation is that the 1993 constitution was written to consolidate Yeltsin's powers,[39] but every constitution has many layers, and our focus is how a constitution addresses labor issues, not governance. Articles 34 and 37 are the relevant ones. Article 34 affirms labor rights within the context of a market-driven economy, defending property rights and repudiating monopolistic practices and unfair competition. Article 37 affirms people's freedom of occupational choice and freedom from forced labor (an implicit reference to the gulags) but also includes traditional pro-

visions for worker safety, a healthy work environment, security against unemployment, the right to strike, and rights to leisure and a paid holiday.
Were we to compare Russia's constitution with almost all that we have discussed so far, we would have to conclude that it fails most to capture the
commitment to worker security. This is amazing in light of its long experiences with collectivization and socialism.

Constitutional History and Labor Provisions in Spain

Spain was united under a personal union of crowns by Ferdinand of
Aragon and Isabella of Castile in the fifteenth century and acquired its borders then. In the nineteenth century, Spain had a constitutional framework
for parliamentary government similar to that of Britain and France, but it
was fractured by the Civil War (1936–1939) and then the dictatorial rule
of Generalissimo Francisco Franco y Bahamonde (1936–1975). In a matter of only a few years, Franco's successor, King Juan Carlos de Bourbon,
and his prime minister, Aldolfo Suárez Gonzalez, transformed Spain into a
pluralistic, parliamentary democracy.

Before Franco, there had been a vigorous Left, with anarcho-syndalism
having a strong following in the late nineteenth century, especially in Cat-
alonia, with a communist party emerging in 1920. Although Franco out-
lawed it, it reemerged in 1975 as a moderate social democratic party, calling
itself the Socialist Party (Partido Socialista Obrero Español, or PSOE). The
constitution was written in 1978, at the beginning of rapid democratization under King Juan Carlos and his prime minister, Suárez. The PSOE
won the election in 1982 and remained in power until 1996, and then
again won the elections in 2004. Thus, socialist principles played a continuous, and sometimes, a dominant role in Spanish modern history. The
constitution reflects this influence although it arguably also reflects the
Catholic tradition that places considerable emphasis on economic security.

Article 35 (1) compactly summarizes a set of policies about economic
rights, specifically that work is a responsibility and a right; people have the
freedom to choose; discrimination is prohibited; and earnings should be
sufficient to satisfy the worker's and the worker's family's needs. Article 36
expresses the intention that professional colleges must ensure democratic
principles that presumably will safeguard against the emergence of a mer-
itocratic elite. Article 37 (1) protects collective bargaining. Article 37 (2) is
especially interesting as it puts the worker–employer relationship into a
larger community context.

We earlier contrasted constitutions that treat workers as free agents,
such as Russia's, as being in an antagonistic relationship with employers and

the state, with the constitutions of Asia and Africa that situate workers in a more organic relationship with employers, the society, and the state. Class antagonisms were not resolved within socialist Russia, and in the aftermath of the breakup of the Soviet Union may have been exacerbated. Whatever the reason, the labor provisions of Russia's constitution contrast with those in constitutions such as Spain's, Jordan's, and the Netherlands', which place a greater emphasis on embedding work and employment within society and the state.

The Americas

The United States has no constitutional guarantees for workers, and we have selected three others from the Americas to illustrate the variation in such guarantees: Brazil, Canada, and Chile. Canada is not included in the UNDP's survey on percent living on $2 a day or less or on percent undernourished because the numbers are negligible. Chile's economy has historically been one of the strongest in Latin America, as reflected in a relatively low value for percent living on $2 a day or less (9 percent) and percent undernourished (4 percent). Brazil has higher values on both of these indicators, 24 percent and 10 percent respectively. Because the constitutional histories of Brazil and Chile are so closely bound up with their political struggles for liberation from their colonizers and for democracy, we abandon the format we have been using and provide brief country overviews along with a summary of constitutional provisions on labor rights.

Brazil

After liberation from Portugal in 1822, Brazil became an empire, which lasted until the First Republic (1889–1930) and its first constitution of 1891. The Great Depression took an enormous toll on the Brazilian economy, and a military coup put Vargas in power in 1933, leading to a new constitution that was very similar to that of the Republic's but reduced the political power of the landed elites. Yet mass political movements and a Communist-led Popular Front emerged and were suppressed, and Vargas consolidated his power even more until demands for a return to democracy led to elections in 1945. The third constitution, under the Second Republic, lasted through economic decline, IMF intervention, and another coup in 1964, followed by high interest rates and high national debts, until the return of democracy in 1985. A new constitution was written and enacted in 1988. Between 1988 and 2002, economic growth was sluggish and corruption was rampant, until Luiz Inácio de Silva ("Lula") became

Brazil's president in 2002. While inequality is high in Brazil, the poverty rate is not high compared with that of many Third World countries. About 10 percent (9.9) live on less than a dollar a day.

The preamble of Brazil's contemporary constitution is worth stating owing to the way it articulates individual rights within a larger societal, national, and international context: "for the purpose of ensuring the exercise of social and individual rights, liberty, security, well-being, development, equality and justice as supreme values of a fraternal, pluralist and unprejudiced society, based on social harmony and committed, in the internal and international spheres, to the peaceful solution of disputes."

Of all the constitutions we have discussed, Brazil's is the most remarkable for its great specificity in outlining workers' rights, and to capture this, we reproduce most of the provisions. In great detail under section 7, it outlines job security (I), unemployment provisions (II and III), compensation (IV–IX), profit sharing (XI), family allowance (XII), hours of work (XIII–XV), and overtime and holiday pay (XVII). It has provisions for maternity and paternity leave (XVIII–XIX); a variety of protections, including risks incurred by technology (XXVII); provisions for equality (XXX–XXXIV); and protection of domestic workers (XXXIV–1). Sections 8 and 9 lay out labor union rights and the right to strike. Sections 10 and 11 provide provision for employee participation in decision making. In sum, the vision for participatory democracy is inseparable from labor rights and a remarkably clear vision of what a good society is.

Canada

The Canadian constitution shares less with the U.S. Constitution than might be imagined, partly because Canada has strong links to British and French, as well as indigenous, traditions. Its first constitution of 1763, while under British rule, affirmed Britain's hegemony over French territory, and its second constitution of 1791 gave greater provincial control to what is now Ontario and Quebec, with Britain's power somewhat reduced. Following rebellions in the 1830s there was further devolution of Britain's power, and another constitution went into effect in 1867, while provincial authorities adopted their own constitutions. However, autonomy from Great Britain was not achieved until 1982, under the Canada Act, and with it a new constitution, and thorough overhaul of the bill of rights, now called the Charter of Rights and Freedoms. This charter clarifies civil and political freedoms, economic rights, and most important to Canadian minority groups, elaborates language rights and many detailed provisions for Canada's aboriginal population.[40]

Canada's provisions for labor rights are quintessentially liberal rights, perhaps owing in part to the difficulties of reconciling differences among the provinces, and the Canadian constitution does not provide the broad safety nets that European constitutions do, while doing more compared with the U.S. Constitution. Canada is one of the most egalitarian of the Organization for Economic Cooperation and Development (OECD) countries, with a Gini coefficient of 25.4. Its poor share more (4.3), its wealthy share less (5.2) than most OECD countries, and its Gini coefficient of 25.4 is nearly as low as those of Denmark and Japan, which have the lowest values, 24.7 and 24.9, respectively.

Chile

After Chile won its independence from Spain in 1818, an early provisional constitution was replaced by the 1833 constitution of the "Portalian State," which remained in force until 1925. It concentrated authority in the national government, more precisely, in the hands of the president, who was elected by a tiny minority. Little punctuated this long period of moderate economic growth, except the acquirement of mineral-rich territory to its North (in the War of the Pacific, 1879–1883). Close ties between the urban elites and wealthy landowners ensured political stability while contributing to the social unrest of workers. However, amazingly as anarchist and syndicalist movements began to take shape, the president, Arturo Alessandri, attempted to integrate them into the government. Coming into power in 1920, he was deposed by the military in 1924, which then enacted his labor and social reforms. Many of these new reforms were included in the 1925 constitution. The 1925 constitution was the second major charter in Chilean history, lasting until 1973. It codified significant changes, including the official separation of church and state, which culminated a century of gradual erosion of the political and economic power of the Roman Catholic Church. The constitution also provided legal recognition of workers' right to organize, a promise to care for the social welfare of all citizens, and an assertion of the right of the state to infringe on private property for the public good.

After 1924 the Chilean economy experienced unending turmoil, exasperated by political instability and American pressure on the Chilean government. This period lasted until 1958, when civilian rule was returned and Jorge Alessandri was reelected as president, making it possible to fully implement the 1925 constitution, which would remain in force until the overthrow of Salvador Allende in 1973. It is Salvador Allende's presidency (1970–1973) that will remain the legend for the progressive pursuit of human rights and reforms, including nationalizing the copper mines, wage increases, expanding health care, and price freezes. General Pinochet staged a military coup, and rather than surrender, Allende committed suicide. Whether the CIA was behind the coup or not is not known,[41] but it is clear that the United States was very much involved in the reign of terror that Pinochet unleashed, with gross human rights violations. The Pinochet constitution of 1980 assured that Pinochet would remain president through 1989 and that a plebiscite in 1988 would determine if he would have an additional eight years in office. The document provided for military domination of the government both before and after the 1988 plebiscite. In 1998–2000 Pinochet was put under house arrest in Britain for his role in the torturing and killing of civilians while in power. In the 2000 presidential elections, socialist Ricardo Lagos Escobar defeated a former adviser of Pinochet. The present constitution restores the democratic provisions.

Even though both Chile and Brazil have nourished comparable socialist traditions, Brazil's constitution more emphatically stresses particular details about labor rights. The poverty rate in Chile is lower than that in Brazil, as indicated by the estimate that less than 2 percent of the population live on less than $1 a day.

Article 6 of Chile's constitution spells out the freedom dimensions of work, namely, the free selection of work and occupation; the prohibition of discrimination; and it spells out some guidelines for qualifications. At the very beginning, Article 6 states that compensation should be just. While stating that workers have a right to engage in collective bargaining, the phrasing of this provision puts the burden on workers, not the firms. Likewise in the final section, it stipulates the restraints on strikers rather than their rights to strike. These work provisions understate the long-standing Chilean tradition of progressive social and economic reforms, and do not reflect Chile's current policies, including the restoration of the public social security program that Pinochet had earlier privatized.[42]

OECD and Non-OECD Country Comparisons

It is useful to compare all OECD countries with the non–OECD countries discussed in this chapter on a variety of economic indicators and on whether or not they have ratified the ICESCR and labor standards. This is a purely descriptive exercise but it does suggest how countries have aligned themselves in the international community, and the challenges that lie ahead for development, eradicating poverty, and narrowing the gap between the rich and the poor.

In these comparisons, presented in tables 6.1 and 6.2, we include the HDI, which is a composite scale based on the following: life expectancy at birth; a country's relative achievement in adult literacy and combined primary, secondary, and tertiary school enrollments; and the GDP.[43] The HDI is, in short, a measure of human development, not economic development per se. We also include whether or not the country has ratified the ICESCR and the number of labor standards (out of the eight fundamental ones) that it has ratified.

Table 6.1.   OECD Countries: HDI Score, Ratifications, and Indicators of Inequality

	1	2	3	4	5	6	7
				Share of Income (or Consumption)			
Country*	HDI Score	Ratified ICESCR	# Labor Standards	Poorest 10%	Richest 10%	Ratio of 5 to 4	Gini Index
Australia	0.95	yes	6	2	25.4	12.5	35.2
Austria	0.93	yes	8	3.1	23.5	7.6	30
Belgium	0.94	yes	6	2.9	22.6	7.8	25
Canada	0.94	yes	5	2.5	25	10.1	33.1
Czech Republic	0.87	yes	7	4.3	22.4	5.2	25.4
Denmark	0.93	yes	8	3.1	21.3	8.1	24.7
Finland	0.94	yes	8	4	22.6	5.6	26.9
France	0.93	yes	8	2.8	25.1	9.1	32.7
Germany	0.92	yes	8	3.2	22.1	6.9	28.3
Greece	0.90	yes	8	2.9	28.5	10	35.4
Hungary	0.85	yes	8	2.6	22.8	8.9	24.4
Ireland	0.94	yes	8	2.8	27.6	9.7	35.9
Italy	0.92	yes	8	2.3	26.8	11.6	36
Japan	0.94	yes	6	4.8	21.7	4.5	24.9
Korea	0.90	yes	4	2.9	22.5	7.8	31.6
Luxembourg	0.93	yes	8	3.5	23.8	6.8	30.8
Mexico	0.80	yes	6	1	43.1	45	54.6
Netherlands	0.94	yes	8	2.8	25.1	9	32.6
New Zealand	0.93	yes	6	2.2	27.8	12.5	36.2
Norway	0.96	yes	8	3.9	23.4	6.1	25.8
Poland	0.90	yes	8	2.9	27.4	9.3	31.6
Portugal	0.90	yes	8	2	29.8	15	38.5
Slovakia	0.84	yes	8	3.1	20.9	6.7	25.8
Spain	0.92	yes	8	2.8	25.2	9	32.5
Sweden	0.95	yes	8	3.6	22.2	6.2	25
Switzerland	0.94	yes	8	2.6	25.2	9.9	33.1
Turkey	0.75	yes	8	2.3	30.7	13.3	40
UK	0.94	yes	8	2.1	28.5	13.8	36
US	0.94	no	2	1.9	29.9	15.9	40.8
Mean				2.86	25.62	10.48	32.17

*Iceland is excluded because of missing values on the economic disparity indicators; its HDI value is 0.94.
SOURCE: *Human Development Report, 2004.*

We also try to capture the extent of poverty, concentration of wealth, and inequality, using data reported by the UNDP for 2004. The indicator of poverty, in column 4, is the total share of the nation's wealth that is divided by the poorest 10 percent. The higher this value, the better off are the poor in a particular country. The indicator of wealth, in column 5, is the total share of the nation's wealth that is shared by the richest 10 percent. The higher this value, the greater is the concentration of wealth in a particular country. One indicator of inequality is the ratio of the value in column 5 to the value in column 4. This ratio reflects the relative share of the richest 10 percent to the relative share of the poorest 10 percent. This is reported in column 6. A superior measure of inequality is the Gini index, because it uses the entire distribution of income. A Gini value reflects the extent to which the distribution of income among individuals or households within a country deviates from a perfectly equal distribution. A value of 0 would indicate perfect equality and a value of 1, perfect inequality.

The overall pattern is quite clear for the OECD countries in table 6.1. European countries, Australia, Canada, Japan, New Zealand, the United Kingdom, and the United States have higher HDI scores than Eastern European countries, Korea, Mexico, and Turkey. This is not surprising because the former went through industrialization earlier. In columns 2 and 3, the United States is the outlier with respect to international agreements about economic rights and labor rights, as we have already indicated. The values in column 4 indicate that the poor are the worst off in Mexico, with the bottom 10 percent sharing only 1 percent of the national wealth, and the poor of Japan the best off, with the bottom 10 sharing 4.8 percent of the national wealth. The contrasts in column 6 are between, on the one hand, Mexico and the United States, where the richest 10 percent share, respectively, 43.1 percent and 15.9 percent of the wealth, and, on the other hand, Japan, where the richest 10 percent share only 4.5 percent. Similar results are obtained with the Gini coefficients, reported in column 7. The highest coefficient value is Mexico's, and it is extremely high, 54.6, but of the remaining countries, Turkey and the United States have the highest values, 40 and 40.8, respectively. These patterns are a powerful indication that the United States departs significantly from other highly industrialized countries, and exhibits wealth inequalities and poverty that are more similar to the poorest of the OECD countries.

Table 6.2 presents comparable information for the non–OECD countries we have discussed in this chapter. The summary indicator for development (HDI) in column 1 shows the great variation, and some countries have values that are equal to or exceed that of Turkey, an OECD state. These include

Table 6.2.   Non-OECD countries: HDI Score, Ratifications, and Indicators of Inequality

	1	2	3	4	5	6	7
				Share of Income (or Consumption)			
Country	Mean HDI Score	Signed ICESCR	# Labor Standards	Poorest 10%	Richest 10%	Ratio of 5 to 4	Gini Index
Bangladesh	0.51	yes	7	3.9	26.7	6.8	31.8
Brazil	0.77	yes	7	0.5	46.7	85	59.1
Cameroon	0.50	yes	8	2.3	35.4	15.7	44.6
Chile	0.84	yes	8	1.2	47	40.6	57.1
China	0.75	yes	3	1.8	33.1	18.4	44.7
Colombia	0.77	yes	7	0.8	46.5	57.8	57.6
Egypt	0.65	yes	8	3.7	29.5	8	34.4
Ethiopia	0.36	yes	6	3.9	25.5	6.6	30
Jordan	0.75	yes	7	3.3	29.8	9.1	36.4
Malawi	0.39	yes	8	1.9	42.2	22.7	50.3
Russia	0.79	yes	7	1.8	36	20.3	45.6
Mean				2.28	36.22	26.45	44.69

SOURCE: *Human Development Report, 2004.*

Brazil (.778), Chile (.84), China (.75), Columbia (.77), Jordan (.75), and Russia (.79). The countries with very low values on the HDI scale are African countries: Cameroon (.50), Ethiopia (.36), and Malawi (.39). Colonization, oppression, the HIV/AIDS epidemic, and tribal conflict and civil strife have all played a role in hampering development.

All of these countries have ratified the ICESCR and each, with the exception of China, has signed at least six of the eight ILO standards. It is evident here that state constitutions do not reflect actual economic conditions. Brazil has an extraordinary constitution in terms of labor rights, while its poor are very badly off, with the bottom 10 percent sharing a miniscule amount of Brazil's wealth, specifically less than 1 percent (.5). The poorest 10 percent of Ethiopia, which has the lowest value on the HDI, do much better, sharing nearly 4 percent of the national wealth. (Bangladesh is comparable.) Brazil, along with Colombia, has an extreme concentration of wealth. The top 10 percent in each of these countries have a huge share of their country's wealth, over 46 percent. Again, the Gini coefficients provide a straightforward indicator of inequality. The least unequal countries are Bangladesh (31.8) and Ethiopia (30), while the most unequal country is Brazil (59.1).

These cross-sectional comparisons do not capture the importance of constitutional provisions for labor and economic security, but comparisons over time do show that constitutions matter.[44] The reasons are clear enough: once a constitution lays out principles for human rights and national goals, the state begins to implement them through newly designed institutions, regulations, taxes, election reforms, and so forth. Of course, developing countries are particularly vulnerable to recessions, IMF sanctions, and high debts. But the purpose of constitutional provisions for labor and economic security is to protect the country's population against these forces, and, more generally, the calamities brought on by the vicissitudes of globalization.

Summary

We have focused in this chapter on constitutional rights for peoples' economic security and labor, retaining the richly textured language to illustrate the aspirations and ideals that motivate the framers who are the spokespeople for their fellow countrymen. They are guided, of course, by earlier models, as well as by their own country's experiences in the regional and global economy, which in the recent decade has seen far more instability than earlier decades. Third World countries have been far more adversely affected by this instability than rich countries.[45] Finally, the nature of work is not everywhere the same. Approximately 80 percent of Ethiopians are peasants, fishers, or nomads, and with Ethiopia's arid climate, subject to severe droughts, the incorporation of Ethiopia into the global economy will be, at best, exceedingly difficult. But Ethiopia must become incorporated into the world economy if it is to provide economic opportunities for its population. Herein lies the importance of its constitution. The country has stated what its bottom line is: specifically, it promises to its citizens that they will be treated with decency and respect and their labor rights will be protected so they can "progressively attain an improved standard of living and in proportion to their productive contribution to the national wealth." The state, on its part "will be guided by this objective in determining its economic and social development policies."

We especially wish to highlight the great differences between older constitutions, most especially the U.S. Constitution, and the newer constitutions that we have discussed in this chapter. These newer constitutions, including Ethiopia's but others as well, do not assume a sharp difference between the interests of the state and those of its citizens, and sometimes even modulate the differences between labor and capital. With the exception of Brazil's constitution, which presupposes that the interests of labor and capital diverge, many constitutions soften this relationship in the interest of promoting solidaristic undertakings. Because the capital–labor antagonistic relation grew out of industrialization and the exploitation of

workers, it is only inevitable that older constitutions reflect this antagonism. However, there has been a shift in the last decades so that now local
capital and workers might usefully form alliances as they are both threatened by international capital. Indeed, this broadens the opportunities for
power sharing and participatory democracy.

Workers in a capitalist economy, according to classical theory, receive a
fair wage *on the market* because of "perfect competition."[46] Joan Robinson
was one of the few twentieth-century economists who argued that the
competition premise was nonsense in labor markets.[47] Rather, she argued,
it is monopolies that play a decisive role in the determination of wages.
Lawyers, accountants, CEOs, and physicians have artificially higher wages
through the monopolies they hold on the supply of their services. To a
layperson, this seems obvious, but chinks in the armor of formal, classical
economics is an important first step in showing that if the economy itself
does not make for the efficient allocation of resources like wages and
wealth, then we must look elsewhere.

In addition to the competition paradigm to account for wages, another
twentieth-century branch of economics that focused on welfare advanced the
principle that an economic (or Pareto) optimum exists whenever it is not possible to make somebody better off without making somebody worse off. Welfare economics played a prominent role in the development of welfare
programs, and included such prominent figures as Arthur Pigou, Lionel Rob-
bins, Alfred Marshall, and Nicholas Kaldor.[48] The problem with welfare economics, as summed up concisely by Amartya Sen, is that "a society in which
some people lead lives of great luxury while others live in acute misery can
still be Pareto optimal if the agony of the deprived cannot be reduced without cutting into the ecstasy of the affluent"; "a state can be Pareto optimal and
still be sickeningly iniquitous."[49] Sen's argument is that interpersonal comparisons of utility and outcomes (wage and income distributions) cannot be justified by any economic principle because monopoly and aggregation lead to
market distortions and, most importantly, intersocietal and intrasocietal unfairness. Sen discards outcomes (utilities) as a decision tool for setting wages
and incomes, but instead uses interpersonal comparisons of peoples' functioning and capabilities, and their circumstances.[50]

Social Economies

We earlier asked whether globalization broke capitalism, but now we make
some tentative inquiries about what a global economy might look like.
Capitalism was a creature of the nation-state, bound up with its producers,
land, workers, and public and private property. Moreover, capitalism was

capable of being regulated within the nation-state, as the Keynsian reforms demonstrated. With globalization, national leaders threw up their hands, hopeless, and let the global economy evolve along a ruthless and destructive path. We have traced the extent to which global capitalism has worsened poverty in many parts of the globe and accelerated consumption in other parts to the point where the planet's varied ecosystems are at risk.

We believe that capitalism is broken because it is out of control. However, we believe that some of the most innovative economists are presenting arguments in the direction that takes them to the same conclusion. Nations cannot tolerate the prevailing extent of cross-national economic transactions that they cannot regulate. Societies cannot tolerate the enormous disparities in wealth and high levels of poverty. A major symptom of these problems is migration, the flow of people in search of work. The United Nations estimated that there were 175 million migrants in the world in 2000.[51]

Capitalist logic, developed within the context of nation-states, underestimates the extent to which economic performance and productivity can yield substantial gains in economic opportunities for all people. It favors short-term speculation by investors; capitalist logic leads to great wealth inequalities that undermine social solidarities; and capitalist logic undermines state capacity to reduce disparities and spread out opportunities generously throughout society.[52] Capitalism is broken because it is destroying biodiversity, environmental resources, and ecosystems, privatizing the commons. The eminent economist Joseph Stiglitz recently stressed the failings of global capitalism as having to do with the dissolution of the social contract involving capital and labor.[53] More specifically, he advocates the renewal of social contracts within firms, involving workers and owners; developing ties of trust between producers, buyers, and sellers; of labor mobilization and collective action, the objective "being one of promoting democratic, equitable, sustainable development."[54]

We are now in a better position to highlight some of the elements of what a radically reformed global economy might look like. We simply advance three. First, as Pierre-Joseph Proudhon earlier believed, and then James Tobin advocated, financial exchanges ("hot money") are actually a form of rent-seeking that exploits the commons and should be taxed to help the nation in which funds are parked for purely speculative purposes. Second, as Adam Smith originally maintained, and Joseph Stiglitz recently elaborated, economic transactions need be embedded in social contracts involving all participants—buyers and sellers, workers and employers, residents and governments. Third, as Amartya Sen advocates, because utilitarian outcomes are always unfair and unbiased, policies need to be aimed toward equalizing peoples' capabilities, to which sociologists would add opportunities as well. We believe that contemporary proponents of human rights would be pleased with these three proposals.

Global markets will not, and should not, diminish. Like universal access to information and knowledge, there must be universal access to markets and commodities. African weavers benefit from world markets as much as do African American rap performers. Everyone is justifiably giddy about what global markets bring. Yet, these global markets disguise ominous trends, and Americans have yet to fully absorb the implications, owing to their central position, being at the hub of a global economy that is more chaotic the more distant from the hub one is. We have outlined many of these symptoms, but there are many indications that the United States will also be caught in the chaos that much of the rest of the world now experiences.

We have described the importance of taxing "hot money," and of renewing and advancing the social contract that involves *ALL* participants of economic exchanges in democratic processes. Without spelling out here how this might work, we need only mention the great potential of the Internet to include widely dispersed participants to mobilize for worker justice, to hold firms to account, and to expose abuses. Finally, we suggested the total upending of the principles of the distribution of resources. Instead of rewarding people by their presumed utility, the aim would be to equalize earning power relative to the cost of living.[55] As sociologists, we further suggest equality of opportunity through universal education and health care.

A social economy, in sum, is democratic, socially inclusive, and economically fair and just. It requires, of course, some thought about how such a social economy can be implemented locally, nationally, and globally. However, this is easier than might be imagined. Two examples help to illustrate this. First, INGOs have demonstrated that they can be democratically governed at the global level as well as carry out their work in local communities. Additionally, they mobilize their collective efforts when they participate in international conferences or work jointly with international organizations, such as the UN Educational, Scientific, and Cultural Organization (UNESCO), the ILO, and other offices of the United Nations.[56] Second, shareholder activism has risen dramatically in the last few years, as shareholders have demanded a say in the way that their funds are invested, such as in military weapons, tobacco, and genetically modified seeds. In the United States, in 2003, over 2.16 trillion dollars were in funds with managed portfolios that can be described as dominated by shareholder activists, either through screens, community investing, or shareholder advocacy.[57]

Paradoxically, economic globalization that appears disastrous in so many respects has also unleashed an enormous potential of global and local co-operation. Many states have quietly advanced forms of democracy at the grassroots level that even the earliest and one of the most thoughtful of socialists, Pierre-Joseph Proudhon,[58] would approve! But these new grassroots democratic forms are tentative, and state support is cautious. Still, one can be hopeful.

Notes

1. L. S. Stavrianos, *The Promise of the Coming Dark Age* (San Francisco: Freeman, 1976).

2. The significance of the UDHR in the context of the two charters is discussed in: United Nations Office of the High Commissioner for Human Rights, *Fact Sheet No. 2 (Rev. 1), The International Bill of Human Rights:* www.ohchr.org/english/about/publications/docs/part1_1.pdf

3. *The International Bill of Rights:* 2.

4. UN Treaty Base: www.unhchr.ch/tbs/doc.nsf/Statusfrset?OpenFrameSet

5. See: www.unhchr.ch/html/intlinst.htm; www.unesco.org/pluralism/diversity/html_eng/decl_eng

6. Universal Declaration of Human Rights: www.un.org/Overview/rights.html

7. UN General Assembly resolution 543 (VI), para 1.

8. Resolution A (XXI), December 16, 1966.

9. As summarized in *Fact Sheet No. 2 (Rev. 1)*.

10. A special procedure exists whereby organizations of employers and workers may file complaints of violations of freedom of association, regardless of whether the relevant ILO conventions have been ratified by the state concerned. For a complete description of these procedures, see the Handbook of Procedures relating to International Labour Conventions and Recommendations. www.ilo.org/ilolex/english/surveyq.htm

11. International Labor Rights Fund: www.laborrights.org/

12. European Constitution Draft: european-convention.eu.int/

13. Youcef Bouandel, *Human Rights and Comparative Politics* (Aldershot, U.K.: Dartmouth Publishing, 1997); also see A. Szymanski, *Human Rights in the Soviet Union* (London: Zed Books, 1984).

14. Bouandel, *Human Rights and Comparative Politics*, esp. 37–40.

15. Max Weber, *The Protestant Ethic and the Spirit of Capitalism* (London: George Allen & Unwin, [1904–1905] 1930).

16. Westerners have criticized Islamic countries for not providing for the rights of individuals, but the other side of the coin is that there is a liberal interpretation of Islamic law (see Abdullahi Ahmed An-Na'im, "Introduction," *Cultural Transformation and Human Rights in Africa,* ed. An-Na'im [London: Zed, 2002], 1–12). However,

Islam engages individual responsibilities and community solidarity more than the Western tradition. See: Emile Sahlyeh, "The Status of Human Rights in the Middle East," in *Human Rights and Diversity: Area Studies Revisited*, ed. David P. Forsythe and Patrice C. McMahon, 252–78 (Lincoln: University of Nebraska Press, 2003); Richard A. Falk, *Human Rights Horizons* (New York: Routledge, 2000), 173–89.

17. Jean-Marc Coicaud, Michael W. Doyle, and Anne-Marie Gardner, *The Globalization of Human Rights* (Tokyo: United Nations University Press, 2003).

18. UNDP, *Human Development Report 2003*, table 7, 258–61.

19. UNDP, *Human Development Report 2000*, table 3, 245–47.

20. UNDP, *Human Development Report 2003*, table 7, 258–61.

21. UNDP, *Human Development Report 2003*, table 3, 245–47.

22. Bangladesh now has a value on the HDI that China had in 1975, a clear indicator of how important it is for Bangladesh to develop its economy and infrastructure. Overall trends are reported in UNDP, *Human Development Report 2003*, table 2, 241–44.

23. http://www.bangladesh.gov.bd/

24. Mary C. Brinton, "From High School to Work in Japan," *Social Service Review* 72 (1998): 442–51.

25. Ito Peng, "A Fresh Look at the Japanese Welfare System," *Social Policy and Administration* 34 (2000): 87–114.

26. Lawrence W. Beer, "Constitutionalism and Rights in Japan and Korea," in *Constitutionalism and Rights*, ed. Louis Henkin and Albert J. Rosenthal, 225–60 (New York: Columbia University Press, 1990).

27. In its preamble, the Chinese constitution states: "The people's democratic dictatorship led by the working class and based on the alliance of workers and peasants, which is in essence the dictatorship of the proletariat, has been consolidated and developed."

28. Shunji Sakai, "Communication and Social Cohesion in Japanese Organizations," *Societies* 38 (1992): 367–72.

29. Albert P. Blaustein and Jay A. Sigler, *Constitutions That Made History* (New York: Paragon House, 1988), 244–56.

30. UNDP, *Human Development Report 2003*, table 7, 258–61.

31. Robert L. Maddex, *Constitutions of the World* (Washington, D.C.: Congressional Quarterly, 1995), 102–5, 149–51, 219–22.

32. The New Partnership for African Development (NEPAD) is now promoting intra-African trade and technological development. See: www.nepad.org/en.html

33. "Fifty years is enough": www.whirledbank.org/development/debt.html

34. Thalif Deen, "US Move to Lift Arms Embargo in Africa Thwarted," *Inter Press Service*, Monday, January 15, 2001: www.commondreams.org/headlines01/0115-01.htm

35. ActionAid Report: IMF Macro-Economic Conditionality Plays Role in Malawi Deaths and Violated the Right to Food: www.actionaid.org/docs/GlobalProgressReport2003.pdf

36. African countries, generally, are extremely poor. On average they now spend about four times more on debt-service payments incurred through IMF intervention than they spend on health care. Had IMF and World Bank loans been spent on education, health care, agricultural improvements, sustainable industries, and pan-African trade instead of financing that chiefly benefited foreign multinationals, these countries' economies would be in much greater shape today. International Forum on Globalization, *Alternatives to Economic Globalization* (San Francisco: Berrett-Koehler, 2002), 38–39.

37. See Henc van Maarseveen and Ger van der Tang, *Written Constitutions: A Computerized Comparative Study* (Dobbs Ferry, N.Y.: Oceana Publications, 1978).

38. George Soros, *George Soros on Globalization* (New York: Public Affairs, 2002).

39. Jan Palmowski, *Oxford Dictionary of Contemporary World History* (Oxford: Oxford University Press, 2003), 555.

40. See discussions in: Maddex, *Constitutions of the World*, 120–22; Francois Venter, *Constitutional Comparison* (Cambridge, Mass.: Kluwer Law International, 2000).

41. In transcripts that were released in May 2004, Kissinger tells Nixon, "We didn't do it. I mean we helped them." www.commondreams.org/headlines04/0527-01.htm

42. Sam Husseini, "25 Years after the Coup, Is Chile a Model for Social Security?" Institute for Public Accuracy, September 8, 1998: www.commondreams.org/pressreleases/Sept98/090898e.htm

43. United Nations Development Programme, *Human Development Report 2004* (New York: Oxford University Press, 2004), 139, 258–59.

44. See, for example: Bouandel, *Human Rights and Comparative Politics*; James C. Strouse and Richard P. Claude, "Empirical Comparative Rights Research," in *Comparative Human Rights*, ed. Richard P. Claude, 51–68 (Baltimore, Md.: Johns Hopkins University Press, 1976); Joseph Wronka, *Human Rights and Social Policy in the 21st Century* (Lanham, Md.: University Press of America, 1992); Niclas Berggren, Nils Karlson, and Joakim Nergelius, eds., *Why Constitutions Matter* (New Brunswick, N.J.: Transaction, 2002).

45. United Nations Conference on Trade and Development, *Escaping the Poverty Trap* (Geneva: UNCTAD, 2002), 161.

46. Perhaps with tongue in cheek, prominent economist Kenneth E. Boulding explains perfect competition in simple terms, using a comparison of lawyers and professors. He explains that whereas lawyers spend less of their time in school, they have lousy working conditions compared with the professor who "lives usually in agreeable surroundings, works among congenial associates, has a good deal of leisure, has long vacations, exercises a little brief authority over his students, and has opportunities for molding young and immature minds." Competitive fairness is at work, he suggests to his readers, for if it were not, the salaries of professors would increase or that of lawyers would decrease. Along these lines, faculty in

American business schools have higher salaries than scholars in arts and sciences, because American corporations are competing with universities for PhDs in accounting, and none are competing with PhDs in philosophy. Boulding, *Economic Analysis*, 3rd ed. (New York: Harper, 1955), 183.

47. Joan Robinson, *The Economics of Imperfect Competition* (London: Macmillan, 1933).

48. Mark A. Lutz, *Economics for the Common Good* (London: Routledge, 1999), 114–16.

49. Amartya Sen, "On the Foundations of Welfare Economics," in *Ethics, Rationality and Economic Behavior*, ed. F. Farina, F. Hahn, and S. Vannucci (New York: Clarendon Press, 1996), 50; cited in Mark A. Lutz, *Economics for the Common Good: Two Centuries of Social Economic Thought in the Humanistic Tradition* (London: Routledge, 1999), 121–22.

50. Amartya Sen, *Development as Freedom* (New York: Knopf, 1999); see also Siddiqur Rahman Osmani, "On Inequality," in *Blackwell Companion to Sociology*, ed. Judith R. Blau, 143–60 (Malden, Mass.: Blackwell, 2001).

51. United Nations, Department of Economic and Social Affairs, cited by Stalker's Guide to International Migration: pstalker.com/migration

52. Dean Baker, Gerald Epstein, and Robert Pollin, "Introduction," in *Globalization and Progressive Economic Policy*, ed. Epstein, Pollin, and Baker, 1–34 (Cambridge: Cambridge University Press, 1998).

53. Joseph E. Stiglitz, *Globalization and Its Discontents* (New York: Norton, 2003).

54. See Robert Albritton, "Socialism and Individual Freedom," in *New Socialisms: Futures beyond Globalization*, ed. Robert Albritton and Richard Westra, 17–32 (London: Routledge, 2004).

55. Osmani, "On Inequality," 151.

56. Through its various Listservs, the Center for Economic, Social, and Cultural Rights draws in participants from around the globe to prepare for international meetings and to disseminate information on specific issues, such as gender equality and the environment.

57. Social Investment Forum, Social Investment Report on Socially Responsibly Investing Trends (2003): www.foe.org/international/shareholder/

58. Pierre-Joseph Proudhon, *Correspondence* (Paris: Lacroix, 1875), II, 296; cited in Dudley Dillard, "Keynes and Proudhon," in *Dissenters*, ed. Mark Blaug, 83 (Aldershot, U.K.: Edward Elgar, 1992); see R. Wade, *Governing the Market Economy* (Princeton, N.J.: Princeton University Press, 1990); Leslie Armour, "The Social Self and the Need for an Alternative to Socialism," *International Journal of Social Economics* 17 (1990): 4–16; for an extensive bibliography see: www.ceedweb.org/iirp

Appendix 6.1
International Covenant on Economic, Social, and Cultural Rights, Approved by General Assembly, 1966; Adopted as Treaty, 1976

Preamble

The States Parties to the present Covenant,

Considering that, in accordance with the principles proclaimed in the Charter of the United Nations, recognition of the inherent dignity and of the equal and inalienable rights of all members of the human family is the foundation of freedom, justice and peace in the world,

Recognizing that these rights derive from the inherent dignity of the human person,

Recognizing that, in accordance with the Universal Declaration of Human Rights, the ideal of free human beings enjoying freedom from fear and want can only be achieved if conditions are created whereby everyone may enjoy his economic, social and cultural rights, as well as his civil and political rights,

Considering the obligation of States under the Charter of the United Nations to promote universal respect for, and observance of, human rights and freedoms,

Realizing that the individual, having duties to other individuals and to the community to which he belongs, is under a responsibility to strive for the promotion and observance of the rights recognized in the present Covenant,

Agree upon the following articles:

Article 1

1. All peoples have the right of self-determination. By virtue of that right they freely determine their political status and freely pursue their economic, social and cultural development.

2. All peoples may, for their own ends, freely dispose of their natural wealth and resources without prejudice to any obligations arising out of international economic co-operation, based upon the principle of mutual benefit, and international law. In no case may a people be deprived of its own means of subsistence.

3. The States Parties to the present Covenant, including those having responsibility for the administration of Non-Self-Governing and Trust Territories, shall promote the realization of the right of self-determination, and shall respect that right, in conformity with the provisions of the Charter of the United Nations.

Article 2

1. Each State Party to the present Covenant undertakes to take steps, individually and through international assistance and co-operation, especially economic and technical, to the maximum of its available resources, with a view to achieving progressively the full realization of the rights recognized in the present Covenant by all appropriate means, including particularly the adoption of legislative measures.

2. The States Parties to the present Covenant undertake to guarantee that the rights enunciated in the present Covenant will be exercised without discrimination of any kind as to race, colour, sex, language, religion, political or other opinion, national or social origin, property, birth or other status.

3. Developing countries, with due regard to human rights and their national economy, may determine to what extent they would guarantee the economic rights recognized in the present Covenant to non-nationals.

Article 3

The States Parties to the present Covenant undertake to ensure the equal right of men and women to the enjoyment of all economic, social and cultural rights set forth in the present Covenant.

Article 4 and Article 5

[General applicability of the Covenant]

Article 6

1. The States Parties to the present Covenant recognize the right to work, which includes the right of everyone to the opportunity to gain his living by work which he freely chooses or accepts, and will take appropriate steps to safeguard this right.
2. The steps to be taken by a State Party to the present Covenant to achieve the full realization of this right shall include technical and vocational guidance and training programmes, policies and techniques to achieve steady economic, social and cultural development and full and productive employment under conditions safeguarding fundamental political and economic freedoms to the individual.

Article 7

The States Parties to the present Covenant recognize the right of everyone to the enjoyment of just and favourable conditions of work which ensure, in particular:

(a) Remuneration which provides all workers, as a minimum, with:
   (i) Fair wages and equal remuneration for work of equal value without distinction of any kind, in particular women being guaranteed conditions of work not inferior to those enjoyed by men, with equal pay for equal work;
   (ii) A decent living for themselves and their families in accordance with the provisions of the present Covenant;
(b) Safe and healthy working conditions;
(c) Equal opportunity for everyone to be promoted in his employment to an appropriate higher level, subject to no considerations other than those of seniority and competence;
(d) Rest, leisure and reasonable limitation of working hours and periodic holidays with pay, as well as remuneration for public holidays.

Article 8

1. The States Parties to the present Covenant undertake to ensure:
   (a) The right of everyone to form trade unions and join the trade union of his choice, subject only to the rules of the organization concerned, for the promotion and protection of his economic and social interests. No restrictions may be placed on the exercise of this right other than those prescribed by law and which are necessary in a democratic society in the interests of national security or public order or for the protection of the rights and freedoms of others;
   (b) The right of trade unions to establish national federations or confederations and the right of the latter to form or join international trade-union organizations;
   (c) The right of trade unions to function freely subject to no limitations other than those prescribed by law and which are necessary in a democratic society in the interests of national security or public order or for the protection of the rights and freedoms of others;
   (d) The right to strike, provided that it is exercised in conformity with the laws of the particular country.

Article 9

The States Parties to the present Covenant recognize the right of everyone to social security, including social insurance.

Article 10

The States Parties to the present Covenant recognize that:

1. The widest possible protection and assistance should be accorded to the family, which is the natural and fundamental group unit of society, particularly for its establishment and while it is responsible for the care and education of dependent children. Marriage must be entered into with the free consent of the intending spouses.
2. Special protection should be accorded to mothers during a reasonable period before and after childbirth. During such period working mothers should be accorded paid leave or leave with adequate social security benefits.
3. Special measures of protection and assistance should be taken on behalf of all children and young persons without any discrimination for reasons of parentage or other conditions.

Children and young persons should be protected from economic and social exploitation. Their employment in work harmful to their morals or health or dangerous to life or likely to hamper their normal development should be punishable by law. States should also set age limits below which the paid employment of child labour should be prohibited and punishable by law.

Article 11

1. The States Parties to the present Covenant recognize the right of everyone to an adequate standard of living for himself and his family, including adequate food, clothing and housing, and to the continuous improvement of living conditions.
2. States Parties to the present Covenant, recognizing the fundamental right of everyone to be free from hunger, shall take, individually and through international co-operation, the measures, including specific programmes, which are needed:

(a) To improve methods of production, conservation and distribution of food by making full use of technical and scientific knowledge, by disseminating knowledge of the principles of nutrition and by developing or reforming agrarian systems in such a way as to achieve the most efficient development and utilization of natural resources;
(b) Taking into account the problems of both food-importing and food-exporting countries, to ensure an equitable distribution of world food supplies in relation to need.

Article 12

1. The States Parties to the present Covenant recognize the right of everyone to the enjoyment of the highest attainable standard of physical and mental health.
2. The steps to be taken by the States Parties to the present Covenant to achieve the full realization of this right shall include those necessary for:
   (a) The provision for the reduction of the stillbirth-rate and of infant mortality and for the healthy development of the child;
   (b) The improvement of all aspects of environmental and industrial hygiene;
   (c) The prevention, treatment and control of epidemic, endemic, occupational and other diseases;

(d) The creation of conditions which would assure to all medical service and medical attention in the event of sickness.

Article 13

1. The States Parties to the present Covenant recognize the right of everyone to education. They agree that education shall be directed to the full development of the human personality and the sense of its dignity, and shall strengthen the respect for human rights and fundamental freedoms. . . .

2. The States Parties to the present Covenant recognize that, with a view to achieving the full realization of this right:

(a) Primary education shall be compulsory and available free to all;
(b) Secondary education in its different forms, including technical and vocational secondary education, shall be made generally available and accessible to all by every appropriate means, and in particular by the progressive introduction of free education;
(c) Higher education shall be made equally accessible to all, on the basis of capacity, by every appropriate means, and in particular by the progressive introduction of free education;
(d) Fundamental education shall be encouraged or intensified as far as possible for those persons who have not received or completed the whole period of their primary education;
(e) The development of a system of schools at all levels shall be actively pursued, an adequate fellowship system shall be established, and the material conditions of teaching staff shall be continuously improved.

3. The States Parties to the present Covenant undertake to have respect for the liberty of parents and, when applicable, legal guardians to choose for their children schools, other than those established by the public authorities . . . to ensure the religious and moral education of their children in conformity with their own convictions.

Article 15

1. The States Parties to the present Covenant recognize the right of everyone:
(a) To take part in cultural life;

    (b) To enjoy the benefits of scientific progress and its applications;

    (c) To benefit from the protection of the moral and material interests resulting from any scientific, literary or artistic production of which he is the author.

3. The States Parties to the present Covenant undertake to respect the freedom indispensable for scientific research and creative activity.

SOURCE: www.unhchr.ch/html/menu3/b/a_cescr.htm

NOTES: Sections relating to implementation are deleted. Adopted and opened for signature, ratification, and accession by General Assembly resolution 2200A (XXI) of December 16, 1966; *entry into force* January 3, 1976. The following states have signed but not ratified the treaty: Belize, Lao People's Democratic Republic, Liberia, Sao Tome and Principe, South Africa, United States of America.

Appendix 6.2
Fundamental Conventions of the International Labour Organization, Brief Description, Number of Ratifying Countries, and U.S. Ratifying Status (175 total state parties, as of July 2004)

Freedom of Association and Protection of the Right to Organize Convention (No. 87); 142 countries—United States, no.

> Workers and employers, without distinction whatsoever, shall have the right to establish and, subject only to the rules of the organisation concerned, to join organisations of their own choosing without previous authorisation.

Right to Organize and Collective Bargaining Convention, 1949 (No. 98), 154 countries—United States, no.

> Workers shall enjoy adequate protection against acts of anti-union discrimination in respect of their employment.

Forced Labor Convention, 1930 (No. 29); 163 countries—United States, no.

> Each Member which ratifies this Convention undertakes to suppress the use of forced or compulsory labour in all its forms within the shortest possible period.

Abolition of Forced Labor Convention, 1957 (No. 105); 161 countries—United States, yes.

> Each Member which ratifies this Convention undertakes to suppress and not to make use of any form of forced or compulsory labour—(a) as a means of political coercion or education or as a punishment for holding or expressing political views or views ideologically opposed to the established political, social or economic system; (b) as a method of mobilising and us-

ing labour for purposes of economic development; (c) as a means of labour discipline; (d) as a punishment for having participated in strikes; (e) as a means of racial, social, national or religious discrimination.

Discrimination (Employment and Occupation) Convention, 1958 (No. 111); 160 countries—United States, no.

Each Member for which this Convention is in force undertakes to declare and pursue a national policy designed to promote, by methods appropriate to national conditions and practice, equality of opportunity and treatment in respect of employment and occupation, with a view to eliminating any discrimination in respect thereof.

Equal Remuneration Convention, 1951 (No. 100); 161 countries— United States, no.

Each Member shall, by means appropriate to the methods in operation for determining rates of remuneration, promote and, in so far as is consistent with such methods, ensure the application to all workers of the principle of equal remuneration for men and women workers for work of equal value.

Minimum Age Convention, 1973 (No. 138); 134 countries—United States, no.

Each Member which ratifies this Convention shall specify, in a declaration appended to its ratification, a minimum age for admission to employment or work within its territory and on means of transport registered in its territory; subject to Articles 4 to 8 of this Convention, no one under that age shall be admitted to employment or work in any occupation. [Age limit varies by type of work, with thirteen being the minimum for "light work"; fifteen otherwise.]

Worst Forms of Child Labour Convention, 1999 (No. 182); 150 countries —United States, yes.

Each Member which ratifies this Convention shall take immediate and effective measures to secure the prohibition and elimination of the worst forms of child labour as a matter or urgency [child defined as under the age eighteen].

SOURCE: International Labour Organization: www.ilo.org

Appendix 6.3
Economic Rights in
Contemporary Constitutions (extracts)

[decorative glyph]

Asia

Bangladesh
13. Principles of ownership.

The people shall own or control the instruments and means of production and distribution, and with this end in view ownership shall assume the following forms—(a) state ownership . . . and nationalized public sector; (b) co-operative ownership . . . (c) private ownership within such limits as may be prescribed by law.

20. Work as a right and duty.
(1)
Work is a right, a duty and a matter of honor for every citizen who is capable of working, and everyone shall be paid for his work on the basis of the principle "from each according to his abilities to each according to his work."
(2)
The State shall endeavor to create conditions in which, as a general principle, persons shall not be able to enjoy unearned incomes, and in which human labor in every form, intellectual and physical, shall become a fuller expression of creative endeavor and of the human personality.

China
42.
(1) Citizens of the People's Republic of China have the right as well as the duty to work.

(2) Using various channels, the state creates conditions for employment, strengthens labor protection, improves working conditions, and, on the basis of expanded production, increases remuneration for work and social benefits. (3) Work is the glorious duty of every able-bodied citizen. All working people in State-owned enterprises and in urban and rural economic collectives should perform their tasks with an attitude consonant with their status as masters of the country. The State promotes socialist labor emulation, and commends and rewards model and advanced workers. The State encourages citizens to take part in voluntary labor.

Japan

27.
(1) All people shall have the right and the obligation to work.
(2) Standards for wages, hours, rest, and other working conditions shall be fixed by law.
(3) Children shall not be exploited.

Middle East

Egypt

4.
The economic foundation of the Arab Republic of Egypt is a socialist democratic system based on sufficiency and justice in a manner preventing exploitation, conducive to liquidation of income differences, protecting legitimate earnings, and guaranteeing the equity of the distribution of public duties and responsibilities.

13.
Work is a right, a duty, and an honor ensured by the State.
Workers who excel in their field of work shall receive the appreciation of the State and the society.
No work shall be imposed on the citizens, except by virtue of the law, for the performance of a public service and in return for a fair remuneration.

Jordan

23.
(i) Work is the right of every citizen, and the State shall provide opportunities for work to all citizens by directing the national economy and raising its standards.

(ii) The State shall protect labor and enact legislation therefore based on the following principles:
   (a) Every worker shall receive wages commensurate with the quantity and quality of his work.
   (b) The number of hours of work per week shall be defined. Workers shall be given weekly and annual days of paid rest.
   (c) Special compensation shall be given to workers supporting families and on dismissal, illness, old age and emergencies arising out of the nature of their work.
   (d) Special conditions shall be made for the employment of women and juveniles.
   (e) Factories and workshops shall be subject to health safeguards.
   (f) Free trade unions may be formed within the limits of the law.

Turkey
48.
Everyone has the freedom to work and conclude contracts in the field of his/her choice. Establishment of private enterprises is free.
The state shall take measures to ensure that private enterprises operate in accordance with national economic requirements and social objectives and in conditions of security and stability.

49.
Everyone has the right and duty to work.
The State shall take the necessary measures to raise the standard of living of workers, and to protect workers and the unemployed in order to improve the general conditions of labour, to promote labour, to create suitable economic conditions for prevention of unemployment and to secure labour peace.

50.
No one shall be required to perform work unsuited to his age, sex, and capacity.
Minors, women and persons with physical or mental disabilities, shall enjoy special protection with regard to working conditions.
All workers have the right to rest and leisure.
Rights and conditions relating to paid weekends and holidays, together with paid annual leave, shall be regulated by law.

Africa

Cameroon

Affirm our attachment to the fundamental freedoms enshrined in the Universal Declaration of Human Rights, the Charter of the United Nations and the African Charter on Human and Peoples' Rights, and all duly ratified international conventions relating thereto, in particular, to the following principles:

—all persons shall have equal rights and obligations. The State shall provide all its citizens with the conditions necessary for their development; . . .
—every person shall have the right and the obligation to work

Ethiopia

40.
4. The right of Ethiopian peasants to free allotment of land and freedom from eviction is guaranteed. Particulars for its implementation shall be determined by law.

41.
1. Every Ethiopian shall have the right to engage in any economic activity and gain his living by work which he freely chooses.
2. Every Ethiopian shall have the right to choose his vocation, work and profession. . . .
4. The State shall allocate progressively increasing funds for the purposes of promoting the people's access to health, education and other social services.
5. The State shall, within the limits permitted by the economic capability of the country, care for and rehabilitate the physically and mentally handicapped, the aged, and children deprived of their parents or guardians.
6. The State shall devise policies designed to create employment of the poor and unemployed; issue programs designed to open up work opportunities in the public sector and undertake projects.
7. The State shall take necessary measures to expand the opportunities of citizens to engage in gainful employment.
8. Peasants shall have the right to be paid a fair recompense for their produce which would enable them to progressively attain an improved

standard of living and in proportion to their productive contribution to the national wealth. The State shall be guided by this objective in determining its economic and social development policies.

Malawi
29.
Every person shall have the right freely to engage in economic activity, to work and to pursue a livelihood anywhere in Malawi.

30.
(1) All persons and peoples have a right to development and therefore to the enjoyment of economic, social, cultural and political development and women, children and the disabled in particular shall be given special consideration in the application of this right.

(2) The State shall take all necessary measures for the realization of the right to development. Such measures shall include, amongst other things, equality of opportunity for all in their access to basic resources, education, health services, food, shelter, employment and infrastructure.

31.
(1) Every person shall have the right to fair and safe labor practices and to fair remuneration.

(2) All persons shall have the right to form and join trade unions or not to form or join trade unions.

(3) Every person shall be entitled to fair wages and equal remuneration for work of equal value without distinction or discrimination of any kind, in particular on basis of gender, disability or race.

Europe

Netherlands
19.
(1) It shall be the concern of the authorities to promote the provision of sufficient employment.
(2) Rules concerning the legal status and protection of working persons and concerning co-determination shall be laid down by Act of Parliament.

(3) The right of every Dutch national to a free choice of work shall be recognized, without prejudice to the restrictions laid down by or pursuant to Act of Parliament.

20.

(1) It shall be the concern of the authorities to secure the means of subsistence of the population and to achieve the distribution of wealth. (3) Dutch nationals resident in the Netherlands who are unable to provide for themselves shall have a right, to be regulated by Act of Parliament, to aid from the authorities.

Russia

34.

1. Everyone shall have the right to freely use his or her abilities and property for entrepreneurial or any other economic activity not prohibited by the law.

2. No economic activity aimed at monopolization or unfair competition shall be allowed.

37.

1. Work shall be free. Everyone shall have the right to make free use of his or her abilities for work and to choose a type of activity and occupation.

2. Forced labor shall be prohibited.

3. Everyone shall have the right to work under conditions meeting the requirements of safety and hygiene, to remuneration for work without any discrimination whatsoever and not below the statutory minimum wage, and also the right to security against unemployment.

4. The right to individual and collective labor disputes with the use of means of resolution thereof established by federal law, including the right to strike, shall be recognized.

5. Everyone shall have the right to rest and leisure. A person having a work contract shall be guaranteed the statutory duration of the work time, days off and holidays, and paid annual vacation.

Spain

35.

(1) All Spaniards have the duty to work and the right to work, to the free election of profession or office career, to advancement through work, and to a sufficient remuneration to satisfy their needs and those of their family,

while in no case can there be discrimination for reasons of sex. (2) The law shall regulate a statute for workers.

37.
(1) The law shall guarantee the right to collective labor negotiations between the representatives of workers and employers, as well as the binding force of agreements.
(2) The right of the workers and employers to adopt measures concerning collective conflict is recognized. The law that shall regulate the exercise of this right, without prejudice to the limitations it may establish, shall include precise guarantees to insure the functioning of the essential services of the community.

The Americas

Brazil

II.
7. (0) The following are rights of city and rural workers, notwithstanding any others that seek to improve their social condition:
I. Employment protected against arbitrary dismissal or against dismissal without cause, according to a supplemental law which shall establish severance payment, among other rights;
II. Unemployment insurance, in the event of involuntary unemployment;
III. Unemployment compensation fund;
IV. A minimum wage nationwide . . .
V. A salary floor in proportion to the extent and complexity of the work;
VI. Irreducibility of salary or wage . . .
IX. Compensation for night work above that for daytime work . . .
XI. Sharing in the profits or results, independent of compensation, and, exceptionally, participation in the management of the company, as defined by law;
XII. Family allowance for their dependents;
XIII. Normal work hours not exceeding eight hours per day and forty-four hours per week . . .
XIV. A work day of six hours for work carried out in uninterrupted shifts;
XV. Paid weekly leave, preferably on Sundays;
XVI. Compensation for overtime work at least fifty per cent above the compensation for normal work;
XVII. Annual vacation with compensation at least one third above the normal salary;

XVIII. Maternity leave without loss of job and of salary, for a period of one hundred and twenty days;

XIX. Paternity leave, under the terms established by law;

XX. Protection of the work market for women through specific incentives according to the law; . . .

XXII. Reduction of work risks by means of health, hygiene, and safety rules;

XXIII. Additional compensation for unhealthy or dangerous work, as established by law;

XXIV. Retirement pension; . . .

XXVII. Protection by virtue of automation, as established by law;

XXVIII. Work accident insurance, under the responsibility of the employer . . .

XXX. Prohibition of any difference in salary, in performance of duties, and in hiring criteria by reason of sex, age, color, or marital status;

XXXI. Prohibition of any discrimination with respect to salary and hiring criteria for handicapped workers;

XXXII. Prohibition of any distinction between manual, technical, and intellectual labor or between the respective professionals;

XXXIII. Prohibition of night, dangerous, or unhealthy work for minors under eighteen years of age, and of any work for minors under fourteen years of age, except as an apprentice;

XXXIV. Equal rights for workers with a permanent employment contract and contract workers.

(1) The category of domestic workers is assured of the rights set forth in [given provisions] and integration into the social security system.

8.
[Labor union rights]

9.
(0) The right to strike is guaranteed . . .

10.
The participation of workers and employers is ensured in the collegiate bodies of government agencies in which their professional or social security interests are the subject of discussion and resolution.

11.
In companies having more than two hundred employees, the election of an employee representative is ensured for the exclusive purpose of furthering direct discussions with their employers.

Canada[1]

(1) Without altering the legislative authority of Parliament or of the provincial legislatures, or the rights of any of them with respect to the exercise of their legislative authority, Parliament and the legislatures, together with the government of Canada and the provincial governments, are committed to promoting equal opportunities for the well-being of Canadians; furthering economic development to reduce disparity in opportunities; and providing essential public services of reasonable quality to all Canadians.

Chile

6.

—Freedom to work and protection of that freedom.

Any person has the right to free employment and free selection of his work, with a just compensation.

—Any discrimination which is not based on personal skills or capability is prohibited, although the law may require Chilean citizenship or age limits in certain cases.

—No type of work can be prohibited except where it is contrary to morals, or public security and health, or where it should be so required by the national interest as declared by the law.

—No type of work can be prohibited except where it is contrary to morals, or public security and health, or where it should be so required by the national interest as declared by the law. No law or provision from the public authority may demand affiliation to any organization or entity whatsoever, as a requirement for undertaking certain activity or work, nor can it demand that any such affiliation be discontinued as a condition to perform such activities or keep such work. The law shall determine which professions require a title or university degree and the conditions to be met in order to engage in them.

—Workmen have the right to collective bargaining with the company for which they work, except where the law should expressly prohibit negotiations. The law shall establish the procedures for collective bargaining and the appropriate procedures for reaching a just and peaceful solution. The law shall provide for the instances in which collective bargaining is to be submitted to mandatory arbitration; this arbitration should be entrusted to special courts of experts, the organization and authority of which shall be established by the law.

---

1. Charter of Rights and Freedoms, Part III.

—Neither State or municipal employees may go on strike; nor may people working for corporations or enterprises, regardless of the nature, objectives or functions thereof, which provide public utility services or the paralysis of which might seriously harm health, the economy of the country, the supplies to the population or the national security. The law shall establish the procedures to determine the corporations or enterprises whose workers will be covered by the prohibition set forth in this paragraph.

SOURCE: Constitution Finder: confinder.richmond.edu

NOTES: Economic rights are sometimes in clauses that include other rights (such as education, social security, etc.). In virtually all cases these provisions were deleted for purposes of parsimony.

In Search of Society

Under the Freedom of Information Act, the American Civil Liberties Union (ACLU) obtained Federal Bureau of Investigation (FBI) records on December 15, 2004, relating to the torture of prisoners held in the jails in Guantánamo Bay, Cuba; Baghdad; and Afghanistan: the ACLU released them to the press a few days later.[1] Below are a few of the personal accounts, emails, and memoranda that were released:

> They tortured me and cuffed me in an act called the scorpion, and pouring cold water on me They tortured me from [one] morning until the morning of the next day, and when I fell down from the severe torture I fell on the barbed wires, and then they dragged me from my feet and I was wounded and, and they punched me on my stomach.

> REDACTED stated that he had been beaten unconscious approximately three or four weeks ago when he was still at Camp X-Ray [Guantánamo]. According to REDACTED, an unknown number of guards entered his cell, unprovoked, and started spitting and cursing at him. . . . REDACTED rolled onto his stomach to protect himself, REDACTED state[d] a soldier named REDACTED jumped on his back and started beating him in the face REDACTED then choked him until he passed out. REDACTED stated that REDACTED was beating him because REDACTED was a Muslim.

> The following information provides initial details from an individual REDACTED who observed serious physical abuses of civilian detainees in REDACTED Iraq during the period of REDACTED. . . . REDACTED observed numerous physical abuse incidents of Iraqi civilian detainees conducted in REDACTED Iraq. He described that such abuses included strangulation,

beatings, placement of lit cigarettes into the detainee's ear openings, and unauthorized interrogations. REDACTED was providing this information to the FBI based on his knowledge that REDACTED cover-up of these abuses. He stated these cover-up efforts included REDACTED.

Already in Spring 2004, news was reported about the abuse of three British repatriated citizens, called the Tipton 3, after their hometown.[2] After their capture in Afghanistan they had been sent to Guantánamo, released only after long negotiations on their behalf by the Center for Constitutional Rights. In interviews they described that they had long periods of isolation, were stripped (especially humiliating for Muslims), were held in stress positions for as many as twelve hours, were threatened by dogs, and were chained hand and foot to a steel ring in the floor, while being bombarded with strobe lights, loud music, and very cold temperatures.

In August 2004 the accounts of Americans torturing prisoners at Abu Ghraib hit the front pages of papers, and received worldwide TV and radio coverage. There were enormous protests around the globe. Yet there was virtual silence among U.S. government officials and certainly no protest from the secretary of defense, the attorney general, the president, the Central Intelligence Agency, the FBI, and the civilian secretaries of the armed services. Yet, in November 2004 the American electorate swept George W. Bush back into office.

The White House had authorized torture a year and a half before the Abu Ghraib story broke. On January 25, 2002, Alberto R. Gonzales, the president's counsel, wrote a memo approving torture techniques that violated the Geneva Conventions,[3] and Bush approved the memo.[4] Later Donald Rumsfeld approved Gonzales's list of interrogation methods. In May 2003, a bill, HR 2224 IH, was introduced to the 108th Congress to prohibit torture or inhumane treatment of prisoners, affirming that U.S. policies must be consistent with the Geneva Conventions and Protocols. It was buried in committee without debate.[5]

The incorporation of Article 5 in the 1948 Universal Declaration prohibiting torture was an explicit response to Hitler's revival of Stalin's methods of torture, and the 1984 Convention against Torture and Other Cruel, Inhumane, and Degrading Treatment or Punishment was a response to the death under torture of Steve Biko in South Africa.[6] There is nothing complicated about such international understandings, and the United States has ratified the 1984 convention.[7] The laws against torture evolved primarily within the framework of Western jurisprudence and are consistent with the principles of U.S. civil and political freedoms.

Given America's extensive power and military presence on all continents, revelations about inhumane treatment of detainees and prisoners were all the more alarming. How dare a country that professes the rule of law with such piety so casually shrug off laws that are universally embraced and have international courts to uphold them?[8] Hannah Arendt teaches us the lesson that when leaders do evil things, it is necessary to probe the sources of legitimacy.[9] While it is important to understand the dynamics of geopolitics and how U.S. political leaders understand what they are doing, Hannah Arendt's question for us is to understand what is happening in American society that explains why Americans acquiescence to U.S. policies.

State Authority

Opinion polls revealed that Americans were sad about the tortures at Abu Ghraib, but they were not angered.[10] One answer as to why is that in times of war, patriotism, combined with peoples' fears of the enemy, heightens identification with national leaders. The more complicated answers, which we will pursue, have to do with the extent to which the U.S. state has preempted society and denied citizens their solidarities and their capacities to oppose the state. One indicator of this is that Americans are much less critical of their government compared with people in most other countries.[11] Some contend that America's weaker society has to do with its population diversity, but this is a myth because many countries have more diverse populations, more languages, more ethnicities.

Consistent with our main thesis, we argue that America's weaker society has to do with pervasive liberalism, which erodes society through the inordinate emphasis on individualism and competition. Additionally, the state derives some of its power from its functional relationship with capitalism, as Nicos Poulantzas argued in the 1960s.[12] This relationship involving the state and capital has since been strengthened in the United States under neoliberal policies that privatize public goods and services, further eroding a sense of the public good and collective interests. Moreover, American materialism, as described by Juliet B. Schor,[13] only strengthens the tenacity of the growing state–capitalist connections, because in the eyes of individual Americans, what keeps the nation strong is the robust connection between capitalist institutions and the state. Best not to rock the boat by challenging what the military is up to in Afghanistan, Abu Ghraib, and Guantánamo.

Besides, under liberal traditions, citizens distinguish between those who are worthy of civil and political rights, and those who are not. Civil and political rights are casually denied to Mexican migrants, and often blacks and routinely to indigenous Americans. When human rights are taken seriously, they are unconditional and inherent to personhood.[14] The thesis that we are pursuing is contrary to one that prevails in America, which is based on the defense of liberal democracy in the interests of impersonal justice, tolerance, and fairness.[15] In support of our thesis we will provide examples of state constitutions that promote societal pluralism.

Finally, contributing to the declining capacity of America's ability to uphold even civil and political rights, as evident in Abu Ghraib, Afghanistan, and Guantánamo, and elsewhere, is the extent to which it has become a military empire, not an upholder of human rights. The United States has troops in 135, or 70 percent, of the world's countries.[16] Militarism breeds secrecy, nationalism, arrogance, and intolerance and contempt of other societies. In the short run, the persons regarded as the enemy lose their fundamental rights, but this is, as history shows us, a slippery slope, with persons regarded as being the suspected enemy denied their rights, domestic opponents of the military denied theirs, and so forth.

Modernization and Development

Modernity, according to Alaine Touraine, is the triumph of an ideology that attributes rationalism to institutions—capitalism and state bureaucracies —and the diminishment of the public sphere.[17] Yes, we agree wholeheartedly, but Touraine, writing in the 1980s, could not fully have anticipated the full onslaught of global, neoliberal capitalism, which co-opts institutions and most especially state bureaucracies. The ideological shift is not trivial, and rationalism is no longer rooted in the Weberian principles of the rational connections between means and ends, but cruder ones having to do with economic returns on investments. If statism had something of a human face (welfare and education), corporatism does not.

Modernity also had its ideational continuities. In spite of differences among John Locke (1632–1704), Adam Smith (1723–1790), Jeremy Bentham (1748–1832), August Comte (1798–1857), Herbert Spencer (1820–1903), and Max Weber (1864–1920), all believed that the pursuit of economic advantage would improve the human condition for individuals, societies, and nations.[18] Economic freedoms were quintessential human freedoms.

The model of worldwide economic development evolved easily from these continuities in Western thought. The key premise of development underlying "modernization" and "development" is that all states (and even societies) follow more or less the same trajectory or path as Western nation-states. In American sociology this idea appeared in the writings of Talcott Parsons,[19] although economists, such as Simon Kuznets, were largely responsible for the theoretical work on development and the technical modeling of developmental trajectories.[20] Alex Inkeles and David H. Smith, based on their cross-national research, concluded that the "modern man" that was emerging in all parts of the world was becoming more and more like Americans. They exercised rationality, were individualists, and were disciplined workers.[21] The epitome of modernity, for American social scientists, was America itself: a capitalist economy, representative democracy, and national unifying culture.[22] The rest of the world would catch up by following in American footsteps. While the development model fell somewhat out of favor in the academy in the 1990s,[23] Francis Fukuyama has recently resurrected it, by contending that there is a general trend toward the universal adoption of capitalism and liberal values.[24] However, there is not much empirical evidence that he is correct; instead there has been ideological divisiveness and increasing economic inequalities.[25] In a later section of this chapter, we will also show that the political and societal values expressed in state constitutions are highly divergent.

It has not turned out the way that developmentalists predicted. American-led capitalism has accelerated economic inequalities, battered local economies, created joblessness, and fueled migration, wrecking families and communities. The conclusion of a 2003 survey by the Pew Research Center carried out in forty-four countries is that large majorities believe that economic globalization, led by Americans, is eradicating their ways of life and distinctive cultures.[26] Especially because we will focus on constitutions, it is helpful to reassess more carefully the varied foundations of nation-states.

The Nation-State

State formation, Jyoti Puri notes, can best be traced to the French Revolution, when the state first defined a civic community of equal citizens with civil equality.[27] His interpretation highlights the political role of the state, but also the importance of national identity, citizenship, and national allegiance. New nation-states, France, the United States, Spain, Holland, and Britain energetically subordinated local loyalties to the larger state. Eviatar Zerubavel provides a wonderful account of how one new nation-state, France, creatively went about its mission of eradicating existing loyalties, not merely local ones but widely shared religious beliefs as well.[28]

Understanding that the main competing loyalty was the Church, French authorities de-Christianized the calendar, making a ten-day week and replacing Sunday with *Décadi*, an official day of rest that occurred on the tenth day. To further secularize and rationalize the calendar, the government divided the year into twelve uniform thirty-day months, and each new thirty-day month was divided into three ten-day weekly cycles called *decades*. On February 4, 1794, the Convention of the Constituent Assembly abolished slavery, which was consistent with the Declaration of the Rights of Man and the French official position of human equality.[29]

America solved the church–state tensions in a way that was different from the way that France did. Instead of attempting to suppress the churches, it simply told them to stay out of state affairs ("the wall of separation") and, essentially, to compete among themselves for adherents.[30]

However, it was later, specifically 1848, that E. J. Hobsbawm argues is the precise moment when the nation-state came into its own.[31] This was the year when the Dictionary of the Royal Spanish Academy drops its definition of *nación* as "aggregate of the inhabitants of a province, a country or a kingdom," and replaces it with a definition that emphasizes the importance of "a common territory, common traditions, and common aspirations, and interests." Benedict Anderson makes a similar argument, contending that the nation rests on a shared understanding of birth and descent, and shared customs, language, and traditions.[32] According to Anderson, 1848 unleashed the forces that would transform Europe and until then, *nation* still meant indigenous, or group that shared the birthplace, customs, language, traditions. While for Anderson the transformation from nation to state accompanied the establishment of a single dominant written language, displacing languages of smaller groups and dialects, for Hobsbawm it meant a political culture that transcended nation.[33] This process began somewhat earlier in the United States because in a real sense the United States started with so few shared group identities, and the truly indigenous were thoroughly marginalized.[34]

Social scientists are familiar with Max Weber's account of the ways that new nation-states adopted a bureaucratic machinery and governance structures, and social institutions that would denaturalize constituent tribes, ethnicities, and races.[35] Bureaucracies and the military in the nineteenth-century nation-state were organized around neutrality, meritocracy, impersonality, unambiguous authority, rules, regulations, a hierarchy, and secular values. As Hobsbawm stresses, the new nation-state rested on a unified body of law and a supreme allegiance that would subordinate the particularistic claims of tribes, ethnicity, and race to a greater good, namely a collectivity whose members shared national loyalties. And we owe to Anderson an understanding of the importance of a single, written language, and to Weber a description of the nation-state's institutions.

Liberal democracy is procedural, not substantive (for example, see Joseph Alois Schumpeter[36]), requiring, therefore, considerable citizen indifference, even apathy.[37] Additionally, a two-party state is especially conducive to such apathy, because both parties compete for the center, washing out ideological differences, aggravated in the United States where the largest share of corporate sources, over which the two parties compete, reinforce political centrism. Even within Congress, the dominant party can manipulate the rules and procedures so that resolutions and bills from the opposing party can get sidelined into committee. Thus, the democratic process, from beginning to end, can marginalize substantive opposition.[38]

Capitalism and Democracy

Capitalism relates to the liberal nation-state in two distinct ways: at the macro and micro level. The theorists of the origins of the state paid relatively little attention to the class divisions within the modern Western state, but we can draw from the work of others to clarify that class divisions, unlike ethnic, religious, or other particularistic ones, became a functional component of the modern nation-state. Here we pick up the argument of Fred Block, namely that there are structural mechanisms—not merely ideological ones—that ensure that the state serves the interests of capitalists.[39] He makes two points. First, capitalists exert power through controlling business and consumer confidence, on which the state depends for legitimacy. That is, capitalists uniquely hold the state hostage through control of the relations involving the economy, workers, and state managers. Second, when capitalists intervene in the economy to create investment opportunities, they only serve the interests of capitalists, not the workers, and thereby further increase their own power. Thus, not only state officials, but also state managers have an incentive to rationalize a capitalist society. Owing to the coherent and close relationship between capitalism and the state, capitalists' need for a large labor pool of minimally educated workers could be met by state's educational policies, yielding a relatively small number of well-educated workers and a relatively large number of minimally educated workers, relaxing the ratio with the growth of the service sector. The argument is partly structural: the process evolves "behind the backs of the actors."[40] Herein we see how the state and the economy erode the underpinnings of society. It is an anonymous capitalist system and an impersonal bureaucratic state that drains the vital juices of society, its varied cultures, and group identifications. Because capitalism is itself driven by obsolescence, it needs to continually drive the public's acquisitive desires, so that materialism fills the vacuum left when society withers away.

Liberalism and the Oppression of Minorities

Lord Acton's defense of the modern state is perhaps the crudest and bluntest ever. He wrote that modernity "improved the inferior races," as they lived "in political union with races intellectually superior."[41] Historically, the liberal nation-state, with all its political and civil freedoms, is less egalitarian than commonly imagined by those who have a good education, are white, and live in white neighborhoods. As we have suggested, such freedoms are discrete—and discretely dispensed.

Evidence suggests that whites believe that rights are theirs to share or not to share. As whites' intolerance of blacks and Latinos is lessening, according to the Southern Poverty Law Center, their intolerance of Arab Americans is increasing.[42] In a December 2004 poll taken by researchers from Cornell University, 44 percent of Americans believed that the civil liberties of Arab Americans should be curtailed, and about 22 percent said the federal government should profile citizens as potential threats based on the fact that they are Muslim or have Middle Eastern heritage.[43] Liberalism is a poor vehicle for the advance of social equality, because it advocates laws and norms that are detached from social and economic realities. In real life, the economic inequalities between whites, on the one hand, and blacks and immigrant Americans, on the other, are enormous, and the liberal can use that as evidence of differential ability, motivation, and deservedness.[44]

State formation in the nineteenth century in the United States thus was achieved through the suppression of distinctive cultures and identities. The Chinese Exclusion Art of 1882, the continued enslavement of blacks until their emancipation to segregation, the ongoing banishment of Native Americans to distant tribal lands, and the ongoing degradation of Mexicans. All this in the name of liberal democracy! We cannot truly understand the extent to which white Americans committed such atrocities, but we can interpret them as part of state formation as described by Hobsbawm, Anderson, and Block. For the story to be complete it is useful to reflect on the experiences of white immigrants. As Ernest Gellner describes, capitalist society excludes local groups, micro groups with particular loyalties and allegiances, by harnessing their loyalties to the state, which in turn makes them loyal and obedient workers.[45] Or as Marshall Berman puts it, bureaucratic rationality of Western institutions, reinforcing an apolitical individualism by sidelining solidarities, undercuts substantive rationality and represses dissent.[46] During the nineteenth century, as nonwhites were excluded from most jobs, the industrial economy was booming, leading to the adoption of an immigration program that attracted many millions of white immigrants from Northern Europe—Ireland in particular—Southern Europe—Italy especially—and a variety of Eastern European countries—Russia, Poland, Latvia, and others. Factory employment, pressures to privatize their own religion and national customs, and English-language schooling resulted in an unprecedented nationalization process that is often described as one of the most successful assimilation experiences in the history of the world.[47]

In other words, the state ensures that individuals lack a reference point for collective allegiances and a focal point for criticism and forging solidarities with others. America is, as is sometimes said, a society of lonely and narcissistic people, preoccupied with their own looks, wealth, material possessions, homes, and personal relations, rather than, say, politics, community life, the environment, and public goods. The fears generated by the Republican administration, including the infamous 2005 duct tape campaign, warnings about foreigners, and the constant manipulation of the alert system, have only reinforced self-centered preoccupations and an ersatz patriotism at the cost of authentic solidarities.[48] Americans do not explore why they are distrusted and feared around the world.

Besides, nation building in the West accompanied the hegemonic political, legal, and cultural control of colonies. The modern world system, ending in the late twentieth century, according to Immanuel Wallerstein, was based on the cultural, political, economic, and legal dominance of the West over the rest of the world.[49] The Third World was never asked whether they liked to be dominated by their colonial powers.[50] Nor were minority groups within Western nations ever asked whether they wanted to give up their identities. They had no choice. Immigrants to America were, as social scientists now say, de-ethnicized ("whitened").[51] Liberalism, for Wallerstein, and us, is the commitment to limited democracy, a commitment to free markets, and the denaturalizing of cultural, societal, religious, and other group identities.[52] Yet increasingly, the channels of protest are becoming clearer, with emergent claims to protect minority and indigenous groups.[53]

Post-Nationalism

Liberalism played an exceedingly important role in early nation building, of course, to free subjects, whether they were Irish or French peasants, English yeomen, Russian surfs, American colonists, or Haitian slaves, and to liberate them *as individuals and as political equals*. That was another century, and the historical conditions in which liberation occurs now are very different. Political equality is a given in liberation movements; it is no longer in contention as it once was. The battles of individual freedom are still fought, of course, but against a background where individual political freedom is taken for granted.

The real battles for liberation are for substantive democracy, religious and cultural equality, the rights to group membership, economic equity, minority group rights, language rights. In none of these battles is individualism at the center of contention, at least not as much as Americans believe it is. Part of the reason individualism has receded to the background in freedom movements is because nation-states no longer have the capacity to command businesses and multinationals or the capacity even to command citizens. Now national borders are porous, and for the purposes of trade and communications of trivial significance.[54]

As the 2004 Report of the United Nations Development Program shows, ethnocultural pluralism is coming to the fore as an issue that faces nation-states, with some states having easily accommodated to pluralism while others are struggling to achieve it.[55] The report cites as examples the older democracies of Spain and Belgium, where multiple and complementary identities are commonplace; the new pluralistic policies evolving in South Africa, India, and Malaysia; South Africa's recognition of eleven official languages; Guatemala, Paraguay, and India developing forms of legal and judicial pluralism; and many countries with large indigenous populations providing them with expanded legal rights, and many countries incorporating minority cultures into the larger one by granting them official recognition by national observance of their religious holidays. To assert human equality these days is not especially to demand equal civil and political rights—that was the battle of yesteryear—but to achieve the rights of being different while being equal at the same time.

The debate between the universalists and pluralists tended to harden during the 1960s and 1970s as the West spoke for universalism, whereas the Third World defended pluralism. Perhaps the most useful contributor to this debate has been Abdullahi A. An-Na'im, who argues for universality of personhood and economic and environmental rights, and also for peoples' rights to their identities that draw from their distinctive cultural and social group memberships.[56] But sociologists can add to this debate. People are not part of one group only; they have cosmopolitan identities, which allows them flexibility, and a predisposition to tolerance.[57] The danger arises when hierarchical class differences are confounded with cultural —racial or ethnic—differences, thereby limiting social associations and creating cultural inequalities.[58] These are the kind of inequalities that dominant groups cannot recognize because they rationalize them away as being due to innate differences. Just as men claim superiority over women, whites claim superiority over nonwhites, and such inequalities as these are harder to eradicate than economic ones.

Human Rights as Relationships

Legal scholars and political scientists have dominated the human rights discourse. As a result, the predominant emphasis has been on how human rights can be codified at the international and national levels. Yet sociologists and anthropologists can make distinct contributions to understanding human rights.

Sociologists and anthropologists recognize that human rights norms and practices, like all norms and practices, depend on the social relations that embed them, and that no society can uphold human rights if they are not valued in relationships and communities. If competition fiercely dominates the marketplace this competition will pervade social relations, imperiling the rights of racial, ethnic, and indigenous minorities. Globalization heightens claims for human rights, as Kiyoteru Tsutsui nicely puts it,[59] but globalization also heightens the awareness of great human variation in values, lifestyles, beliefs, and so forth. It is important that this happens if for no other reason than that it will loosen the deep cleavages of economic inequality that underlie cultural differences.

There are many ways of squaring the celebration of cultural differences with the advance of an international ethics of universalism. One is simply pragmatic. As Jack Donnelly points out, we have to build solidarities across lines of difference so that groups will cease intergroup rivalries, especially the kind that leads to oppression and, worse, genocide.[60] He cites Serbs massacring Muslims in Bosnia and Kosovo; Sudanese Muslims massacring non-Muslims in the south of Sudan; and the governments of Guatemala and Paraguay killing their indigenous peoples. We could add to his examples the marginalization of the Roma in Europe, blacks in the contemporary United States, and Muslims in France. There are degrees of cultural intolerance, rooted in complex struggles for social, political, and economic rights. Second, we could stress the obvious. Cultural diversity is akin to biodiversity. It is as necessary for the survival of human societies, which requires internal variation or else they wither and stagnate. Third, what underlie cultural diversity are, of course, human identities, and without those, people themselves could not survive.

By highlighting the social relational aspects of diversity we also highlight the ethics of human relations. This is a key component of virtually all religious traditions.[61] Perhaps the first formalization of relational ethics can be traced back to the ancient texts of the Vedas and Upanishads, written over three thousand years ago. These early scriptures enjoined followers to practice selfless concern for the sick, the homeless, and the unfortunate. The principle, as codified in the *Manava Dharma Sutra* (Treatise on Human Duties), stressed that only through relationships with others who were different in some respects was it possible to promote equality. This Hindi tradition may have been the oldest, but later major religious traditions highlighted similar relational ethics, including Buddhism and Judaism (both around 2,500 years ago), Christianity (about 2,000 years ago), and Islam (1,500 years ago).[62] To *stand by one's own rights* is still considered in some religious traditions to be antisocial and selfish.[63]

Yet religious traditions also have inherent tendencies to privilege believers over nonbelievers, which is aggravated by disputes over land or water, when the resources of one exceed those of the other, and the ethical principle that stresses regard for the other loses out to the moral principle of ideological self-righteousness.[64] Globalism has increased intersocietal contact, but it also has brought about interdependencies and commonalities not conceivable a few decades ago. These realities increase the ways that we can think of globalized ethical practices and interpersonal ethical regard.

Ideology, Human Rights, and Group Rights

Universal human rights and particular group rights intersect in different ways from one society to another. In Africa the danger has been that whereas constitutions promote societal fluidity to preserve customary laws and national laws, particular ethnic or religious groups hijack privileges for themselves. It is important to consider that economic rights, though not in themselves ideological and divisive, can become so when they are manipulated to benefit one group over another. This is particularly the case in African states, owing to the horizontality of customary law and the verticality of formal human rights doctrine.[65] Yet this plays out very differently in Western societies. As Ulrich Willems notes, liberal states, notably the United States but also France, contend that the wall of separation between the state and religion guarantees the rights of all, while in fact, dominant cultural and religious groups repress the rights of minority groups.[66]

When the cultural minority is indigenous, provisions for group rights are especially important, because typically they have been pushed into the least desirable and least sustainable parts of a country. They are particularly subject to the abuses of the cultural majority, the state, and private enterprise. Recent constitutional changes in many Latin American countries and Canada have buttressed the rights of indigenous groups.[67] Grave threats to group rights are posed by those states that ideologize the state, as the former Soviet Union did, and which Israel continues to do.[68] Islamic states are comparable to Israel in some respects, but Israel has no constitution that clarifies the role of religion whereas Islamic states all do.[69]

Notwithstanding the threats posed by the ideologized state, in our view, the two gravest threats to cultural rights on a global scale emanate, first, from commodification and the suppression of local culture by markets, and, second, from the Western realist doctrine that evolves around principles of power and geopolitical dominance. A great deal has been written about the extent to which Western commodities have invaded and swamped local communities and societies. This is often described as the "homogenization of culture."[70] However, we also stress the insidious political perspective that subordinates human rights to economic practices. The realist doctrine pragmatically treats all human rights as "soft" and "flexible," as when the United States links food aid to whether a country votes the "right way" on an issue before the United Nations, or dumps its subsidized agricultural products, undercutting the country's agriculturalists' ability to sell, and therefore, produce. The U.S. government thereby sets the norms for multinationals, which engage in the same realist pursuit of self-interest when they swamp other countries with cheap imports, driving out local producers and local products.

The Pluralistic Underpinnings of the Modern Nation-State

All of the early nation-states—the United States, Britain, the Netherlands —suppressed their indigenous populations to create homogenous nations. This coherence helped to serve the interests of capital and entrepreneurs who could count on a disciplined, homogenous labor force. As Benedict

Anderson described, the early nation states de-ethnicized their populations in the interest of political coherence, while labor historians have also drawn attention to the ways that this served the interests of capital.[71]

During the acceleration of industrialization in America, the whitening and assimilation of European immigrants created one enormous labor pool for industry while the "unassimilable" blacks, Hispanics, and Asians were put to work in farms and railroads, and Native Americans were excluded altogether from employment in white-owned and managed industries. This segmented the labor force and hastened the assimilation of white immigrants, who privatized their cultures and religions. A state that is demographically diverse is not necessarily pluralistic. Demographic social and cultural diversity is very different from social and cultural pluralism; the former refers only to categories of group membership, while the latter refers to a collective recognition of the legitimacy of social and cultural differences.

Group and Cultural Rights

The 2003 UNESCO (UN Educational, Scientific, and Cultural Organization) Universal Declaration on Cultural Diversity (UDCD) is the first formal statement by the international community to affirm cultural pluralism and the importance of culture for individual and group identity.[72] The declaration highlights the importance of inclusiveness, cultural exchange, and interaction, and implies, as we have, that such diversity is based on equality so that group membership is not confounded with differences in wealth and power. It also stresses that cultural diversity is essential for democracy, and the flourishing of creativity in public life. We can understand why cultural diversity enriches public life, but in this section we hope to clarify why cultural pluralism enriches democracy as well.

This new emphasis on cultural diversity is in response to economic globalization and the realistic doctrine, which lead to the destruction of cultural, social, and language differences. Economic globalization also fuels high rates of migration from one nation to another, and migrants' cultures are at particular risk. Having a history, a language, group customs, and traditions is the core of personhood, and Americans are apt not to see that, as the ideology of liberalism is a denial of the distinctive importance of cultural differences. Because liberalism emphasizes rationality, and efficiency, it minimizes the importance of culture. (Liberalism is, of course, a culture into itself.) To highlight how states can affirm the cultural rights of citizens, we draw here from the African

Cultural Charter, the European Social Charter, and the American Declaration of the Rights and Duties of Man.

The Cultural Charter for Africa

Although as we have seen, UNESCO has recently promulgated the first international declaration that affirms the rights of groups to their culture, the Organization of African Unity (now the African Union) made the first such formal declaration. It was drafted in 1976 and entered into force in 1990. Its uniqueness and elegance lie in the way that it harmonizes cultural identity with political, social and economic rights, and with philosophical and spiritual ideas. Excerpts are reproduced in appendix 7.1.

The Cultural Charter for Africa is especially striking for the way it clarifies how colonization dehumanizes people by appropriating their cultural identities, the core of human dignity. It also clarifies that a pan-African identity is essential for restoring particular cultural identities. For example: "the unity of Africa is founded first and foremost on its History, that the affirmation of cultural identity denotes a concern common to all peoples of Africa, that African cultural diversity [is] the expression of a single identity." It is through solidarity and brotherhood that cultural unity is restored, which "transcends ethnic and national divergencies."

The charter also clarifies that ethical regard of others is achieved through the recognition of human differences as well as human similarities, and that the achievement of human rights is inseparable from the expression of cultural identity. This charter has far-reaching implications for understanding that the marketization of societies, as it is now accelerating, also has devastating effects on cultural dignity, just as colonization did. It precociously anticipates the UNESCO Declaration, and goes further than the other two charters that we will discuss in clarifying the relationship between cultural differences and cultural unity, and the way that culture is the articulation of group memberships in their societies.

The European Social Charter and European Union Constitution

African peoples grapple with the enormous problem of relocating their societies, cultures, and identities in the aftermath of decolonization and in the midst of a new world economy that further imperils them. Africa as a continent, as well as individual African nations, are far ahead of other continents and nations in articulating the relationships between culture, society, and the state in other than the dominant paradigm of the nation-state. Yet, Europe is beginning to recognize the importance of cultural diversity, approaching this as a human rights issue, and Latin America is likewise framing diversity in terms of human rights for indigenous populations. What underlies all these conceptions is the principle, as Abdullahi A. An-Na'im puts it, that cultural rights are universal rights, but still take a myriad of forms.[73]

Human rights doctrine of the European community has formally evolved within the context of the Council of Europe and is independent of the European Union (EU). Established in 1949, it oversees the evolution of human rights provisions, codified in the European Social Charter, and oversees the European Court of Human Rights (ECHR) and the European Commission of Human Rights. In this context we are interested in those 1966 provisions of the charter that address issues pertaining to diversity and pluralism.[74]

Formally, the European Social Charter does less than the Cultural Charter for Africa in addressing the issues of social and cultural diversity. For example, while the European Social Charter (Article 19) does emphasize the legal and economic rights of migrants, it pays only slight attention to the importance of migrants maintaining cultural connections with their home country and to the importance of language retention, unlike the Cultural Charter for Africa. The European Social Charter has a clause on nondiscriminatory hiring practices (Article 20), and more emphatically states in Part V, Article E: "The enjoyment of the rights set forth in this Charter shall be secured without discrimination on any ground such as race, colour, sex, language, religion, political or other opinion, national extraction or social origin, health, association with a national minority, birth or other status." Nevertheless, while minimally asserting social and cultural rights, the European Social Charter is exemplary in the ways it articulates the basic freedoms of people, including their rights to a job, a decent wage, health care, and so forth. We will return to these in the next chapter.

Comparativists stress that while the European human rights system fails to come fully to terms with cultural rights, it has advanced what Eva Brems terms "a margin of appreciation doctrine," namely a legitimization of the conception of cultural differences, but in the absence of legal provisions.[75] She argues that this margin of appreciation doctrine has been possible because European human rights are generally not interpreted in such strongly individualistic terms as American human rights are. The guiding principles are derived from a commitment to allow differences to flourish so long as particular practices do not violate the human rights of others. For

example, she shows how the European Court has upheld religious pluralism over state objections and in the absence of formal codes. She makes
the important point that individual and group morals are quite different
from the ethical issues that arise from intergroup relations. No better an example perhaps is the ongoing debate in France about the rights of members of religious minorities to wear clothing that sets them apart from the
more secular French majority.

However, if the European constitution is approved, cultural rights in
the EU would be greatly advanced over what is specified in the charter.
The relevant sections of the constitution are Articles II-21 and II-22,
which affirm that the Union upholds peoples' rights to their culture, language, and religion and forbids discrimination on the basis of sex, race,
color, ethnicity, social origin, genetic features, language, religion or belief,
political or any other opinion, membership, property, birth, disability, age,
or sexual orientation.[76] Thus, there is not only the ban against discrimination, but also the affirmation of the importance of difference and of peoples' rights to their identity.

American Declaration on the Rights and Duties of Man

A further basis of comparison is the 1948 American Declaration of the
Rights and Duties of Man, which is under the jurisdiction of the Inter-
American Commission on Human Rights (IACHR) of the Organization
of American States (OAS) of which the United States is a member.[77] In
many ways the declaration is similar to the European Social Charter in its
emphasis on nondiscrimination. However, in its evolving doctrine, the
IACHR has dealt specifically with the rights of indigenous peoples, both
advocating for group as well as individual rights, casting both as "collective
rights." In cases that have come before the court, it has often ruled that indigenous or tribal customary law takes precedence over state laws.[78] For
example, in a case where a matriarchal tribe won a settlement, the court
has ruled that the women of the tribe receive the payment and tribe members then decide the distribution of the settlement claim. Indigenous
groups also have certain rights to self-rule and have self-determination
within their own territory.

Summary

Cultural rights are difficult to subject to the logic of judicatory reasoning,
since culture is not only particular, but also dynamic, suggesting that
formal courts of law may not be the best tribunals. Nondiscrimination is

certainly the place to start, but beyond this human rights considerations highlight that people are embedded in communities of identity, race, ethnicity, and language. As we recognize, categorization of people by their race or ethnicity or tribe is fraught with difficulties, the source of intergroup conflict rather than solidarity. Yet we have argued that in these cases it is not culture that is to blame, but rather the confoundedness of cultural differences with differences in power and resources.

To elaborate a bit, and propose a comparison with the United States, the philosophical implication of the African Cultural Charter is that pluralism creates solidarities while also undermining the economic and bureaucratic forces that depersonalize people and their groups of membership. In contrast, a component of the hegemonic assimilationist myth in the United States is that when people become "non-foreign," they become citizens. Moreover, we argue, that when foreigners became non-foreigners and became citizens, they also achieved the American dream of becoming consumers. This is a plausible speculation because it helps to make sense of the way that consumer products were marketed in America. Until quite recently consumers were Anglos (at least in the media). We might say that the assimilationist myth in America was manipulated, if not partly created, by capitalists and depended on robbing people of their cultural identities, whether they were Irish, Russian, Italian, Hungarian, or whatever else.

The materials we have covered in this chapter imply a radical break with the way that the United States frames culture and cultural differences. Only on college campuses has there been an engagement with cultural diversity and pluralism. Otherwise the paradigmatic way that cultural differences are dealt with continues to be a variation on the theme of assimilation; specifically, what is emphasized in the United States is nondiscriminatory treatment of minorities. Employers and institutions are advised not to discriminate against racial and ethnic minorities, but rather to recognize their aspirations to be part of the mainstream.

Although this implied emphasis in the United States on a single culture is similar to the understandings expressed in the European Social Charter, it is very different from the vision of the UNESCO UDCD, of the African Cultural Charter, that of the proposed EU Constitution, and to some extent, the vision in the OAS American Declaration of the Rights and Duties and in the European constitution. Speculatively, as global connections continue to proliferate, it is likely that there will be greater emphasis on the positive role that culture plays in people's identities and in societies. Our reasoning is circular. More connections make people aware of cultural differences, and because of their cultural differences people want more connections.

Notes

1. www.aclu.org/torturefoia/released/fbi.html; www.aclu.org/Safeandfree/Safeandfree.cfm?ID=17216&c=206

2. David Rose, "US Afghan Allies Committed Massacre," *Observer/UK*, March 21, 2004: www.commondreams.org/headlines04/03211-03.htm

3. Michael Ratner, "The Road to Abu Ghraib: Paved with the Legal Opinion of Alberto R. Gonzales," Thursday, November 18, 2004: http://commondreams.org/views04/1118-32.htm; also see Gregory Hooks and Clayton Mosher, "Outrages against Personal Dignity," *Social Forces* (forthcoming).

4. Andrew Rosenthal, "Legal Breach: The Government's Attorneys and Abu Ghraib," *New York Times*, published on Thursday, December 30, 2004: www.commondreams.org/views04/1230-14.htm

5. On June 25, 2003, it was referred to committee, which is to say, buried in the Subcommittee on Immigration, Border Security, and Claims. thomas.loc.gov/cgi-bin/bdquery/z?d108:h.r.02224:

6. Geoffrey Robertson, *Crimes against Humanity* (New York: New Press, 1999), 247.

7. In 2004, there was widespread understanding of the rules of war and the consequences of violating them, due in large measure to the highly publicized cases involving Augusto Pinochet, Slobodan Milôsević, General Krstić, Garcia Meza, and Jean Kambanda.

8. Google searches turn up national surveys—for example, 99 percent of sampled Malaysians opposed Bush's policies.

9. Hannah Arendt, *The Origins of Totalitarianism* (New York: Harcourt Brace, 1951).

10. John Ritter, "Poll: War Opposition Up amid Iraqi Abuse Scandal," *USA Today*, May 11, 2004: www.commondreams.org/headlines04/0511-05.htm

11. Ronald Inglehart, *Modernization and Postmodernization: Cultural, Economic, and Political Change in 43 Societies* (Princeton, N.J.: Princeton University Press, 1990); K. Newton and P. Norris, "Confidence in Public Institutions," in *Disaffected Democracies,* ed. S. Pharr and R. Putnam (Princeton, N.J.: Princeton University Press, 2000).

12. Nicos Poulantzas, "The Problems of the Capitalist State," *New Left Review* 58 (1969): 67–78.

13. Juliet B. Schor, *The Overspent American* (New York: HarperPerennial, 1998); also see Herbert J. Gans, *Middle American Individualism* (New York: Oxford University Press, 1988).

14. The Freedom House, which ranks countries on human rights, is disingenuous. It really focuses on political rights, and even so, does not mention U.S. backing

of oppression in China, trivializes the post-9/11 detention and deportation of thousands of foreign nationals without a trial, and glosses over the abuses in Guantánamo and at Abu Ghraib: www.freedomhouse.org/ratings/index.htm. It closely follows the U.S. State Department's rankings: See U.S. Department of State, Country Reports on Human Rights Practices, www.state.gov/g/drl/rls/hrrpt/

15. Robert Nozick, *Anarchy, State and Utopia* (New York: Basic, 1974); John Rawls, *A Theory of Justice* (Oxford: Oxford University Press, 1971); Michael Walzer, *On Toleration* (New Haven, Conn.: Yale University Press, 1997).

16. U.S. Department of Defense, "Active Duty Military Personnel Strength by Regional Area and by Country," quoted in "A 'Long Walk to Freedom' and Democracy: Human Rights, Globalization and Social Injustice," Havidán Rodriquez, *Social Forces* 83 (2004): 413–22.

17. Alain Touraine, *Critique of Modernity* (Cambridge, Mass.: Blackwell, 1995).

18. John U. Nef, *Western Civilization since the Renaissance* (New York: Harper and Row, 1963), 343.

19. Talcott Parsons, *Essays in Sociological Theory* (New York: Free Press of Glencoe, 1954), 412–15.

20. Simon Kuznets, *Modern Economic Growth: Rate, Structure and Spread* (New Haven, Conn.: Yale University Press, 1966).

21. Alex Inkeles and David H. Smith, *Becoming Modern: Individual Change in Six Developing Countries* (Cambridge, Mass.: Harvard University Press, 1974), 289–316.

22. See Kenneth Bollen, "Political Democracy and the Timing of Development," *American Sociological Review* 48 (1979): 572–87; Dietrich Rueschemeyer, Evelyne Huber Stephens, and John D. Stephens, *Capitalist Development and Democracy* (Chicago: University of Chicago Press, 1992).

23. Yujiro Hayami, *Development Economics* (Oxford: Clarendon Press, 1997).

24. Francis Fukuyama, *The End of History and Last Man* (New York: Free Press, 1991).

25. Juan Díez-Nicolás, "Two Contradictory Hypotheses on Globalization," in *Human Values and Social Change*, ed. Ronald Inglehart, 235–64 (Leiden, The Netherlands: Brill, 2003); James K. Galbraith, "A Perfect Crime: Global Inequality," *Daedalus: Journal of the American Academy of Arts & Sciences* 131, 1 (2002): 11–25.

26. The Pew Research Center for People and the Press, "Views of a Changing World 2003: War with Iraq Further Divides Global Publics," June 3, 2003: people-press.org/reports/display.php3?ReportID=185

27. Rogers Brubaker, *Citizenship and Nationhood in France and Germany* (Cambridge, Mass.: Harvard University Press, 1992); Jyoti Puri, *Encountering Nationalism* (Malden, Mass.: Blackwell, 2004).

28. Eviatar Zerubavel, *Hidden Rhythms: Schedules and Calendars in Social Life* (Chicago: University of Chicago Press, 1981).

29. Georges Lefebvre, *The French Revolution, Vol. II* (London: Routledge & Kegan Paul, 1964), 358.

30. Judith Blau, Kent Redding, Walt Davis, and Kenneth C. Land, "The Duality of Church and Faith," *Sociological Perspectives* 4 (1997): 557–80.

31. E. J. Hobsbawn. *Nations and Nationalism since 1780* (Cambridge: Cambridge University Press, 1990), 14–15.

32. Benedict Anderson, *Imagined Communities: Reflections on the Origin and Spread of Nationalism* (London: Verso, 1991).

33. Anderson, *Imagined Communities*.

34. As early as 1789, an American nationalism was so powerful that it spawned an "official (anti-British) language" based on Noah Webster's *Dissertation on the English Language*; see Kenneth Cmiel, *Democratic Eloquence* (Berkeley: University of California Press, 1990).

35. Max Weber, *Economy and Society*, 2 vols. ed. Guenther Roth and Claus Wittich (Berkeley: University of California Press, 1978).

36. Joseph Alois Schumpeter, *Capitalism, Socialism, and Democracy*, 3rd ed. (New York: Harper, [1942] 1962), 269.

37. For an overview see: Giovanni Sartoni, "Democracy," in *International Encyclopedia of the Social Sciences, Vol. 4*, ed. David L. Sills, 112–22 (New York: Macmillan, 1968).

38. Public Citizen, a legislative watch group, diligently reports on actions taken by Congress that harm the public: corporate welfare, benefits for pharmaceutical companies, racialized prison policies, declining funding for poor schools, unaffordable housing, the weakening of federal regulations in the areas of occupational safety, and so forth. See: www.citizen.org/

39. Fred Block, *Revising State Theory: Essays in Politics and Postindustrialism* (Philadelphia: Temple University Press, 1987).

40. Block, *Revising State Theory*, 67.

41. John Emerich Edward Dalberg-Acton (Lord Acton). *The History of Freedom and Other Essays* [1862], excerpts in *Nations and Identities: Classic Readings*, ed. Vincent P. Pecora, 153 (Malden, Mass: Blackwell, 2001).

42. Southern Poverty Law Center: www.splcenter.org/index

43. Also see, "44 Percent of Americans Queried in Cornell National Poll Favor Curtailing Some Liberties for Muslim Americans": www.news.cornell.edu/releases/Dec04/Muslim.Poll.bpf.html; www.comm.cornell.edu/msrg/report1a.pdf

44. Adamantia Pollis, "A New Universalism," in *Human Rights: New Perspectives, New Realities*, ed. Admantia Pollis and Peter Schwab, 9–31 (Boulder, Colo.: Rienner, 2000). Michael Freeman, "Liberal Democracy and Minority Rights," in *Human Rights*, 31–52.

45. Ernest Gellner, *Nations and Nationalism* (Ithaca, N.Y.: Cornell University Press, 1983), 57.

46. Marshall Berman, *All That Is Solid Melts into Air* (New York: Penguin, 1982).

47. Milton Gordon, *Assimilation in American Life: The Role of Race, Religion, and National Origins* (New York: Oxford University Press, 1964).

48. Robert Jay Lifton, *Superpower Syndrome* (New York: Thunder's Mouth Press/Nation Books, 2003).

49. Immanuel Wallerstein, *After Liberalism* (New York: New Press, 1995).

50. Wallerstein, *After Liberalism*, 13.

51. Ilan Peleg, "Ethnic Constitutional Orders and Human Rights," in *Human Rights and Diversity*, ed. David P. Forsythe and Patrice C. McMahon, 279–96 (Lincoln: University of Nebraska Press, 2003).

52. Judith Blau and Alberto Moncada, *Human Rights: Beyond the Liberal Vision* (Lanham, Md.: Rowman & Littlefield, 2005).

53. Jack Donnelly, "Ethics and International Human Rights," in *Ethics and International Affairs: Extent and Limits*, ed. Jean-Marc Coicaud and Daniel Warner, 128–60 (Tokyo: United Nations University Press, 2001).

54. Will Kymlicka, *Multicultural Citizenship* (Oxford: Oxford University Press, 1995); Allen Buchanan and Margaret Moore, eds., *States, Nations, and Borders* (Cambridge: Cambridge University Press, 2003).

55. UNDP, *Human Development Report 2004* (New York: United Nations and Oxford University Press, 2004).

56. Abdullahi A. An-Na'im, "Introduction: 'Area Expressions' and the Universality of Human Rights," in *Human Rights and Diversity: Area Studies*, ed. David P. Forsythe and Patrice C. McMahon, 1–24 (Lincoln: University of Nebraska Press, 2003).

57. Rose Laub Coser, *In Defense of Modernity: Role Complexity and Individual Autonomy* (Stanford, Calif.: Stanford University Press, 1991); Georg Simmel, "The Web of Group Affiliations," in *The Sociology of Georg Simmel*, ed. Kurt Wolf (New York: Free Press, 1955).

58. Peter M. Blau and Joseph E. Schwartz, *Crosscutting Social Circles* (Orlando, Fla.: Academic Press, 1984).

59. Kiyoteru Tsutsui, "Global Civil Society and Ethnic Social Movements in the Contemporary World," *Sociological Forum* 19 (2004): 63–87.

60. Jack Donnelly, "Ethics and International Human Rights."

61. Bertrand Russell, *Human Society in Ethics and Politics* (London: Routledge, 1954), 28.

62. For an excellent summary see: Paul Gordon Lauren, *The Evolution of International Human Rights: Visions Seen* (Philadelphia: University of Pennsylvania Press, 2003).

63. T. W. Bennett, *Human Rights and African Customary Law under the South African Constitution* (Bellville, South Africa: Community Law Centre, University of the Western Cape and Juta & Co., 1995); Henning Melber, "Namibia's Constitution: Vision and Reality," in *The State and Constitutionalism in Southern Africa*, ed. Owen Sichone, 15–22 (Harare, Zimbabwe: Sapes Books, 1998).

64. Understanding the relational underpinnings of diversity is an important objective in international human rights discussions. In 2003 Report of the UN Secretary-General on Strengthening Human Rights, the relational underpinnings

of diversity were stressed. General Assembly, United Nations, *Strengthening United Nations Action in the Field of Human Rights through the Promotion of International Cooperation and the Importance of Non-Selectivity, Impartiality, and Objectivity* (Geneva, Switzerland: Office of the UN High Commissioner for Human Rights, 2003).

65. Bennett, *Human Rights and African Customary Law under the South African Constitution*. Vera Sachs, "Can Law Protect Language? Law, Language and Human Rights in the South African Constitution," *International Journal of Discrimination and the Law* 4 (2000): 343–68; Assefaw Bariagaber, "The Politics of Cultural Pluralism in Ethiopia and Eritrea," *Ethnic and Racial Studies* 21 (1998): 1056–73; Henning Melber, "Namibia's Constitution: Vision and Reality," in *The State and Constitutionalism in Southern Africa*, ed. Sichone, 15–22.

66. Ulrich Willems, "Religion as a Private Matter? A Critique of the Liberal Principle of a Radical Separation between Politics and Religion," *Politische Vierteljahresschrift* 43, supplement (2002): 86–112.

67. Donna Lee Van Cott, "Andean Indigenous Movements and Constitutional Transformation," *Latin American Perspectives* 30 (2003): 49–69.

68. Ruth Gavison, "Constitutions and Political Reconstruction? Israel's Quest for a Constitution," *International Sociology* 18 (2003): 53–70; also see Said Amir Arjomand, "Law, Political Reconstruction and Constitutional Politics," *International Sociology* 18 (2003): 7–32; Grazyna Skapska, "Moral Definitions of Constitutionalism in East Central Europe," *International Sociology* 18 (2003): 199–218.

69. Keyvan Tabari, "The Rule of Law and the Politics of Reform in Post-Revolutionary Iran," *International Sociology* 18 (2003): 96–113.

70. For example, see John Tomlinson, *Globalization and Culture* (Chicago: University of Chicago Press, 1999).

71. Anderson, *Imagined Communities*.

72. UNESCO UDCD: www.unesco.org/culture/pluralism/diversity/html_eng/dec1_en

73. An-Na'im, "Introduction: 'Area Expressions' and the Universality of Human Rights."

74. European Social Charter (1996): conventions.coe.int/Treaty/en/Treaties/Html/163.htm

75. Eva Brems, "The Margin of Appreciation Doctrine of the European Court of Human Rights," in *Human Rights and Diversity*, ed., David P. Forsythe and Patrice C. McMahon, 81–110 (Lincoln: University of Nebraska Press, 2003).

76. European Convention. Secretariat, *Draft Treaty Establishing a Constitution for Europe*, Brussels: July 18, 2003: european-convention.eu.int/docs/Treaty/cv00850.en03.pdf

77. www.cidh.oas.org/Basicos/basic2.htm

78. Chapter III. Doctrine and Jurisprudence of the IACHR on Indigenous Rights (1970–1999): www.cidh.org/indigenas/chap.3.htm#6

Appendix 7.1
Excerpts from the Preamble of the
Cultural Charter for Africa

Organization of African Unity
Drafted July 3, 1976; Entered into force, September 19, 1990

CONVINCED that all cultures emanate from the people, and that any African cultural policy should of necessity enable the people to expand for increased responsibility in the development of its cultural heritage;

AWARE OF THE FACT that any people has the inalienable right to organize its cultural life in full harmony with its political, economic, social, philosophical and spiritual ideas;

CONVINCED that all the cultures of the world are equally entitled to respect just as all individuals are equal as regards free access to culture;

RECALLING that, under colonial domination, the African countries found themselves in the same political, economic, social and cultural situation; that cultural domination led to the depersonalization of part of the African peoples, falsified their history, systematically disparaged and combated African values, and tried to replace progressively and officially, their languages by that of the colonizer, that colonization has encouraged the formation of an elite which is too often alienated from its culture and susceptible to assimilation and that a serious gap has been opened between the said elite and the African popular masses;

CONVINCED that the unity of Africa is founded first and foremost on its History, that the affirmation of cultural identity denotes a concern common to all peoples of Africa, that African cultural diversity, the expression of a single identity, is a factor making for equilibrium and development in the service of national integration; that it is imperative to edify educational systems which embody the African values of civilization, so as to ensure the rooting of youth in African culture and mobilize the social forces in the context of permanent education; that it is imperative to resolutely ensure the promotion of African languages, mainstay, and media of cultural heritage in its most authentic and essentially popular form, that it is imperative to carry out a systematic inventory of the cultural heritage, in particular in the spheres of Traditions, History and Arts;

GUIDED by a common determination to strengthen understanding among our peoples and cooperation among our States in order to meet the aspirations of our peoples to see brotherhood and solidarity reinforced and integrated within a greater cultural unity which transcends ethnic and national divergencies;

AWARE that culture constitutes for our peoples the surest means of overcoming our technological backwardness and the most efficient force of our victorious resistance to imperialist blackmail;

CONVINCED that African culture is meaningless unless it plays a full part in the political and social liberation struggle, and in the rehabilitation and unification efforts and that there is no limit to the cultural development of a people;

CONVINCED that a common resolve provides the basis for promoting the harmonious cultural development of our States . . .

SOURCE: http://www.africa-union.org/home/Welcome.htm

Cornucopia of Rights

8

We have frequently drawn from Mahmood Mamdani and Mary Wollstonecraft to illustrate human rights principles. The *slap* is the archetypical violation of human rights. Mamdani clarifies that everyone round the world recognizes what human dignity and agency are, and there is a universal, intuitive understanding of when and how a person's dignity and agency are being transgressed and when and how they are upheld.[1] Dignity and agency are the very foundations of human rights, thereby highlighting too the importance of empathy that accompanies social connectedness and reciprocity. We have stakes, in other words, in the human rights of others.

Mary Wollstonecraft's scathing letter to Edmund Burke has provided us with a conceptual handle on the ways that poverty degrades the human condition and economic inequalities estrange humans from one another. The grounds for her attack were not only that capitalism fuels poverty and enormous economic inequalities, but that inequalities alienate humans from one another. Thus, Wollstonecraft brings us back full circle to human rights. In detail, it is impossible to prioritize given rights—the rights of children, of minorities, of immigrants, of women, and so forth. They are interdependent and mutually reinforcing. Nevertheless, in today's world, global economic inequalities pose the greatest threat to human rights and human societies. The self-interest of a tiny global economic elite threatens the security of billions. This imperils the quality of human life, jeopardizes development, and impedes the advance of democracy. Wollstonecraft's understanding of the human costs of capitalism is just as relevant today as it was when she wrote in the late eighteenth century.

Only when people have economic security can they cooperate to achieve their political, social, cultural, and environmental rights. For that reason, we have highlighted economic rights. However, as we have stressed, human rights entail more than economic security, and in this chapter we provide details about other human rights, drawing from state constitutions. We initially digress somewhat because in the course of our research we discovered the importance of a constitutional language about solidarity, and we believe this is relevant for the ways that states clarify the importance both of decentralized democracy and human rights. The very idea of solidarity implies something about social relations among people, not simply individuals' relations to the state.

The Language of Solidarities

The central premise of the Western, liberal constitution is one that highlights individual sovereignty and personal autonomy, and thereby circumvents society. This is still the premise of the oldest constitution, namely, the American one. Human rights provisions, which have been introduced into constitutions in the last few decades, are at odds with this premise, since human rights depend as much on society as they do on the nation-state. The state can promulgate constitutional provisions for, say, the rights of migrants, but to make a genuine difference, citizens, nonprofits, and businesses must adopt new practices, and this requires public discussions, cooperation, and shared commitments. We could say that the civil society needs to be enlivened and engaged for constitutional provisions to be implemented.

A serendipitous discovery in our research was the use of "solidarity" and "solidarities" in recently revised constitutions.[2] We believe this is significant because it portends a new vision, a radical departure from the eighteenth-century model, and one that relates to the growing importance of human rights and to a set of closer relations involving citizens, society, and the state. Appendix 8.1 provides extracts of all constitutions that employ this language. We attempt to provide a classification of the ways in which *solidarity* is employed in these constitutions, although there is no single best way of doing that and we encourage readers to identify other patterns. We highlight the following: (1) Solidarity as Equality and National Unity; (2) International Solidarity; (3) Solidarity against Adversity; (4) Solidarity as Democratic Civil Society; and (5) Solidarity as Human Rights.

Constitutional provisions that fall in category 1, as Equality and National Unity, stress either the importance of national unity through reciprocity (Congo-Brazzaville) or the importance of promoting more equitable interregional development. This is illustrated by Argentina's constitution. A variation on this theme is that the nation-state embodies a set of values that unify the people in solidarity. Macedonia is the prime example of this, while Mozambique specifies this in greater detail, namely that national unity is bound up with progress and peoples' rights as well as solidarity in liberation struggles and with all African peoples. Spain's constitution captures varied ideas about solidarity, including interregional ties and the importance of sharing ecological resources.

Category 2 pertains to expressions of international solidarity. We have taken that portion of Cameroon's constitution that addresses this issue as a continental solidarity (as we have already seen that the Mozambique constitution does). Yet two relatively isolated countries—Cuba and Paraguay—also stress such solidarity. Solidarity against Adversity (category 3) resonates with the idea of regional and international solidarity, but is more explicit that solidarity must override self-interest when disaster strikes. The three examples that we found that cluster in category 3 are in different parts of the world: Colombia, Kuwait, and Morocco. Category 4 is illustrated by the constitutions of two countries—Cape Verde and Tibet—that highlight the importance of solidarity as it relates to civil society, shared goals, and democracy. The final group, category 5, makes explicit the connections between solidarity, cooperation, and human rights or justice.

The reason why we begin this chapter highlighting this very new constitutional language of *solidarity* is that it is a departure from traditions and reflects new thinking about what a nation-state is and what it does. More explicitly, it is a marked departure from the liberal nation-state, which emphasizes self-interest, and instead provides a framework for understanding the nation-state as the active supporter of the human rights of its citizens, and for understanding citizens as being engaged in promoting collectively valued goals.

In the remainder of this chapter we will consider various human rights and how they are treated in state constitutions. Again, at the cost of being comprehensive we select constitutions so that we can provide the specific framework and language in which rights are clarified. However, we do provide a tabular summary of all constitutions that have provisions for particular rights, specifically, economic rights, women's rights, provisions for maternity, and minority rights. Finally, it has only been very recently that states have revised their constitutions to take into account environmental protections and safeguards for their populations. However, enough states have for us to review some constitutional provisions for environmental rights.

However, first, we wish to make some conceptual connections between our discussion in the last chapter regarding diversity and pluralism with social solidarities, with which we began this chapter. To be sure diversity and pluralism are not the antecedents to solidarities, because as we are painfully aware, ethnic and religious diversity can easily trigger animosities and strife. But diversity is the bedrock of identity and human dignity, and social pluralism is the foundation of a vital civil society. We have also suggested that solidarities that cross lines of difference are at the core of recognizing and advancing human rights. Constitutions help us to understand how nation-states are advancing these ideas.

Constitutions and Diversity

State constitutions, we concluded, deal with diversity in each of four different ways, but each is conditioned by demographic, historical, and ecological features. The first approach is to simply ignore it. This essentially is what the U.S. Constitution does, by stating in Article XV that rights cannot be denied or abridged on "account of race, color, or previous condition of servitude." Without acknowledging the importance of institutionalized racial hierarchies, affirming differences in culture, or attempting to rectify the disadvantages that African Americans and indigenous Americans have long experienced, the U.S. Constitution simply authorizes inequalities. We might refer to this as *singularism*. This is not all that dissimilar from religious orthodoxy required in some fundamentalist Islamic states.

In contrast, some state constitutions actively protect the rights of minorities, recognizing their special vulnerabilities, but do nothing to affirm their distinctiveness. We term this *minimalism*. It is quite common in European constitutions that have provisions making it illegal to discriminate against minorities. (So does the U.S. Civil Rights Act of 1964, but it is a law, and lacks constitutional authority.) A third approach is more in line with the genuine embrace of pluralistic differences and advocates the active recognition of differences. We term this *pluralism*. A variant of this is the recognition of regional concentrations of particular groups, but this does not pose the challenges that a highly diverse population does. We term this *regional diversity*. To capture this variation, we selected constitutions from Asia and Asia Pacific, the Middle East, Europe, and the Caribbean and Latin America. These constitutional extracts are reproduced in appendix 8.2.

Asian States

Bangladesh, one of the poorest countries in the world, enduring extremely high population densities and calamitous droughts and seasonal monsoons, is nevertheless exemplary in its formal guarantees of toleration. Of course, Bangladesh has less ethnic diversity than most countries, with 98 percent of the population ethnic Bengalis, but there are considerable religious differences, with a sizeable Hindi population and smaller Buddhist and Christian populations. (Its national calendar recognizes the holidays of all these groups.) Its constitution underscores that it is important to "conserve the cultural traditions," which we characterize as affirming *pluralism*.

India, many times the size of Bangladesh, advances an unusual combination of *minimalism* and *pluralism*. India is a country of overwhelming societal complexity. There are over sixteen hundred different languages and dialects, and over two hundred scripts. Although the country is predominately Hindi, small and important religious minorities include Muslims, Buddhists, and Christians. It was only in the 1950 constitution that a Union of India was established, an integration of 562 autonomous princely states. Castes are relentlessly divisive, dividing Hindis by occupations, residence, complex customs, marriage rules, and especially economic differences. There are five castes, with the fourth being the Sudras, or peasants and laborers, and the fifth, the Panchamas, the untouchable caste (formally abolished in Article 17 of the constitution).

The Indian constitution attempts to deal with these diversities in different ways. First, it extensively outlines the grounds prohibiting discrimination (Article 15), which we have termed *minimalism*. Second, it raises the possibility that the state can pass laws to advance the rights of Scheduled Castes and Tribes (Article 15), while abolishing the lowest caste (Article 17). Third, in Article 29 it affirms the rights of citizens to their own language and culture, a *pluralistic* right.

New Zealand's constitution is more straightforward, affirming the *pluralistic* rights of any ethnic, religious, or linguistic minority to their culture, religion, and language. Here the point might be made that New Zealand may be especially interested in upholding the rights of the Maori, but once a country reaches the point of dealing in a straightforward way with any particular minority group, logic compels the country to extend cultural rights to other groups, which in the case of New Zealand would include Asian immigrants as well.

Middle East

The U.S. spotlight on Muslims since 9/11 has not especially enhanced Americans' understanding of Islam and has done nothing to reassure Muslims that U.S. interests are benign. This has complicated reformist efforts within Islamic states, intensifying the voices of traditionalists in many instances. According to Iftikhar H. Malik, Islamic intellectuals have carved out three distinct positions since the first Gulf War. The first is that Islam is in disaccord with modernity and will have to abandon its religious traditions to accommodate global realities. The second, also extreme, is that Muslim societies and states must reassert an Islamicization in opposition to the West. The third is that Islam is, at its core, a humanistic and progressive tradition, and can balance secular trends while retaining many of its traditions.[3]

Constitutions provide a clue about the likelihood of each of these possibilities. The Bangladeshi constitution, as we have shown, has adopted what Malik terms a humanistic and progressive tradition, with its espousing pluralism. The three Islamic states in the Middle East that we include in our sample of states illustrate a range of responses to the realities of population heterogeneity. Egypt emphasizes ethnicity (Arab) and downplays Islam, while adopting a policy of nondiscrimination, which we have labeled as a *minimalist* approach to diversity. Iran, in contrast, affirms traditional Islam, which is a variant of *singularism.* Jordan, like Egypt (and somewhat like India), emphasizes nondiscrimination in Article 6, but affirms religious pluralism provided it is consistent with "public order or morality" (Article 14).

Africa

We have selected three African states: Ethiopia, South Africa, and Uganda. Ethiopia is extraordinarily diverse, with around eighty different ethnicities, distinguished by language, culture, lifestyle, and religion (Orthodox Christians and Muslims). Ethiopian's flexibly accommodates this extraordinary diversity by legitimizing it, indeed granting cultural communities their full right to distinctiveness. This right also encompasses the right to secede (Article 39.1). Few states embrace *pluralism* to the extent that Ethiopia does. South Africa likewise supports cultural, religious, and linguistic *pluralism,* although not to the extent that Ethiopia does. Uganda, with a history of African and Indian hostility, is less effusive about diversity, but nevertheless affirms ethnic, religious, ideological, political, and cultural diversity. Generally, these three cases amplify the extent to which most African countries are stressing that diversity is a source of strength, and this is likewise emphasized in the African Charter that we discussed in the last chapter. Some of the more homogeneous, and predominately Muslim states, such as Algeria and Morocco, are less committed to supporting the rights of their cultural minorities, but Africa, as a continent, tends to highlight social processes that support cultural diversity, in contrast with both liberal states, such as the United States, and traditionally religious states, such as Iran.

Europe

There is great variation among European countries, with many of the former communist ones, such as Armenia, Russia, and Poland, advancing *pluralism*, whereas many of the western European countries maintain a liberal tradition in which minorities are protected against discrimination. However, as we know, communism is not a guarantor of cultural tolerance; the Bosnia Civil War and the breakup of the diverse state of Yugoslavia are brutal reminders of the ways that communism may have repressed ethnic hierarchies by confounding them with political ones. When the political hierarchies crashed, the bottled up ethnic hostilities could no longer be contained. Readers are more familiar with patterns in the rest of Europe, including regional cultural diversity in Spain and policies about religious scarves in France. Therefore, we did not include these and instead selected the constitution of Finland, which emphasizes *pluralistic language rights* and the rights of the Roma and the indigenous Sami. Finland's constitution recognizes the needs of the disabled as well as those of the hearing impaired; Italy's the importance of "groups' personality."

The Caribbean and Latin America

What is *not* said in a constitution about cultural difference is often as interesting as what is said. What is often stressed in Caribbean and Latin American constitutions is the importance of the preservation of indigenous groups and their cultures. On the other hand, constitutions of Caribbean and Latin American countries rarely refer to religion, although they sometimes highlight the importance of the Catholic tradition over others, and rarely refer to the black population, the descendents of slaves. An exception is Brazil, which states in Article 215: "The State protects manifestations of popular, Indian, and Afro-Brazilian cultures and those of other groups participating in the Brazilian civilization process."[4]

Both Paraguay and Colombia provide special protections for their indigenous populations, as do other Latin American states, and in the case of both, indigenous peoples are protected as vulnerable populations. The Colombia constitution explicitly links self-governance with cultural identity, and the Paraguay constitution makes the link between the preservation of indigenous habitats and the preservation of their ethnic identity. Paraguay, like many African countries, recognizes pluralistic legal systems, by granting indigenous populations their rights to draw on customary law. These two Latin American countries both epitomize a *pluralistic* approach to diversity, or as the Colombia constitution nicely states it, "Culture in its diverse manifestations is the basis of nationality."

Jamaica's constitution reflects more the influence of its former colonial power than do either Colombia's or Paraguay's. The implication of the wording is that rights cannot be denied for reasons of race, religion, political ideology, or gender, which is more than the U.S. Constitution allows, and is similar to the nondiscriminatory clauses found in many European constitutions. We would describe this as the *singular* approach to diversity.

Pluralism in Constitutions

Any society in which the state constitution does not make provisions for diversity easily succumbs to the politics of racial, ethnic, or cultural hierarchy. It is inevitable and universally the case. Such provisions never insure that there will be no discrimination or intergroup strife, but having provisions, accompanied by a political culture of solidarity, will in the long run reduce discrimination and strife.

We feel that these varied state constitutions, which deal in many different ways with diversity of all sorts, clarify how individual states create an inclusive umbrella for the varied segments of their populations. As we have already discussed, the language of solidarity provides such an umbrella while also helping to preserve groups whose distinctive cultures are endangered. The authorization of cosmopolitan pluralism also helps to empower groups to participate in democracy, and, indeed, to foster a grounded, grassroots democracy. We have contrasted pluralism with minimalist expressions of mere tolerance of minority groups, or at best, formal guidelines about nondiscriminatory treatment. However, as we know from experiences in the United States, discrimination against blacks and Latinos is subtle and insidious, and is below the radar of antidiscrimination laws.

Economic and Social Rights

On November 30, 2004, a nongovernmental (NGO), the Egyptian Center for Housing Rights (ECHR), sent word through an international Listserv of the Center for Economic, Social, and Cultural Rights, an international nongovernmental organization (INGO), that the Egyptian government had demolished housing for eighteen families. It stated, in part, "This also constitutes a blatant violation of international law, particularly with relation to the conditions laid down by Economic, Social, and Cultural Rights Committee's general comments number 7 issued on 16 May 1997 with relation to involuntary evacuation." Egypt's Center for Housing Rights could legitimately call on the international community to put additional pressure on the Egyptian government, because Egypt had signed the International Covenant on Economic, Social, and Cultural Rights (ICESCR). Article II. 1 states: "the right of everyone to an adequate living for himself and his family, including adequate food, clothing and housing," and the subsequent ruling, which applies to all parties of the ICESCR, protects people from involuntary evacuation. (Appendix 6.1 reproduces this covenant.) Anyone who has traveled in Egypt knows that Egypt has not successfully eradicated poverty, successfully housed all of its population, or complied with the ICESCR in other respects. Yet, as countries are overcoming debt and beginning to eradicate poverty, efforts to comply with the ICESCR best ensure equity and fairness. The United States, which has not signed the ICESCR, confronts moral hazards with its minimalist approach to social and economic security.

The ICESCR is reproduced in appendix 6.1. Simply to note here, ensuring gender equality is the purpose of Article 3, the rights to work and economic security of Articles 6 and 7; Article 9 deals with social security; Article 10 deals with protecting mothers and children; Article 11 is on maintaining an adequate standard of living; Article 12 is on health; and Article 13 is on education. We cannot possibly review all of these, but we have selected five to illustrate how widely these provisions have been adopted by states and formalized in their constitutions. Appendix 8.3 summarizes information for whether or not each state constitution has provisions for economic rights, women's rights, maternal rights, minority rights, and the right to health care.

Constitutional Provisions

Economic Rights

The decision rule for whether or not a constitution guarantees economic rights was simply whether it stated that people had rights to a job or employment. Appendix 8.3 provides the information on whether each constitution formalizes such rights.

Virtually all states do have such provisions. At the risk of some overlap with materials presented earlier, it is important to at least again briefly illustrate the way that economic rights are framed in constitutions. When simply stated, they are universally applicable, but each country positions them in ways that are compatible with their societies and traditions. We have selected a few states to provide an indication of this variation.

> **Albania:** The state, within its constitutional powers and the means at its disposal, aims to supplement private initiative and responsibility with: employment under suitable conditions for all persons who are able to work.
>
> **Bulgaria:** Citizens shall have the right to work. The state shall take care to provide conditions for the exercising of this right;
>
> **Denmark:** In order to advance the public weal efforts should be made to afford work to every able-bodied citizen on terms that will secure his existence.
>
> **Italy:** The republic recognizes the right of all citizens to work and promotes conditions to fulfill this right; According to capability and choice, every citizen has the duty to undertake an activity or a function that will contribute to the material and moral progress of society.
>
> **Laos:** Lao citizens have the right to work and engage in occupations which are not against the law. Working people have the right to rest, to receive medical treatment in time of ailment to receive assistance in case of incapacity and disability, in old age, and other cases as prescribed by law.

In other words, although there is a range of approaches to work—as a guaranteed good, as a principled good, as a duty, and as intimately connected with other rights—almost all states have decided that they share in the responsibility for insuring the economic well-being of their citizens.

Women's Rights and Maternal Rights

We were surprised to find that gender or women's rights are somewhat rarer in constitutions than are economic rights. Appendix 8.3 shows this variation. Again, to clarify how constitutions vary in the way that gender equality or women's rights are stated in constitutions we provide a few illustrations.

> **Argentina:** Actual equality of opportunities for men and women to elective and political party positions shall be guaranteed by means

of positive actions in the regulation of political parties and in the electoral system. . . . To legislate and promote positive measures guaranteeing true equal opportunities and treatment, the full benefit and exercise of the rights recognized by this Constitution and by the international treaties on human rights in force, particularly referring to children, women, the aged, and disabled persons.

Eritrea: Without consideration to the gender wording of any provision in this Constitution, all of its articles shall apply equally to both genders. Any act that violates the human rights of women or limits or otherwise thwarts their role and participation is prohibited. Men and women of full legal age shall have the right, upon their consent, to marry and to found a family freely, without any discrimination and they shall have equal rights and duties as to all family affairs.[5]

Mozambique: Men and women shall be equal before the law in all spheres of political, economic, social and cultural affairs. All citizens are equal before the law. They shall enjoy the same rights, and shall be subject to the same duties regardless of color, race, sex, ethnic origin, place of birth, religion, educational level, social position, the legal status of their parents, or their profession.

United States of America: The right of citizens of the United States to vote shall not be denied or abridged by the United States or by any State on account of sex.

We did not include the United States in appendix 8.3 as affirming women's rights, owing to the highly circumscribed rights that women are constitutionally guaranteed. Other states go much further by formally stating in their constitutions that women are (in the negative sense) protected from discrimination, and (in a positive sense) have equal political, economic, and social rights. Out of these 159 countries, 129 have specific provisions for women's rights. In addition, we identified constitutions that specified maternal rights for women, notably paid leaves for childbirth and early childcare. A total of sixteen have such specific rights.

The language is very similar, which is not surprising, since the purpose is to insure that women have political, economic rights equal to men, and that they need assistance, or support, when they themselves are caring for infants. Countries from all regions of the world support women's and maternal rights, and some countries have provisions for both.

Minority Rights

Out of the 159 countries, the majority, 101, have provisions for minority rights, sometimes in the affirmative, namely to enhance the dignity and robustness of minority cultures to enhance pluralism, and sometimes as a liberal (negative) right, to protect minorities from discrimination. Minorities are usually specified as racial, ethnic, linguistic, tribal, or indigenous minorities, and sometimes as religious groups.

Health Care Rights

As already implied, health care rights are quite common in constitutions, usually linked with social and housing rights provisions. We indicate in appendix 8.3 those countries that do have constitutional provisions that guarantee health care rights. It is useful to point out that there are not strong regional patterns, and states from all regions (but not every state in a given region) do have them. Again, it is useful to provide some idea of the variation in the ways that health care rights are framed.

> **Belarus:** Citizens of the Republic of Belarus shall be guaranteed the right to health care, including free treatment at state health-care establishments. The right of citizens of the Republic of Belarus to health care shall also be secured by the development of physical training and sport, means to improve the environment, the opportunity to use fitness establishments, and improvements in occupational safety.
>
> **Finland:** The public authorities shall guarantee for everyone, as provided in more detail by an Act, adequate social, health and medical services and promote the health of the population. Moreover, the public authorities shall support families and others responsible for providing for children so that they have the ability to ensure the well-being and personal development of the children.
>
> **Mozambique:** All citizens shall have the right to medical and health care, within the terms of the law, and shall have the duty to promote and preserve health.
>
> **Tibet:** The Tibetan Administration shall endeavor to promote adequate health, medical and sanitation services, and provide free medical treatment. It shall conduct special medical care programs for immunization and chronic illnesses; and educate people on environmental issues.

In sum, appendix 8.3 and these illustrations provide a fairly good summary of socioeconomic rights, which are increasingly incorporated into new constitutions. The United States was ideologically opposed to such rights through the Cold War, but with globalization, many countries realize that they are imperative to protect their populations. Now, after so many decades of repudiating such rights, the United States not only stays the course, but adamantly insists that firms in the private sector must compete among themselves for "customers" of health care, social security, education, and housing. We will conclude this chapter with a section on environmental rights. They epitomize collective goods, as well as individual rights, and they demand global cooperation because the environment is always a shared resource. All people benefit from well-maintained collective goods (such as transparent governments, global communications, sensible laws about the use of the oceans, and preservation of rain forests and ecosystems). Most nations are dealing realistically with the threats posed by global warming: for example, by ratifying the Kyoto Protocol and enacting its provisions. Not the United States.

The Walk to the Scaffold

King Charles I of England reputedly said on his way to the scaffold, "the prospect concentrates the mind wonderfully."[6] The prospect of multiple pending global crises has also concentrated the minds of many people today. It would be an understatement to say that the United States has been irresponsible, and the list goes on and on: not adopting policies that other states have to reduce environmental toxins, to reduce CO_2 emissions, to provide for biodiversity and preserve marshlands. The United States is leading the world into environmental catastrophe. That is not an exaggeration.

There is so much that could be cited in this connection, but one recent report suffices to sum up what scientists know about environmental risks in the United States. In July 2004 the National Priorities Project issued a press release that included the following conclusions: 64 percent of Americans breathe air classified as "unhealthy"; nearly twenty-two million people drink water that violates health codes; 11 percent of surface waters are impaired or threatened; the U.S. government has issued nearly three thousand fish consumption advisories; 97 percent of the population live in an area with one hundred times the cancer risk goal set by the Clear Air Act; 80 percent of its people live in an area with a worse risk of non-cancer health problems than the goal set by the Clear Air Act; and seven million American children have asthma.[7]

If we take a global perspective, it is easier to pinpoint the main culprits of environmental decline and degradation. The ambitious report *Global Environmental Outlook 3*, timed to contribute to the World Summit on

Sustainable Development, summarizes what progress has been made since the first environmental summit in 1992 and the Stockholm Conference on the Human Environment in 1972. Environmental degradation, the report concludes, has three main causes. They exemplify what lies at the core of the world's crisis today—overconsumption, on the one hand, and poverty, on the other. Overconsumption—oversized cars, energy inefficient homes—is a main culprit related to the increasing concentration of CO_2 or greenhouse gases, which heats up the planet, creates acid precipitation that kills fish, warms the oceans, and melts the polar ice cap. Urban and industrial development reduces biodiversity. Consumption levels in rich countries are unsustainable. To illustrate, growing ozone exposure is responsible for crop loss, widespread health problems and deaths, stratospheric cooling, and dramatic loss in biodiversity. Some parts of the ocean can no longer absorb CO_2, and coral reefs, which make up an integral part of the oceans' ecosystem, are dying at a rate far exceeding predictions a few years ago.

A Positive Scenario

Amazingly, a reprieve is possible for the environment. Not entirely, of course, but a slowing of environmental decline. At least the UN Educational, Scientific, and Cultural Organization (UNESCO) optimistically reports that there is an emerging new consensus on dramatic reforms that will reduce deterioration in the ozone layer, carbon monoxide emissions, and overall deforestations. Although the United States has not signed several environmental treaties, including the Kyoto Protocol, it has been a cooperating partner, according to UNESCO, on an international coalition, the Earth Observation Summit.[8] The Summit included panels of scientists from UNESCO and from thirty-three countries and the European Commission.

Assuming the best-case scenario, where U.S. scientists prevail over U.S. corporate interests, it is likely that major international treaties will be approved that will greatly slow the release of carbon dioxide and other greenhouse gases into the environment, reduce airborne particulates, and stop the deterioration of biodiversity and deforestation. These are costs that will be borne primarily by the world's top consuming countries, not the poorest ones, because it is the richest countries in the world (plus China) that are largely responsible for emissions. It is not impossible to imagine that, for example, the United States, the European Union countries, Canada, Australia, and New Zealand will implement legislation for fuel-efficient cars and houses, requiring simple technologies, and with tax credits, not an onerous burden for consumers. Renewable energy sources, such as wind and solar power, are rapidly being developed and implemented in Europe.

Virtually all responsibilities for environmental policies in the United States lie with the Environmental Protection Agency (EPA). If we want to understand U.S. policies on water, forests, air, pesticides, and wetlands, it would be to the EPA we would turn. Consistent with its liberal legalistic tradition that is reinforced by capitalists' interests to use the state for their own purposes, the United States has taken a defensive posture on environmental issues. There are few environmentally friendly policies in the EPA. It is a rule-ridden agency, devoting much of its efforts to helping industries continue to exploit the environment within the limits of the law, putting the burden on members of the public when they have little power to make much of an impact. The United States does not have a clear policy on environmental sustainability, because the EPA, a creature of Congress and beholden to the president, is in no position to develop a policy.

U.S. Federal Policies

Within the past decade countries have revised their constitutions to establish priorities and guidelines for environmental policies. Other countries have agencies that are the counterparts of the EPA, but they operate under the umbrella of constitutional provisions. In appendix 8.4 we present a great variety of—although by no means all—constitutional provisions for environmental rights.

We do not present the full provisions in most cases because we are interested in the variation in approaches that states take. Many states emphasize an overall philosophy about preserving the environment for the future (for example, Albania, Papua New Guinea, Peru), sometimes in connection with other values (e.g., Croatia and Cuba). More frequently, constitutions specify that environmental safeguards are the responsibility of the state: Afghanistan, Bulgaria, Cambodia, China, Kazakhstan, North Korea, Latvia, Nepal, Nigeria, Slovenia, and others.

Another way of considering the environment is to cast protections as the rights of citizens, emphasizing that they are among a larger collection of human rights. This approach is illustrated by such country constitutions as the following, often linking the rights of humans, including future generations, with the responsibilities of the state: Belgium, Cameroon, Chile, Colombia, Congo-Brazzaville, Georgia, South Korea, South Africa, and Sri Lanka. Some state constitutions place great weight on obtaining information and keeping the public informed: Azerbaijan, Belarus, Moldova, and Norway. This implies that the state will undertake comprehensive surveys in order to monitor environmental changes.

Other states focus on culpability and the responsibility of repairing environmental damage—Argentina, Austria—and while most stress that citizens and the state have the duty to preserve the environment, a few states mention the direct responsibilities of property holders and economic agents—Brazil, Iran, Moldova, Northern Cyprus, Romania, Slovakia, Sri Lanka. A few constitutions mention the special importance of the natural habitat for indigenous communities. These include Brazil, Chechnya, and Madagascar. One state—Ethiopia—considers environmental issues, at least in part, to be part of public, democratic discussions.

As we indicated, some of these are extracted from longer discussions on the environment, because our purpose is not a comparative analysis of state policies, but rather a sampling of conceptual differences. However, we reproduce most of Brazil's section on the environment to illustrate how one state deals comprehensively with environmental issues. It covers all of the issues we have reviewed, and it does so in ways that link the environment with health and peoples' quality of life. Moreover, it highlights the role that the economic sector must play in order to achieve environmental objectives.

States draw from implicit understandings about societies—not necessarily as entities with close-knit ties, but as entities where there is abundant bonhomie, feelings of comradeship and loyalty, but most of all a sense of informal and casual trust. This is different from nationalism and patriotism. There is no need to cement a society together; it is more naturally organic.

American Democracy

Constitutions provide the overall framework from which laws and statutes are derived. They are the starting point for laying out the key values and aspirations of a people. To give two examples from the United States, civil rights for minorities and equal rights for women are laws, but that is all. These laws are not grounded in a language of justice and commitment, but rather in very technical legalese that reveals anticipation of lawsuits and contentiousness. We describe these as "negative rights," because they are framed as being rights of citizens that have been, in a certain sense, wrenched from the powerful state. They are not positive rights that are woven into the fabric of the country and its society. Other constitutions stress people's positive rights, along with the duties of the state and all citizens to uphold them. The U.S. Constitution does not allow for the expression of shared ideals, cooperation, and solidarities, and by not allowing for such, privileges individual over human rights, thereby privileging those that have wealth and superior resources.

In these chapters we laid out some preliminary considerations that we believe need to be debated within public forums, as a first step to revising the U.S. Constitution. There are reasons to believe that Americans might be amenable to such debates. The first is that ordinary Americans are becoming concerned that they will lose Social Security for their old age and access to medical care, and feel threatened by chronic plant closings and mergers, which lead to joblessness. The second is that Americans are becoming cynical about the close ties of lobbyists, the super-rich, and multinationals to government. In international comparisons of established democracies, Americans rank exceptionally high on an indicator of perceptions that government is tainted by corruption.[9] The third is that many Americans are recognizing that to have a genuinely pluralistic society,[10] it is important to abolish the racialized hierarchies that marginalize the non-white population, not only African Americans, but also Latinos and many Asian groups. Finally, women recognize that they are denied economic and political rights that men take for granted. At least, we view these as the main mobilizing forces, besides the mobilization around environmental issues, that are likely to contribute to the voices for constitutional reform.

Notes

1. It is plausible that humans are hardwired this way because the reciprocity that accompanies empathy has survival value not only for individuals but for aggregates.

2. Although "solidarity" was made internationally famous in Poland's Solidarność movement, the constitutions employ the language more in the sense of social cohesion, in contrast with the constitutional tradition of privileging individual rights.

3. Iftikhar H. Malik, *Islam and Modernity* (London: Pluto Press, 2004), esp. 5–8.

4. Brazil constitution: www.oefre.unibe.ch/law/icl/

5. Eritrea's constitution, however, is not in force.

6. David Harvey, "Considerations on the Environment of Justice," in *Global Ethics and Environment*, ed. Nicholas Low, 109–30 (London: Routledge, 1999), 114.

7. National Priorities Project, *Environment Threatened in the United States* (Northampton, Mass.: 2004): www.nationalpriorities.org/

8. Susan Schneegans, Amy Otchet, Robert Missotten, and Maria Hood, "A System for Managing the Planet by 2015," *A World of Science* 2 (2004): 2–7.

9. Americans have exceptionally high scores on the Transparency International Global Corruption Barometer. Transparency International compiles survey data from forty-four countries to estimate citizen perceptions of corruption in a variety of areas. The United States rates as one of the highest on perceptions of corruption in political parties. Over 39 percent of the sampled adults in America are concerned that their politicians are corrupt, referring largely to the inordinate influence of corporate lobbyists over legislative decisions. The mean percentage for all countries is 29.7. Transparency International: www.transparency.org/

10. Andrew S. Mcfarland, *Neopluralism: The Evolution of Political Process Theory* (Lawrence: University Press of Kansas, 2004).

Appendix 8.1
The Language of Solidarity

1. Solidarity as Equality and National Unity

Angola: Economic, social and cultural *solidarity between all regions* of the Republic of Angola shall be promoted and intensified, with a view to the common development of the Angolan nation as a whole.

Argentina: The distribution among the Nation, the provinces and the City of Buenos Aires, and among themselves, shall be carried out in direct relation to the jurisdictions, services and functions of each one of them taking into account objective sharing criteria; it shall be based on principles of *equity and solidarity* giving priority to the achievement of a similar degree of development, of living standards and equal opportunities throughout the national territory.

Cameroon: The State shall ensure the harmonious development of all the regional and local authorities on the basis of *national solidarity,* regional potentials and *inter-regional balance.*

Congo-Brazzaville: We, the Congolese People, concerned to: . . . cooperate with all peoples who share our ideals of peace, liberty, justice, *human solidarity,* on the basis of principles of equality, reciprocal interest and mutual respect, sovereignty, and territorial integrity;

Greece: The State has the right to claim of all citizens to fulfil the *duty of social and national solidarity.*

North Korea: Citizens shall firmly safeguard the political and ideological *unity and solidarity* of the people.

Macedonia: The fundamental *values* of the constitutional order of the Republic of Macedonia are: . . . humanism, social justice and *solidarity*;

Mozambique: The family and the State shall ensure that children receive a comprehensive *education*, bringing them up in the values of national unity, love for their country, human equality, social respect and *solidarity*.

> . . . shall be in *solidarity with the struggle* of the African peoples and states for unity in respect of their freedom, dignity, and right to economic and social progress.
> . . . shall support and be in *solidarity* with the struggles of peoples for their *national liberation*.

Pakistan: Inspired by the resolve to protect our *national and political unity and solidarity* by creating an egalitarian society through a new order;

Spain: The Constitution is based on the indissoluble unity of the Spanish nation, the common and indivisible homeland of all Spaniards, and recognizes and guarantees the right to autonomy of the nationalities and *regions* which make it up and the *solidarity* among all of them . . . rational use of all natural resources for the purpose of protecting and improving the quality of life and protecting and restoring the *environment*, supporting themselves on an indispensable *collective solidarity*.

2. Solidarity as International

Cameroon: *Jealous* of our hard-won independence and resolved to preserve same; convinced that the salvation of Africa lies in forging ever-growing *bonds of solidarity* among African Peoples, affirm our desire to contribute to the advent of a united and free Africa, while maintaining peaceful and brotherly relations with the other nations of the World, in accordance with the principles enshrined in the Charter of the United Nations;

Cuba: *Basing ourselves* on proletarian internationalism, on the fraternal friendship, aid, cooperation and *solidarity of the peoples of the world*, especially those of Latin America and the Caribbean;

Paraguay: . . . accepts international law and endorses the following principles: *international solidarity* and cooperation;

3. Solidarity against Adversity

Colombia: [It is the duty of citizens] To strive in accordance with the principle of social *solidarity, to respond with humanitarian actions* when faced with situations that endanger the life or health of individuals.

Kuwait: The State shall ensure the *solidarity of society in shouldering burdens* resulting from public disasters and calamities,

Morocco: All shall, *in solidarity, bear the costs* resulting from *disasters* suffered by the Nation.

4. Solidarity as Democratic Civil Society

Cape Verde: To promote *social solidarity*, the autonomous organization of *civil society*,

Tibet: Whereas in particular, efforts shall be made in promoting the achievement of Tibet's common goal as well as to strengthen the *solidarity* of Tibetans, both within and out of Tibet, and to firmly establish a *democratic system*, suitable to the . . . ideals of the Tibetan people.

5. Solidarity as Human Rights

Cuba is an independent and sovereign socialist state of workers, organized with all and for the good of all as a united and democratic republic, for the enjoyment of political freedom, social justice, individual and collective well-being and *human solidarity*.

Italy: The republic recognizes and guarantees the inviolable *human rights*, be it as an individual or in social groups expressing their personality, and it ensures the performance of the unalterable duty to political, economic, and *social solidarity*.

Paraguay: The [educational] system is designed to promote the full development of human personality, to foster freedom and peace, to promote social justice, *solidarity, cooperation, and integration of all peoples*, the respect for the human rights and the principles of democracy, to confirm the commitment to the fatherland and to strengthen the cultural identity.

Poland: paying respect to the inherent dignity of the person, his or her right to freedom, the *obligation of solidarity* with others, and respect for these principles as the unshakeable foundation of the Republic of Poland . . . social *market economy*, based on the freedom of economic activity, private ownership, and *solidarity*, dialogue and cooperation between social partners, shall be the basis of the economic system of the Republic of Poland.

Turkey: The Republic of Turkey is a democratic, secular and social state governed by the rule of law; bearing in mind the concepts of public peace, *national solidarity* and justice; respecting *human rights*;

Emphasis added.

SOURCE: State Constitutions, University of Richmond Constitution Finder: confinder.richmond.edu/

Appendix 8.2
Pluralism in Contemporary Constitutions

Asia and Asia Pacific

Bangladesh
Article 23. National Culture.

The State shall adopt measures to conserve the cultural traditions and heritage of the people, and so to foster and improve the national language, literature and the arts that all sections of the people are afforded the opportunity to contribute towards and to participate in the enrichment of the national culture.

India
Article 15. Prohibition of discrimination on grounds of religion, race, caste, sex or place of birth

(1) The State shall not discriminate against any citizen on grounds only of religion, race, caste, sex, place of birth or any of them.
(2) No citizen shall, on grounds only of religion, race, caste, sex, place of birth or any of them, be subject to any disability, liability, restriction or condition with regard to—
(a) access to shops, public restaurants, hotels and places of public entertainment; or
(b) the use of wells, tanks, bathing ghats, roads and places of public resort maintained whole or partly out of State funds or dedicated to the use of general public.

(3) Nothing in this article shall prevent the State from making any special provision for women and children.

(4) Nothing in this article or in clause (2) or article 29 shall prevent the State from making any special provision for the advancement of any socially and educationally backward classes of citizens or for the Scheduled Castes and the Scheduled Tribes.

Article 17. Abolition of Untouchability
"Untouchability" is abolished and its practice in any form is forbidden. The enforcement of any disability arising out of "Untouchability" shall be an offence punishable in accordance with law.

Article 29. Protection of interests of minorities
(1) Any section of the citizens residing in the territory of India or any part thereof having a distinct language, script or culture of its own shall have the right to conserve the same.

New Zealand

Section 20. A person who belongs to an ethnic, religious, or linguistic minority in New Zealand shall not be denied the right, in community with other members of that minority, to enjoy the culture, to profess and practice the religion, or to use the language, of that minority.

Middle East

Egypt
Preamble. Second Section
Union: the hope of our Arab Nation, being convinced that Arab Unity is a call of history and of the future, and a demand of destiny; and that it cannot materialise except through an Arab Nation, capable of warding off any threat, whatever the source or the pretexts for such a threat.

 Article 40. All citizens are equal before the law. They have equal public rights and duties without discrimination between them due to race, ethnic origin, language, religion or creed.

Iran
Preamble. First Section
The Constitution of the Islamic Republic of Iran advances the cultural, social, political, and economic institutions of Iranian society based on Islamic

principles and norms, which represent an honest aspiration of the Islamic Ummah. This aspiration was exemplified by the nature of the great Islamic Revolution of Iran, and by the course of the Muslim people's struggle, from its beginning until victory, as reflected in the decisive and forceful calls raised by all segments of the populations. Now, at the threshold of this great victory, our nation, with all its beings, seeks its fulfillment.

Jordan
Article 6. (i) Jordanians shall be equal before the law. There shall be no discrimination between them as regards to their rights and duties on grounds of race, language or religion.
Article 14. The State shall safeguard the free exercise of all forms of worship and religious rites in accordance with the customs observed in the Kingdom, unless such is inconsistent with public order or morality.

Africa

Ethiopia
Article 39. The Right of Nations, Nationalities and Peoples
1. Every nation, nationality or people in Ethiopia shall have the unrestricted right to self determination up to secession.
2. Every nation, nationality and people shall have the right to speak, write and develop its language and to promote its culture, help it grow and flourish, and preserve its historical heritage.
5. For the purposes of this constitution, the term "nationality" shall mean a community having the following characteristics: people with a common culture reflecting considerable uniformity and a similarity of custom, a common language or (minority) languages of communication, a belief in a common bond and identity, the majority of whom live in a common territory.
6. Affiliated nationalities who share common characteristics but exhibiting varying cultures, common political and economic interests and believe in establishing, on the basis of the free choice of their peoples, a common administration may together decide to be recognized as a single nation or as one people.

South Africa
6. (1) The official languages of the Republic are Sepedi, Sesotho, Setswana, siSwati, Tashivenda, Xitsonga, Afrkaans, English, isiNdebele, isiXhosa and isiZulu.

6. (5) A Pan South African Language Board established by national legislation must (a) promote and create conditions for the development and use of (i) all official languages; (ii) the Khoi, Nama and San languages; and (iii) sign language; and (b) promote and ensure respect for (i) all languages commonly used by communities in South Africa . . . and Arabic, Hebrew, Sanskrit, and other languages used for religious purposes in South Africa.

31. (1) Persons belonging to a cultural, religious or linguistic community may not be denied the right, with other members of that community—(a) to enjoy their culture, practice their religion and use their language; and (b) to form, join and maintain cultural, religious and linguistic association and other organs of civil society; (2) The rights in subsection (1) may not be exercised in a manner inconsistent with any provision of the Bill of Rights.

Uganda
III. National Unity and Stability.
(i) All organs of State and people of Uganda shall work towards the promotion of national unity, peace and stability.

(ii) Every effort shall be made to integrate all the peoples of Uganda while at the same time recognizing the existence of their ethnic, religious, ideological, political and cultural diversity.

Europe

Poland
35. (1) The Republic of Poland shall ensure Polish citizens belonging to national or ethnic minorities the freedom to maintain and develop their own language, to maintain customs and traditions, and to develop their own culture.
(2) National and ethnic minorities shall have the right to establish educational and cultural institutions, institutions designed to protect religious identity, as well as to participate in the resolution of matters connected with their cultural identity.

Italy
2. The republic recognizes and guarantees the inviolable human rights, be it as an individual or in social groups expressing their personality, and it en-

sures the performance of the unalterable duty to political, economic, and social solidarity.

Russia
26. Everyone shall have the right to determine and state his national identity. No one can be forced to determine and state his national identity. Everyone shall have the right to use his native language, freely choose the language of communication, education, training and creative work.

Armenia
37. Citizens belonging to national minorities are entitled to the preservation of their traditions and the development of their language and culture.

Finland
Section 17. Right to one's language and culture
(1) The national languages of Finland are Finnish and Swedish.
(2) The right of everyone to use his or her own language, either Finnish or Swedish, before courts of law and other authorities, and to receive official documents in that language, shall be guaranteed by an Act. The public authorities shall provide for the cultural and societal needs of the Finnish-speaking and Swedish-speaking populations of the country on an equal basis.
(3) The Sami, as an indigenous people, as well as the Roma and other groups, have the right to maintain and develop their own language and culture. Provisions on the right of the Sami to use the Sami language before the authorities are laid down by an Act. The rights of persons using sign language and of persons in need of interpretation or translation aid owing to disability shall be guaranteed by an Act.

Caribbean and Latin America

Colombia
Article 68. The members of ethnic groups will have the right to training that respects and develops their cultural identity.

Article 70. The state has the obligation to promote and foster the equal access of all Colombians to their culture by means of permanent education and scientific, technical, artistic, and professional instruction at all stages in the process of creating the national identity. Culture in its diverse manifestations is the basis of nationality. The state recognizes the equality and dignity of all those who live together in the country. The state will promote research, science, development, and the diffusion of the nation's cultural values.

Article 246. The authorities of the indigenous (Indian) peoples may exercise their jurisdictional functions within their territorial jurisdiction in accordance with their own laws and procedures provided these are not contrary to the Constitution and the laws of the Republic. The law will establish the forms of coordination of this special jurisdiction with the national judicial system.

Article 330. In accordance with the Constitution and the laws, the indigenous (Indian) territories will be governed by councils formed and regulated according to the customs of their communities and will exercise the following functions: (1). Supervise the application of the legal regulations concerning the uses of land and settlement of their territories; (2). Design the policies, plans, and programs of economic and social development within their territory, in accordance with the National Development Plan. (3). Promote public investments in their territories and supervise their appropriate implementation. (4). Collect and distribute their funds; (5). Supervise the conservation of natural resources; (6). Coordinate the programs and projects promoted by the different communities in their territory; (7). Cooperate with to maintain public order within their territory in accordance with the instructions and provisions of the national government; (8). Represent the territories before the national government and the other entities within which they are integrated; and (9). Exploitation of natural resources in the indigenous (Indian) territories will be done without impairing the cultural, social, and economic integrity of the indigenous communities. In the decisions adopted with respect to the said exploitation, the government will encourage the participation of the representatives of the respective communities.

Paraguay

62. The Constitution recognizes the existence of Indian peoples, defined as ethnic groups whose culture existed before the formation and constitution of the State of Paraguay.

63. The right of Indian peoples to preserve and to develop their ethnic identity in their respective habitat is hereby recognized and guaranteed.

They also have the right to freely apply their systems of political, socio-economic, cultural and religious organization, and to voluntarily observe customary practices. . . . Indian customary rights will be taken into account when deciding conflicts of jurisdiction.

64. Indian peoples have the right, as communities, to a shared ownership of a piece of land, which will be sufficient both in terms of size and quality for them to preserve and develop their own lifestyles.

65. The right of Indian peoples to participate in the political, socioeconomic, and cultural life of the country in accordance with their customary practices, the Constitution, and the national laws is hereby guaranteed.

66. The State will respect the cultural heritage of Indian peoples, especially regarding their formal education. At their request, the State will also defend them against demographic decline, the degradation of their habitat, environmental contamination, economic exploitation and cultural alienation.

Jamaica
Section 24.3. Whereas every person in Jamaica is entitled to the fundamental rights and freedoms of the individual, that is to say, has the right, whatever his race, place of origin, political opinions, colour, creed or sex, but subject to respect for the rights and freedoms of others and for the public interest, to each and all of the following, namely—
a. life, liberty, security of the person, the enjoyment of property and the protection of the law;
b. freedom of conscience, of expression and of peaceful assembly and association; and
c. respect for his private and family life, the subsequent provisions of this Chapter shall have effect for the purpose of affording protection to the aforesaid rights and freedoms, subject to such limitations of that protection as are contained in those provisions being limitations designed to ensure that the enjoyment of the said rights and freedoms by any individual does not prejudice the rights and freedoms of others or the public interest.

SOURCE: Constitution Finder: confinder.richmond.edu/#A

Appendix 8.3
Constitutional Provisions for Economic Rights, Women's Rights, Maternal Rights, Minority Rights, and Health Care Rights

Country	Economic Rights	Women's Rights	Maternal Rights	Minority Rights	Health Care Rights
Afghanistan		YES	YES	YES	
Albania	YES	YES			YES
Algeria	YES	YES			
Andorra	YES	YES			
Angola	YES	YES			YES
Antigua and Barbuda	YES	YES			
Argentina	YES	YES		YES	
Armenia	YES	YES		YES	YES
Australia	YES				
Austria	YES	YES		YES	YES
Azerbaijan	YES	YES		YES	YES
Bahamas		YES			
Bahrain	YES	YES			
Bangladesh	YES	YES		YES	
Barbados	YES				
Belarus	YES	YES		YES	YES
Belgium	YES	YES		YES	YES
Belize	YES				
Bosnia and Herzegovina				YES	
Brazil	YES	YES	YES	YES	YES
Bulgaria	YES	YES	YES	YES	YES
Cambodia	YES	YES	YES	YES	

Appendix 8.3 (*Continued*)

Country	Economic Rights	Women's Rights	Maternal Rights	Minority Rights	Health Care Rights
Cameroon	YES	YES		YES	
Canada	YES	YES		YES	
Cape Verde	YES	YES		YES	YES
Chechnya	YES	YES		YES	YES
Chile	YES			YES	YES
China	YES	YES		YES	YES
Colombia	YES	YES	YES	YES	YES
Congo-Brazzaville	YES	YES		YES	YES
Cook Islands		YES		YES	
Costa Rica	YES	YES			YES
Croatia	YES			YES	YES
Cuba	YES	YES			YES
Cyprus	YES	YES		YES	
Czech Republic				YES	
Denmark	YES	YES			
Dominica		YES			
Egypt	YES	YES		YES	YES
Eritrea	YES	YES		YES	YES
Estonia	YES	YES		YES	YES
Ethiopia	YES	YES	YES	YES	
Fiji	YES	YES		YES	
Finland	YES	YES		YES	YES
France	YES	YES			
Georgia	YES	YES		YES	YES
Germany	YES	YES	YES	YES	
Ghana		YES	YES	YES	
Greece	YES	YES		YES	
Grenada	YES	YES			
Guinea	YES	YES		YES	
Guyana	YES	YES			
Haiti	YES	YES		YES	YES
Hong Kong		YES		YES	
Hungary	YES	YES		YES	YES
Iceland	YES	YES			

(*continued*)

Appendix 8.3 (*Continued*)

Country	Economic Rights	Women's Rights	Maternal Rights	Minority Rights	Health Care Rights
India	YES	YES		YES	
Indonesia	YES			YES	
Iran		YES	YES	YES	
Iraq (Interim Government)	YES			YES	
Ireland	YES	YES			
Italy	YES	YES		YES	
Jamaica		YES			
Japan	YES	YES		YES	
Jordan	YES			YES	
Kazakhstan	YES	YES		YES	
Kenya		YES		YES	
Kiribati		YES			
Korea (North)	YES	YES		YES	
Korea (South)	YES	YES			
Kuwait	YES				
Kyrgyzstan	YES	YES		YES	YES
Laos	YES	YES			
Latvia	YES	YES		YES	YES
Lebanon					
Liberia	YES	YES			
Libya	YES	YES			YES
Liechtenstein	YES	YES			
Lithuania	YES	YES		YES	
Luxembourg	YES				YES
Macedonia (Former Yugoslav Rep.)	YES	YES		YES	YES
Madagascar	YES	YES		YES	
Malawi	YES	YES		YES	YES
Malaysia	YES			YES	
Maldives					
Mali	YES	YES		YES	
Malta	YES	YES			
Marshall Islands				YES	YES
Mauritania	YES	YES		YES	

Appendix 8.3 (*Continued*)

Country	Economic Rights	Women's Rights	Maternal Rights	Minority Rights	Health Care Rights
Mauritius		YES			
Mexico	YES	YES			
Micronesia	YES	YES		YES	YES
Moldova	YES	YES		YES	YES
Monaco	YES			YES	
Mongolia	YES	YES		YES	YES
Morocco	YES	YES			
Mozambique	YES	YES	YES		YES
Namibia	YES	YES		YES	
Nauru		YES			
Nepal	YES	YES		YES	
Netherlands	YES	YES			
New Zealand				YES	
Nigeria	YES	YES			YES
Niue					
Norway	YES			YES	
Oceania	YES	YES		YES	
Oman					
Pakistan	YES	YES		YES	
Palau					
Palestinian Authority		YES	YES	YES	
Paraguay	YES	YES		YES	
Peru	YES	YES		YES	YES
Philippines	YES	YES		YES	YES
Poland	YES	YES	YES	YES	YES
Portugal	YES	YES	YES	YES	YES
Puerto Rico	YES	YES			
Qatar		YES		YES	
Romania	YES	YES		YES	
Russia	YES	YES	YES	YES	YES
Rwanda	YES	YES			
St. Kitts and Nevis		YES			

(*continued*)

Appendix 8.3 (*Continued*)

Country	Economic Rights	Women's Rights	Maternal Rights	Minority Rights	Health Care Rights
St. Lucia		YES		YES	
Saint Vincent and Grenadines		YES			
Samoa		YES		YES	
Saudi Arabia	YES				YES
Sierra Leone				YES	
Singapore				YES	
Slovakia	YES	YES		YES	YES
Slovenia		YES		YES	YES
Solomon Islands		YES		YES	YES
South Africa	YES	YES		YES	YES
Spain	YES	YES		YES	
Sri Lanka	YES	YES		YES	
Suriname	YES	YES		YES	YES
Swaziland		YES		YES	
Sweden	YES	YES			
Switzerland	YES	YES		YES	YES
Syria	YES	YES			YES
Taiwan	YES	YES	YES		
Tajikistan	YES	YES		YES	YES
Thailand	YES	YES			YES
Tibet	YES	YES		YES	YES
Trinidad and Tobago		YES			
Tonga					
Tunisia				YES	
Turkey	YES	YES		YES	
Turkmenistan				YES	
Tuvalu		YES			
Uganda	YES	YES		YES	YES
Ukraine	YES	YES	YES	YES	YES
United Kingdom		YES		YES	
United States					
Uzbekistan					
Vanuatu		YES		YES	

Appendix 8.3 (*Continued*)

Country	Economic Rights	Women's Rights	Maternal Rights	Minority Rights	Health Care Rights
Venezuela	YES	YES		YES	
Vietnam	YES	YES		YES	
Yemen	YES	YES		YES	
Zambia	YES	YES			
Zimbabwe		YES			

SOURCE: State constitutions; confinder.richmond.edu

NOTES: Israel does not have a constitution; and the following countries are excluded because their constitutions are not available in English: Benin, Bolivia, Burkina Faso, Burundi, Chad, Comoros, Congo-Kinshasa, Dominican Republic, Ecuador, El Salvador, Guatemala, Honduras, Nicaragua, Panama, Senegal, and Uruguay.

Appendix 8.4
Environmental Rights:
Extracts from Selected Constitutions

Afghanistan: the state shall create suitable environment.

Albania: rational exploitation of forests, waters, pastures and other natural resources on the basis of the principle of sustainable development.

Andorra: preserving the integrity of the Earth and guaranteeing an environment fit for life for the coming generations.

Angola: All citizens shall have the right to live in a healthy and unpolluted environment.

Argentina: As a first priority, environmental damage shall bring about the obligation to repair it according to law.

Armenia: The state shall ensure the protection and reproduction of the environment and the rational utilization of natural resources.

Austria: [The state will take] measures to counter factors hazardous to the environment.

Azerbaijan: Everybody shall have the right to collect information on environmental situation and to get compensation for damage rendered to the health and property due to the violation of ecological rights.

Belarus: [The public] shall be guaranteed the right to receive, store, and disseminate complete, reliable, and timely information on the activities of state bodies and public associations, on political, economic, and international life, and on the state of the environment.

Belgium: The right to enjoy the protection of a healthy environment.

Belize: [The state will promote] policies which protect the environment.

Brazil: All persons are entitled to an ecologically balanced environment, which is an asset for the people's common use and is essential to healthy life, it being the duty of the Government and of the community to defend and preserve it for present and future generations. The economic order . . . will protect the environment. [It is the state responsibility] to protect the environment and fight pollution; to preserve forests, fauna and flora; . . . and the single health system shall cooperate in the preservation of the environment, including that of the work place; and the economic order . . . [will] control the production, marketing, and use of techniques, methods, and substances which represent a risk to life, to the quality of life, and to the environment; Lands traditionally occupied by Indians are those on which they live on a permanent basis, those used for their productive activities, those which are indispensable to preserve the environmental resources required for their well-being and those necessary for their physical and cultural reproduction, according to their sues, customs, and traditions.

Bulgaria: The State shall ensure the protection and reproduction of the environment, the conservation of living nature in all its variety, and the sensible utilization of the country's natural and other resources.

Cambodia: The State shall protect the environment and balance of abundant natural resources and establish a precise plan of management of land, water, air, wind geology, ecologic system, mines, energy, petrol, and gas, rocks and sand, gems, forests and forest products, wildlife, fish and aquatic resources.

Cameroon: Every person shall have a right to a healthy environment. The protection of the environment shall be the duty of every citizen.

Cape Verde: To protect the landscape, nature, the natural resources and the environment, as well as the historical, cultural and artistic national heritage; everyone shall have the right to a healthy life and ecologically balanced environment and the duty to defend and conserve it. Economic activities shall not jeopardize the eco-system, nor should they contribute to the disequilibrium of the relations between man and the environment.

Chechnya: [The state will promote] protection of the original environment and traditional way of life of small ethnic communities.

Chile: The right to live in an environment free from contamination.

China: The state protects and improves the living environment and the ecological environment, and prevents and remedies pollution and other public hazards. The state organizes and encourages forestation and the protection of forests.

Colombia: Citizens will be educated in the respect for human rights, peace, and democracy, and in the use of work and recreation for cultural, scientific, and technological improvement and for the protection of the environment. [It is the duty of the] State to protect the integrity of public space and its assignment to common use, which has priority over the individual interest.

Congo (Brazzaville): Each citizen shall have the right to a healthy, satisfactory, and enduring environment and the duty to defend it.

Croatia: Freedom, equal rights, national equality and equality of genders, love of peace, social justice, respect for human rights, inviolability of ownership, conservation of nature and the environment, the rule of law, and a democratic multiparty system are the highest values of the constitutional order of the Republic of Croatia and the ground for interpretation of the Constitution.

Cuba: It recognizes the close links they have with sustainable economic and social development to make human life more rational and to ensure the survival, well-being and security of present and future generations.

Estonia: Everyone shall be obligated to preserve human and natural environment and to compensate for damages caused by him.

Ethiopia: The people concerned shall be made to give their opinions in the preparation and implementation of policies and programs concerning environmental protection.

Georgia: Everyone shall have the right to live in a healthy environment and enjoy natural and cultural surroundings. Everyone shall be obliged to care for natural and cultural environment. A person shall have the right to receive complete, objective and timely information as to the state of his/her working and living environment.

Greece: The protection of the natural and cultural environment constitutes a duty of the State and a right of every person. The State is bound to adopt special preventive or repressive measures for the preservation of the environment in the context of the principle of sustainability. Matters pertaining to the protection of forests and forest expanses in general shall be regulated by law.

Guyana: Every citizen has a duty to participate in activities designed to improve the environment and protect the health of the nation. In the interests of the present and future generations, the State will protect and make rational use of its land, mineral and water resources, as well as its fauna and flora, and will take all appropriate measures to conserve and improve the environment.

Haiti: Since the environment is the natural framework of the life of the people, any practices that might disturb the ecological balance are strictly forbidden.

Hong Kong: . . . pay regard to the protection of the environment.

Hungary: The Republic of Hungary recognizes and shall implement the individual's right to a healthy environment . . . the protection of the urban and natural environment.

Iran: The preservation of the environment, in which the present as well as the future generations have a right to flourishing social existence, is regarded as a public duty in the Islamic Republic. Economic and other activities that inevitably involve pollution of the environment or cause irreparable damage to it are therefore forbidden.

Italy: . . . protection of the environment, of the ecosystem and of the cultural heritage.

Kazakhstan: The government sets as its goal the protection of an environment which is conducive to life and human health.

Kiribati: . . . of persons generally or any class of persons that are reasonably required in the interests of defense, public safety, public order, public morality, public health, environmental conservation or in fulfillment of the international treaty obligations.

North Korea: The State shall adopt measures to protect the environment in preference to production, preserve and promote the natural environment and prevent environmental pollution so as to provide the people with a hygienic environment and working conditions.

South Korea: All citizens have the right to a healthy and pleasant environment. The State and all citizens shall endeavor to protect the environment.

Laos: All organizations and citizens must protect the environment and natural resources: land, underground, forests, fauna, water sources and atmosphere.

Latvia: The State shall protect the right of everyone to live in a benevolent environment by providing information about environmental conditions and by promoting the preservation and improvement of the environment.

Lithuania: The exhaustion of land and entrails of the earth, the pollution of waters and air, the production of radioactive impact, as well as the impoverishment of fauna and flora, shall be prohibited by law.

Macedonia: [Instill] values—proper urban and rural planning to promote a congenial human environment, as well as ecological protection and development.

Madagascar: The Fokonolona (minorities) may take appropriate measures to prevent destruction of their environment, loss of their land, seizure of herds of cattle, or loss of their ceremonial heritage, unless these measures jeopardize the common interest or public order.

Malawi: To manage the environment responsibly in order to—(i) prevent the degradation of the environment; (ii) provide a healthy living and working environment for the people of Malawi; (iii) accord full recognition to the rights of future generations by means of environmental protection and the sustainable development of natural resources; and (iv) conserve and enhance the biological diversity of Malawi.

Mali: The protection and defense of the environment and the promotion of the quality of life is a duty of everyone and of the State.

Moldova: The State guarantees every citizen the right of free access to truthful information regarding the state of the natural environment. . . . Private individuals and legal entities shall be held responsible before the law for any damages they may cause to personal health and property due to an ecological offense.

Mongolia: [Peoples'] right to healthy and safe environment and to be protected against environmental pollution and ecological imbalance.

Mozambique: The State shall promote efforts to guarantee the ecological balance and the conservation and preservation of the environment for the betterment of the quality of life of its citizens.

Nepal: The State shall give priority to the protection of the environment and also to the prevention of its further damage due to physical development activities.

Nigeria: The State shall protect and improve the environment and safeguard the water, air and land, forest and wild life of Nigeria.

Northern Cyprus (Turkey): No real or legal person shall drain or dump into the sea or into any dam, lake or river, for any purpose whatsoever, any liquid, gas or Solid matter which is of such a nature as to cause harm to human health or to endanger marine life and resources.

Norway: In order to safeguard their right in accordance with the foregoing paragraph, citizens are entitled to be informed of the state of the natural environment and of the effects of any encroachments on nature that are planned or commenced.

Papua New Guinea: We declare our fourth goal to be for Papua New Guinea's natural resources and environment to be conserved and used for the collective benefit of us all, and be replenished for the benefit of future generations.

Paraguay: Those activities that are likely to cause environmental changes will be regulated by law.

Peru: . . . [to promote] to peace, tranquility, enjoyment of leisure time and rest, as well as to a balanced and suitable environment within which he may conduct his life.

Poland: . . . shall safeguard the independence and integrity of its territory and ensure the freedoms and rights of persons and citizens, the security of the citizens, safeguard the national heritage and shall ensure the protection of the natural environment pursuant to the principles of sustainable development.

Portugal: to promote the prevention, the suppression and the prosecution of offences against public health, consumer rights, the quality of life, the preservation of the environment and the cultural heritage.

Qatar: . . . shall work to protect the environment and ecological balance so as to achieve sustainable development for the generations to come.

Romania: The right of property compels to the observance of duties relating to environmental protection and assurance of neighborliness, as well as of other duties incumbent upon the owner, in accordance with the law or custom.

Saudi Arabia: The state works for the preservation, protection, and improvement of the environment, and for the prevention of pollution.

Slovakia: By exercising ownership, no harm must be done to human health, nature, cultural monuments, and the environment beyond limits set by law.

Slovenia: The state shall promote a healthy living environment. To this end, the conditions and manner in which economic and other activities are pursued shall be established by law.

Somaliland: The state shall give a special priority to the protection and safeguarding of the environment which is essential for the well-being of the society and the care of the natural resources. Therefore, the care of and the damage to the environment shall be determined by law.

South Africa: Everyone has the right (a) to an environment that is not harmful to their health or well-being; and (b) to have the environment protected, for the benefit of present and future generations, through reasonable legislative and other measures that (i) prevent pollution and ecological degradation; (ii) promote conservation; and (iii) secure ecologically sustainable development and use of natural resources while promoting justifiable economic and social development.

Spain: Everyone has the right to enjoy an environment suitable for the development of the person as well as the duty to preserve it.

Sri Lanka: Every citizen is entitled to own property alone or in association with others subject to the preservation and protection of the environment and the rights of the community.

Suriname: . . . social objectives of the State shall aim at: the identification of the potentialities for development of their own natural environment and the enlarging of the capacities to ever more expand those potentialities.

Switzerland: . . . shall collect the necessary statistical data on the status and evolution of the population, the economy, the society, the territory, and the environment in Switzerland.

Tajikistan: [take] measures to improve the condition of the environment, formation and development of mass athletics, physical fitness, and other sports.

Tibet: . . . shall conduct special medical care programs for immunization and chronic illnesses; and educate people on environmental issues.

Turkey: Everyone has the right to live in a healthy, balanced environment.

Turkmenistan: The government is responsible for preserving the national historico-cultural heritage and natural environment, as well as for ensuring equality between social and national groups.

Uganda: . . . shall be managed in such a way as to meet the development and environmental needs of present and future generations of Ugandans; and in particular, the State shall take all possible measures to prevent or minimize damage and destruction to land, air and water resources resulting from pollution or other causes.

Ukraine: Everyone is guaranteed the right of free access to information about the environmental situation, the quality of food and consumer goods, and also the right to disseminate such information. No one shall make such information secret.

Uzbekistan: Citizens must treat the natural environment with care.

A Socratic Dialogue

I n chapter 10, to spark classroom discussions, we present a draft revised
U.S. Constitution. As a way of providing a transition to chapter 10, we
felt that providing a mock conversation would put readers into the
frame of mind to consider how they themselves might discuss these issues.
Nothing is better suited than adapting a Socratic dialogue for our purposes,
since this is a method that is widely used to develop critical thinking and
to hone in on the ramifications of given premises. As a model, we use
Book I of *Plato's Republic*.[1]

As a refresher, Socrates is not a contemporary of Plato, but Plato puts
him in nearly all of his works. He is present in Book I of *The Republic*, as
well as in our dialogue (Soc). Plato is himself not present, but his two
brothers, Glaucon and Adeimantus, speak on his behalf in *The Republic*. It
being the twenty-first century, we invented instead a sister for Plato—
Adimantara (Adi). We do not keep all of Plato's Sophist personages, but re-
tain two, Thrasymachus (Thras, a temperamentally conservative Sophist)
and Cephalus (Ceph, an elderly Sophist of some wealth). We also add a
waiter, and invent a name for him, Phainomena[2] (Phai). He is an immigrant from Morocco. Because Plato freely deconstructs history (by, for example, adding Socrates to Book I), we do so as well. The dialogue implies
that Pierre-Joseph Proudhon is a contemporary, when he is, in fact, a
nineteenth-century journalist, who advocated socialism. We also needed
an empirical sociologist, and found a close match in Herodotus (Hero),
who according to historical accounts of Ancient Greece was a rather careful collector of facts. That Plato was about two years old when Herodotus
died will not bother us here.

Book I of *The Republic* opens in the comfortable home of Polemarchus, where a lively discussion unfolds. Instead of asking the readers to conjure a scene with toga-clad people, reclining on cushions, eating grapes, drinking wine from clay goblets, we instead cast the scene in a contemporary place, the lounge of the Algonquin, an old midtown Manhattan hotel, an enduring favorite of authors, painters, and journalists. Its settees and antique desks, floral arrangements, make a perfect setting, with jazz piano off in the background.

The Scene Opens

Narrator: Thrasymachus arrives first on a warm summer evening at the Algonquin, and having ordered himself a bourbon, lounges with the Sports section of the New York Times, *when Adimantara arrives.*

Thras: Welcome! I look forward to our conversing here. It is more uplifting than reading about the Chicago Cubs beating the Yankees again. Sit down. Sit down. *She pulls up a comfortable leather chair to join him.*

Narrator: Cephalus is now seen outside, tipping the cab driver. He takes the few steps slowly with a cane, slowly enough that Socrates, walking, reaches the huge mahogany doors first, and opens them for Cephalus. They come in together.

Adi: (Getting up, and pulling up a chair for Cephalus, while Socrates pulls up one for himself.) It is so wonderful you could both join us. Cephalus, you don't come often enough from the Hamptons into town.

Soc: Yes, indeed, we learn from you, as you have reached what the poets call, "the threshold of old age."

Ceph: Yes, by Zeus, I miss the pleasures of my youth—of sex, drink, and feasts, and some other things that go with them. But. . . . *(sighing)* I have just returned from the Chelsea Spas. I feel refreshed with all the attention the young lads give me.

Soc: (Wink at the others, with a smile, but continues.) It may not be for me to say this, but some remark that your mind endures your old age easily because of your wealth.

Ceph: As the poet Pindar said, it is hope and generosity that make a good man bear his years easily.

Adi: But does a poor man sing this tune so easily?

Soc: Adimantara, you are speaking of justice, are you not?

Thras: Justice is nothing but the advantage of the stronger.

Soc: You then say that the rugby player Danny McGuire has the advantage over all of us because he is stronger. Is that justice?

Thras: Well, I didn't mean physical strength.

Adi: Well, let us talk about the just State here too. If America is stronger than the entire European Union, does America have justice on her side?

Ceph: How can you talk about a just State? It is rulers who are just or un-just.

Soc: You are all going over too many things at once. Let us first consider the just ruler. Does not the just physician put the patients' interests ahead of his? Does not the just ship captain put the interests of her crew before her own? Consider, then, the ruler.

Ceph: Just rulers do what is best for their people just like the just ship captain does what is best for his crew. But the ship captain knows more than his crew, and the ruler knows more than his people.

Thras: Yes, exactly. How can the people know what is in their interest? The ruler has the mandate to do what he thinks is best and what he thinks is just.

Adi: HE, HE, HIS, He. . . .You have earlier acknowledged in our conversations that women are the equals of men in matters of social, mental, economic, and political capacities. (*Laughs.*) Please do not regress when you have made so much progress. (*Waves to the waiter.*) And you have thrown democracy out of the window. You ignore that the crew of trained and talented people cooperate to keep the ship on course. The enlightened captain always seeks the advice of the navigator, the deck officers, the communications experts, the steward crew, the people in the engine room, and the Scientific Computer System (SCS) specialists. When there is a decision to be made, the enlightened captain takes all their expert advice into account. The best decisions flow from a process that is just and democratic. The same goes for society.

Adi: (*Turning to the waiter.*) A Campari, please, on the rocks, for me. Socrates, will you have the usual, a sherry fino? Cephalus, a martini, straight up? Thrasymachus, another bourbon for you? All right, now Thrasymachus, please be clear about what you mean by the "just ruler."

Thras: My naïve friend, and I don't mean that just because you are a woman. I mean that you have never been on the crew of a large battleship and haven't the vaguest idea of how things work.

Soc: Now, Thrasymachus, we all have respect for conservative thinkers like yourself, who want to see how things can be done most efficiently, ignoring the complexities. You would prefer a formula or, even better, a machine to run everything, from ships to the polis itself. . . . I mean Manhattan. But not having that, you want a master who will decide things. If the captain of a large ship—you can call it a battleship if you want—if the captain ignores the experts—the navigator and others—the ship can go on the wrong course, or run out of fuel, or founder and sink. The captain cannot merely give orders, but needs to consult with the crew. But in the case of our fair city, and maybe—especially—our Empire, a ruler can usurp power, ignoring what the people want and what they need for their security.

Ceph: By Jove. You have a point, Socrates. But you forget that in the case of our Empire, people vote for the ruler. If they get a corrupt ruler, it is their own fault.

Adi: All of you, even you, Socrates, talk about governance and leadership in terms of people who govern and rule. Is it not true that we have institutions and procedures for governance? If so, we can think of many arrangements for governance. There can be democratic arrangements for elections, to elect a ruler directly, by popular vote, without restrictions on party participation. Or we could have a democracy by starting from the bottom and working up to the top. What do they call that? Sidewalk democracy? Oh, no, grassroots democracy. . . . Everyone would benefit from sharing perspectives, and solving problems collectively. There are many decisions that affect citizens, and they have a stake in those decisions. People know their own interests better than others do.

Let us say, here in New York City, the rich want subsidized private schools, tax breaks, airport conveniences for their private airplanes. They want fancy shops so they can impress their friends in London, Paris, and Tokyo with their latest fashions and jewelry. This is foolish when the workers need decent public transportation, parks, jobs, good public schools, health care, affordable housing. And, the really poor have no housing whatsoever. In January of this year the Coalition for the Homeless counted 36,200 homeless men, women, and families in New York City alone![3] And, then there are—

Soc: (Interrupting.) My dear, now you are on too many topics at once.

Adi: Socrates, I was getting to my point, namely, that governance should be inclusive and democratic. If all who reside now in New York City—mostly workers and now increasingly the working poor and those without a job—had a voice in governance New York City would be a more humane and civilized place. It is barbarically unequal now. The rich, who have few stakes in our city, except for their shopping sprees, now control the rulers because the rulers depend mostly on capitalist developers for revenues, and the capitalist developers keep building and renovating for the rich and for corporations—not for the people.

Soc: Cephalus: You might see in Adimantara's argument that when people merely vote for their representatives it is not true democracy. People now have a choice between the Zenocrats and the Repucrats, and both are beholden to the rich, the lobbyists, and the capitalist developers. Because of the way the entire economy is set up—and politics depends on the economy—the Zenocrats and the Repucrats behave the way they do.

Ceph: Do you mean we should abandon voting?

Soc: Not at all! We should have more voting, more public forums, more community meetings, and more things to vote on. We should vote on fundamental issues, such as the minimum wage for workers and a jobs creation policy, vote on public priorities, vote on priorities in the city budget. With a small subsidy, everyone in the city could have a laptop, and with everyone online, there could be real democracy. Of course, there are technical issues to be solved, but we certainly have the programming and computer technology to make that possible.

Adi: Yes, the real meaning of democracy is citizen participation, or codetermination, or empowerment—whatever you wish to call it. There is a paradox now, with capitalists the globe-trotters, ravaging the earth, and our rulers simply at their mercy. That is why the rulers do not represent the people.

Ceph: I will cede the point that rulers are liable to errors and it is presumptuous of rulers to think that they speak for all citizens.

Soc: Do you agree, then, that rulers can make laws that are ill conceived and go against the interests of the citizens?

Ceph: Yes. I can agree with that.

Thras: Cephalus is an agreeable old fellow who is falling for your trap. The strong ruler makes laws that are good for the entire polis—I mean city. Being a ruler gives that person access to the wisest counsel, which makes him both more powerful and wiser.

Adi: (*Impatient.*) Dear friend, Thrasymachus, you have not been listening and lost the gist of our discussion. If democracy would become simply a part of everyday life, it follows that the best ruler—she or he—would implement what the citizens decide.

Soc: Cephalus also raises the questions of laws. Every democracy needs a legal framework as a structure for decision making. Now we have what people call a liberal democracy, which privileges procedures over substance, economic rights of corporations over the rights of the people. To create a new democracy based on given rights of humans and to encourage citizen participation, we would need a new legal framework.

Thras: Now you make sense! We need order for the chaos you are proposing. The masses are basically not to be trusted. If the people do not have laws they will run around willy-nilly in every different direction. What are you going to call this legal framework?

Soc: Ok, let's call it a *Constitution.* It will lay down the basic principles about governance and the fundamental rights of the people.

Adi: What people? I think I can illustrate my point right here. (*She waves to the waiter.*)

The waiter comes over to the table. His name is Phainomena.

Phai: Yes ma'am, may I serve you something?

Adi: No, no, I am fine. Maybe the others would like something? (*Looking around, but not giving them a chance to order.*) I have something to ask you, if you don't mind.

Phai: No, I do not mind. Please ask.

Adi: Are you a citizen of our city?

Phai: I have a green card, if that is your question. I am from Marrakesh, where I attended a very fine high school and received a fellowship to study at the Sorbonne. There I finished my thesis, but received an entry permit to the United States in the lottery system. Most lottery winners from Africa drive a taxi, but because I speak fluent English, Spanish, and French, my chances were better in the hotel and restaurant business. I send money back to my family, but from what I have saved, I hope to go to school here, perhaps CUNY Graduate School. The degree from the Sorbonne does not mean anything here.

Adi: Can you vote?

Phai: Of course not. I am not a citizen.

Adi: Do you have health insurance?

Phai: No, of course not.

Adi: But you pay Social Security taxes and income tax?

Phai: Of course, these come out of my wages and my tips are reported as income.

Adi: And where do you live?

Phai: In Brooklyn, with twenty immigrants in one room. We sleep in shifts according to our occupation. Some drive taxis at night; others work as janitors in the day, and some like me, have two jobs. As a night watchman I am allowed to sleep some while on duty, and sometimes on the weekend, I sleep in the room in Brooklyn.

Adi: This is an outrageous injustice! It is like a slave system. Although you pay taxes and are subject to the laws of the city, you have no medical insurance and no citizenship rights to vote. By the way, according to recent reports, 40 percent of New York City's population are disenfranchised because of their immigrant status.[4]

Thras: Yes, I agree this is unfair.

Phai: I would love to be a teacher in the public schools; my education was in Spanish and Latin American literature. I think I have something to offer. I speak five languages and read and write easily in three of them. My family is scattered all over the globe. I have a brother in Germany, a sister in Argentina. We search for good opportunities for ourselves so that we can support our family in Morocco, and Morocco, as you know, is an extremely poor country. But now with the multinationals and financiers in Morocco, wealth is highly concentrated, just like it is here. We need more citizen alliances around the globe to advance peoples' rights.

I enjoyed talking with you, but now I must get back to work. (*Socrates unobtrusively slips him a large bill, as an appreciation for his contributions to the discussion, and mindful of the poverty both in Brooklyn and in Morocco.*)

Phai: Let me know when you need something else.

Ceph: Thank you, young man. Another bourbon, please—when you get to it.

(*Turning to the others.*) Terrible, terrible. Such talent, such a waste.

Adi: All people have talents. Some are good in crafts; others have talents for the theater, others are good speakers, and so forth and so on. The schools do nothing but test, test, test, and do not have time to help children develop their talents.

Soc: I think we are all agreed that residents of New York should vote, whether they are citizens or not.

Adi, Thras, Ceph: (*Nearly in unison.*) Yes.

Soc: And are we also agreed that all people have talent that needs only to be discovered and nourished, and it is the job of the teachers and the child's families and neighbors and relatives to help them discover their talents?

Ceph: Yes, of course. Even the people in Piraeus—I meant Paramus—know that.

Soc: Come now, Cephalus, don't be the urban elitist. Let us then talk about the laws and where they come from.

I proposed a framework that is a *Constitution.* It will lay down the basic principles about governance and the fundamental rights of the people.

Thras: I have no quarrels with that. But governments have a way of becoming corrupt. The real estate crowd alone gave Bushicon $4,346,136 in 2004 for his election,[5] and any sociologist knows that when money passes from one hand to another hand it is expected that the receiver gives back favors. It is a bad form of reciprocity. It's nothing but a corrupt exchange for power.[6]

Adi: The same crowd gave Goremption $1,560,686.[7] Is he less corrupt than Bushicon?

Thras: Let us say I was at a party, a pretty lively party, and a woman or a man asked me if I would sleep with them for a million dollars. And, I said, "Sure, for a million dollars." Then this woman or man said, "Well, what about ten dollars?" And, I would say, "No way. What do think I am? A prostitute?" Of course, it was already established in my first answer that I was very willing to be a prostitute. The amount does not matter. Both Goremption and Bushicon are corrupt.

Soc: If we examine the question, we can hold that this is not an analogy. Under the current laws we have, it is inevitable that corporations and wealthy lobbyists will buy off politicians, and make politicians indebted to them. Politicians will do their bidding. This is aside from issues about people's integrity, although these days politics does attract many people who see nothing wrong with the way that governance is entangled in the capitalist economy. Your analogy, Thrasymachus, is about individuals who make choices, given certain opportunities. Is it not? I am talking about systems.

Thras: Yes, I see your point. But I see too you are leading up to a view that supports nothing but anarchy.

Adi: Pierre-Joseph Proudhon could not join us this afternoon, but I know what he would say about the fundamental principles of any constitution, and, then, my friend, tell me what you say in reply.[8] He would say that economic factors must serve the interests of democracy by promoting the public good and through equalization of wealth, mutualism in credit and insurance, and reciprocalism in exchange. He would abolish private property, of course, so that people will want to participate in governance and in decisions about the operations of collectively owned enterprises. For Pierre-Joseph, human security is the sole purpose of government, and the people run their affairs democratically, while the—

Soc: (*Interrupting Adimantara.*) My dear, excuse me for interrupting you, but our friend, Pierre-Joseph should speak for himself, and I am sure he will be joining us another day. But we can speak for ourselves on this important point. Cephalus, you yourself have eloquently defended this idea at the Forum: namely that human security is the sole purpose of government. Do you still agree with that?

Ceph: Yes, certainly, the government of the City of New York must ensure the security of its citizens. But that means that we must also defend ourselves from Washington that imposes its policies on us. Its privatization policies make us all less secure. I am personally rich from my best-selling books on sophistry in computer programming and do not rely much on my Social Security, but many of my friends see nothing ahead but poverty as they face retirement with privatized Social Security accounts. I may not agree with Pierre-Joseph about abolishing private property, but I do agree with him about the purpose of government.

Thras: Our chariots—I mean—our mopeds, bikes, and cars—are one kind of private property that we should have as individuals, but Washington's laws give corporations, as property holders, the rights of persons, and give them huge tax breaks. That is a grave injustice.

Adi: And as they say, the rich get richer and the poor get poorer. This does not allow people their full dignity. Jobs do not pay enough to live on. This is a violation of personhood. The wealthy live in houses behind walls, perhaps to shield themselves from looking at poverty. And, poverty comes in a rainbow of colors. Maybe the wealthy live in houses behind walls because they are . . . "color-blind." Perhaps eye surgery would be a solution. After eye surgery, the wealthy would vote for the redistribution of wealth across all the colors of the human rainbow.

Ceph: Specious reasoning, my dear.

Thras: I am neither poor nor rich. But, yes, government is by the people and for the people. I cede that point. Government should promote human security, and it should do so through redistribution or shared ownership. That may mean war with Washington.

Adi: Dear Thrasymachus, you always seize on war as a simple way out of things. As we are now waging war on the Iraqi people! And did you feel secure when we were waging war on the Vietnamese people? And before that on the Korean people?

Thras: (Annoyed.) I would not put it that way. We are waging war on the Iraqis *for* the Iraqis and *for* their security. We want to spread our own freedoms around the world.

Adi: That is condescending, my dear friend. It is also naïve. Don't you believe we want their oil? Would it not be better to provide them with food aid and grants so they can be secure enough to establish their own democracy?

Soc: Let us leave this discussion about war for another day. Would you not say that if the government were to be solely devoted to the security of the people that it would wisely carry out the democratic will of the people?

Adi: Yes, we have established that democracy is our goal and it is realistic to expect broad participation. The government then provides the services efficiently, and that means everything from improving the services on the Number 1 and 9 subway lines to ensuring that everyone has a job, housing, education, social security, to maintaining parks and a healthy environment. I would say the government is accountable to the people for promoting their security, and people participate directly in governance decisions.

Herodotus, an empirical comparativist and historian, enters through the front doors, obviously, out of breath from rushing.

Hero: My friends, my friends. I am so sorry to be late. I was collecting so many documents, and now I have just returned from Persia, I mean, Iran, catching a late flight, and then the bus from JFK, and then the subway. I am really tired, but very excited to join you.

Narrator: Adimantara gets up, gives Herodotus a big hug, and pulls up another chair.

Soc: Greetings old friend.

Ceph: Yes, old chap. Your data and comparisons always enlighten us.

Thras: Welcome.

Phai: (Approaching the table.) Sir, may I take your bags and put them in the checkroom? And, may I take your order?

Hero: Gin and tonic, please. In Rome we do as the Romans do, and in Iran we do as the Iranians do. In Iran we don't drink, but we can smoke. Here, we can't smoke, but we can have a drink.

Phai: Happy to bring that, Sir. Would anyone like a refill?

Soc: Please bring us all Perrier, oh yes, and some nuts or pretzels, please.

Ceph: And so Herodotus, your trip was a success?

Hero: Oh yes, I have collected now all of the information on the way that governments provide security for their people.

Adi: (*Very excited.*) Amazing. And especially so because that is what we were just talking about—the government's role in providing security for the population.

Phai: (*With the tray.*) Here you are. Anything else?

Soc: The check please, when convenient.

Hero: I need to be clear that all of the data that I have is about what constitutions have to say about the role of government in providing security. In practice, it can be difficult, but constitutions clarify the intentions of the people and the goals for the state. As you know Washington's laws say little about people's security, but depending on the mood of a particular president, and who happens to get elected to Congress, sometimes people have no security at all. People try to impress others with all their possessions to convey to others that they are secure. And it can be a dog fight to get to the top.

Thras: So what did you learn? Name one such provision.

Hero: You know the world treaty aiming to abolish the death penalty?[9]

Ceph: Yes, of course, we all know it. Several of us participated in drafting it, and we happily did so. But I am not an empiricist. I do not keep track of the details of who did what and who didn't.

Hero: Well, you need your empiricists, or you would never know whether your good logic and reasoning amounts to anything. A total of fifty-four countries have ratified it, and seven others have signed it.

Thras: What! That is not the majority.

Hero: I have queried the leaders.[10] Almost all whose countries have not ratified it say they agree with it but that there must be exceptions during wartime. According to the most recent developments there are only two countries in Europe and Central Asia that permit the death penalty at all, and discussions are moving forward to abolish it.[11]

Soc: Your scientific evidence is helpful. What, and to whom does your craft give what we call justice?[12]

Hero: Some call it political science. Some call it sociology. Whatever it is, it shows us how to measure behavior and decisions about justice. It does not tell us what justice is.

Adi: Well, I am interested in the empirical details. We were talking about security of the people. What does the Washington law say about security?

Hero: I have done a content analysis and it does not mention "security," but it does mention "securities."

Soc: That is very good then.

Ceph: Now we are getting somewhere. What does the Washington law say about securities?

Hero: Section 8 says: "Congress has the power to provide for the 'Punishment of counterfeiting the *Securities* and current Coin.'"

Thras: That's all!!? Just money securities?

Hero: I told you. You may look it up for yourself. You are not only a Sophist, but you are also a Skeptic.

Adi: What then do other state constitutions say about security?

Hero: (*Reaching into his briefcase for his BlackBerry.*) I will send you my file that has all of the information. But I can tell you that the majority of state constitutions have detailed provisions about the securities of their people— for jobs, housing, protection of minorities, cultural rights, and so forth.

Soc: I have not invested in a BlackBerry, or a machine that Googles, for that matter. Please just send me your report.

Hero: Of course.

Ceph: What do these constitutions say about justice for the various tribes of their countries? In many places, even in our fair city, Athens, huh, I mean New York, not all of the tribes are treated equally.

Hero: (*Concentrates on sending e-mail to himself.*) Ceph, I will send you that file as well. Some places have provisions that we would call reparations, and many places have constitutions that deal with this through provisions of equality and language preservation. Washington's policies sometimes polarize us, rather than pluralize us, if you forgive the circumlocution.

Phai: (*Returns with bill, and Socrates pays, and hands Phainomena his card.*) Thank you, sir.

Soc: (*To Phai.*) You may call me Socrates. Please ring me up at that number if you would like employment. I could use some assistance translating. The new constitution should be in Spanish and English. Then we will see about other languages.

Phai: Thank you ever so much. I do enjoy translating.

Soc: Not at all. It's my good fortune to find a multilingual translator. (*Turning to the others.*) Now that we spoken of justice, war, the death penalty, and many things, we will apply our knowledge and Herodotus's empirical findings to write a new draft constitution. Encourage your friends to try their hand at it as well. Cephalus and Thrasymachus can do whatever they can do to revise the one Washington has given us already, and Adimantara and I will work on new provisions. We will all consult Herodotus, whose compendium of constitutions will be helpful.

Our present discussion shows that the capacity for justice, learning, and engaging in just practices is universal, and even shared by the subtle Sophists and the Skeptics amongst our selves. When we have abolished poverty and deprivation and have achieved a state founded on the principles of justice, equality, and the recognition of our plural cultures and traditions, democracy will flourish, along with our collective development.

All gather their things together, bid their farewells, and exit the Algonquin Hotel.

Notes

1. *Plato's Republic,* trans., G. M. A. Grube (Indianapolis: Hackett, 1974).

2. *Phaninomena* means something that is in a perpetual state of flux or change, which is akin to the condition of a migrant.

3. www.coalitionforthehomeless.org/—47k—February 4, 2005.

4. www.migrationinformation.org/

5. www.opensecrets.org/2000elect/select/AllCands.htm

6. A pun on Peter Blau's book, *Exchange and Power in Social Life* (New Brunswick, N.J.: Transaction, 1986), which he would approve.

7. www.opensecrets.org/2000elect/select/AllCands.htm

8. Pierre-Joseph Proudhon, *What Is Property? Or, An Inquiry into the Principle of Right and of Government* (Cambridge: Cambridge University Press, [1840] 1994).

9. Second Optional Protocol to the International Covenant on Civil and Political Rights, aiming at the abolition of the death penalty (December 15, 1989: http.ohchr.org/english/law/ccpr-death.htm).

10. That is not necessary; state reservations are posted on the UN webpage: www.ohchr.org/english/countries/ratification/12.htm#reservations

11. web.amnesty.org/pages/deathpenalty-041004-petition-eng

12. Nearly verbatim from *The Republic,* 7.

Draft Revision of the U.S. Constitution

Preamble

WE THE PEOPLE of the United States, in Order to form a more perfect Union, establish Justice, insure domestic Tranquility promote the human rights of its people, promote the general Welfare, and secure the Blessings of Liberty to ourselves and our Posterity, do ordain and establish the Constitution for the United States of America.

I. Revision of Amendments to the Constitution

Provisions contained in Articles I through VII of the 1788 Constitution and Articles [XX], [XXV], [XXVI], and [XXVII] of the Amendments are retained and not copied here. The revised proposed amendments refer to the Articles amended to the Constitution and are conventionally bracketed, to distinguish them from the Constitution.

1. Citizens, residents, and foreign nationals have the right to speak their conscience, the right to their opinions, the right to exercise their religion, the right to peaceful assembly, the right to petition the Government for a redress of grievances, the right to form associations, and the right to exercise their religion. There are no limitations to these rights except insofar as they infringe on the rights of others.[1]

2. All persons born or naturalized in the United States are citizens of the United States. Citizens, persons with resident permits, and persons detained in jail have the right to vote. All citizens have the right to run for any elected office, although residence requirements may be established by law.[2]

3. Discrimination for reasons of gender, sexual orientation, race, ethnicity, religion, political opinion, disability, and age, or any other personal or social condition or circumstance is prohibited. The State recognizes efforts to rectify existing inequalities as commendable. The enumeration in the Constitution of certain rights shall not be construed to deny or disparage other rights retained by the people.[3]

4. A well-regulated military, being necessary to the securities of the people, shall defend the United States and its hemispheric allies. A regional plan will be implemented that includes all member states of the Organization of American States that will coordinate defense and the maintenance of peace in the Americas. No private citizen or private contractor can carry out activities granted by law to the military. Conscientious objection for ethical or religious reasons is recognized. Private ownership of guns is illegal, and the Federal government will establish a program for lending guns for the purpose of hunting.[4]

5. The right of the people to be secure in their persons, houses, papers, communications, and effects, against unreasonable searches and seizures, shall not be violated, and no Warrants shall issue, but upon probable cause, supported by Oath or affirmation, and particularly describing the place to be searched, and the persons or things to be seized.[5]

6. No person shall be held to answer for a capital, or otherwise infamous crime, unless on a presentment or indictment of a Grand Jury, including cases arising in the military. No person shall be tried for the same offence twice; put in jeopardy of life or limb; nor be compelled in any criminal case to be a witness against himself or herself; nor be deprived of life, liberty, or property, without the process of law; nor shall private property be taken for public use, without just compensation. Detention is equitable and fair, always with the goal of reintegrating the offender back into the community. There is no death penalty.[6]

7. In all criminal prosecutions, the accused shall enjoy the right to a speedy and public trial, and to be informed of the nature and cause of the accusation; to be confronted with the witnesses against him; to have compulsory process for obtaining witnesses in his own favor and to have the assistance of counsel for the defense.[7]

8. In suits at common law, where the value in controversy shall exceed a reasonable amount set by law, the right of trial by jury shall be preserved, and no fact tried by a jury shall be otherwise reexamined in any court of the United States than according to the rules of the common law.[8]

9. Excessive bail shall not be required, as determined by law, nor excessive fines imposed, as determined by law, nor cruel and unusual punishment inflicted.[9]

10. The powers not delegated to the United States by the Constitution, nor prohibited by it to the States, are reserved to the States respectively, or to the people. This does not preclude power sharing with other countries, and regional and international bodies, for the purposes of promoting world peace and security.[10]

11. The judicial power of the United States does not extend to citizens or subjects of any foreign state who were not residents of the United States involving a case of law. The United States promotes international law, and is party to the International Court of Justice and the International Criminal Court.[11]

12. Slavery, involuntary servitude, the abuse or torture of prisoners, and child labor shall not exist in the United States or any place subject to its jurisdiction, or by American businesses and corporations regardless of their location—in the United States or elsewhere.[12]

13. Election of the President and Vice President, Senators, and members of the House of Representatives shall be by direct ballot with the State being the smallest geographical unit in the elections for both the Senate and House. Washington, D.C., Guam, Puerto Rico, and the Virgin Islands are treated as any State. No legally certified political party can be excluded from national elections, with certification rules set by an independent commission. Simple majorities decide the outcomes.[13]

14. The Federal and State governments will launch projects to encourage direct democracy, with the first step being citizens participating in decisions at the Local level and referenda at the State and Federal levels. Low-interest loans and subsidies for broadband technology will be made available to citizens and permanent residents for this purpose. It is the duty and the responsibility of all people to participate in these processes.[14]

15. All persons born or naturalized in the United States are subject to the jurisdiction thereof, are citizens of the State wherein they reside. No State shall make or enforce any law which shall abridge the privileges or immunities of citizens of the United States; nor shall any State deprive any person of liberty or property without due process of law; nor deny to any person within its jurisdiction the equal protection of the laws.[15]

16. Representatives shall be apportioned among the States according to their respective numbers, counting the whole number of persons in each State. No person who has committed acts of genocide or violated international humanitarian law can be elected to Federal office or State office or hold a position as officer of the United States or of any State.[16]

17. It is the responsibility of Congress to enforce, by appropriate legislation, the provisions of the Federal debt, and to hold annual public hearings to access the public debt, and to disseminate to the public the substance and terms of indebtedness.[17]

18. The Congress shall have the power to lay and collect taxes on incomes, from whatever source derived, without apportionment among the several States, and without regard to any census or enumeration. Tax policies will be progressive, with the tax rate increasing with personal and business incomes. Public hearings are required, along with media coverage of congressional debates on tax policies.[18]

19. The Senate of the United States shall be composed of two Senators from each State, elected by the people thereof, for six years, with no term limits. When vacancies happen in the representation of any State in the Senate, the executive authority of each State shall issue writs of election to fill such vacancies. The legislature of any State may empower the executive thereof to make temporary appointments until the people fill the vacancy by election.[19]

20. One year after the ratification of this article, the manufacture, sale, or transportation of known harmful drugs—for example, heroin, cocaine, crack, and meth—within, the importation thereof into, or the exportation thereof from the United States for personal use is hereby prohibited. It is the duty of families, communities, and schools to educate young people about the dangers of these drugs, and high priority is given to the humane rehabilitation of people who are addicted to these drugs.[20]

Additional Amendments
II. Private Sector and Nongovernmental Organizations (NGOs)

Private sector establishments do not have constitutional protections or rights, except as specifically stated. Otherwise, they are subject to laws specified in the U.S. Legal Code, and regulatory laws enacted by Congress and regulatory guidelines of the Federal government and States.

2. All workers are paid no less than a Living Wage, and private-sector establishments, NGOs, and government will comply with this provision. Living Wage guidelines will be established by the Department of Labor through a process involving public hearings and consultation with unions.

3. Private sector establishments are chartered by the Federal U.S. government, and subject to the laws of the U.S. government and State governments, and to international laws. They are taxed in accordance with these laws, and are strictly subject to zoning and environmental laws that promote sustainable development. Responsible investment policies are encouraged so that producers are not violating international human rights laws and treaties, and abide by Local labor laws and international labor standards. Private sector actors will be provided with incentives to partner with governments and NGOs in development projects.

4. The stock exchange, commodities markets, and financial markets will comply with government guidelines, and oversight committees will include members of the public. The Armex Defense Indexed stocks will be abolished.

5. The right to property of all citizens is guaranteed, its contents and limitations established by law. Expropriation, use, or restriction of private property by any government from public necessity requires just compensation.

6. Unchecked local commercialization threatens the environment of communities and detracts from the quality of life for residents. Local planning authorities will regulate commercial development so that establishments provide jobs while not leading to the deterioration of the environment and the quality of life of residents.

7. Nongovernmental and not-for-profit entities are part of society, and include political parties, foundations, charitable organizations, advocacy organizations, and unions. Churches, to the extent that they provide public services, may qualify as NGOs. As comprising civil society, they operate under special tax codes, and, unlike businesses and corporations, have free-speech protections. Media will donate time to these entities to broadcast programs that are in the interest of the public.

8. All corporate entities are publicly owned.

III. Science, Knowledge, Intellectual Rights

1. Scientific research that promotes medical and technological advance, as well as basic science, must be protected from domination by the private sector, and Federal guidelines will be established to prevent profit goals from contaminating research carried out in partnerships involving universities, research institutes, government agencies, NGOs, and the private sector.

2. Laws will establish provisions for the protection of human subjects in all scientific research.

3. The rights of authors, inventors, composers, scientists, engineers, and artists are protected by law. These rights may not be used by corporate entities to establish harmful monopolies, either in the United States or elsewhere.

4. In the interest of the public good, provisions will be made so that copyrights and patents are short-term and, in some cases, inapplicable.

IV. Religion, Language, and Cultural Heritage

1. The United States promotes no religion over others, and people have rights to their private beliefs, much like rights to an ideology, and secularism is the guiding principle in legislation, scientific policy, and medical practice. The "wall of separation" refers to the toleration of religion in society and public life, and the exclusion of religious doctrine within Federal and State governments.

2. The independence and autonomy of all churches and religious denominations, as well as nonprofit organizations, charitable organizations, and trade unions are guaranteed, without restrictions other than those imposed by law.

3. English is the official language of government, but Federal agencies, State and Local governments are encouraged to provide documents and post information in other languages whenever there is sufficient need to do so. Schools will require the study of a second language at the primary, secondary, and tertiary levels.

4. Government authorities will protect the national and cultural heritages through preservation and documentation, and maintain public sites and museums.

5. Indigenous people will be granted unconditional rights over their land, and will receive reparations for past harms that will allow them to overcome the poverty they now face. They will be given the opportunity of forming a united nation within the United States, but having independent statehood rights.

6. As reparations to the descendents of slaves, a Trust Fund, valued at 5 percent of the Gross Domestic Product, will be established. Corporations that continue to exist and that are found liable for earlier commercial exploitation of slaves will likewise be assessed 5 percent of their annual profits for a period of not less than five years. The sole purpose of this Trust Fund will be to benefit descendents through, for example, upgrading of schools, scholarships for students, restoration of agricultural lands, neighborhood renovation, and business start-up costs.

V. Human Rights

1. Everyone has the right to live in a healthy, ecologically balanced environment, and the duty and responsibility to contribute to promoting such an environment. The law will define and establish sanctions for ecological crimes, and regulate activities that are likely to cause environmental changes. Tax incentives will encourage the implementation of ecologically sound technologies and practices, such as biodegradable products, solar and wind energy technologies, and hybrid automobiles.

2. Everyone has the right to an identity, including a gender and sexual identity, as well a cultural, racial, ethnic, indigenous, and religious identity. All native and naturalized citizens have an American identity. National pluralism and unity depends on recognizing these pluralistic identities, and the State will encourage communities, schools, private sector organizations, and governmental units to promote such recognition.

3. Freedom of residence is a right, and the Federal, State, and Local governments will promote that freedom through nondiscriminatory housing and development policies, and in other ways promote neighborhood and community diversity.

4. Every American has the right to reside in the United States, to move freely within the United States, to leave the United States and to return to it. Foreigners, other than tourists, may apply for residence, study, and work.

5. Everyone is free to join associations and unions.

6. Housing is a human right. The Federal and State governments will monitor the housing supply and costs to ensure that the private sector is providing affordable housing, and will provide subsidized housing to supplement the private supply. None will be homeless or be living in temporary shelters.

7. Clean water is a human right. The Federal and State governments will monitor the water supply and ensure that drinking water is safe. It is the duty of people, private and not-for profit and private sector establishments, and the government to preserve water supplies.

8. Everyone has the right to sufficient food, and if people are unable to support themselves and their dependents, Federal, State, and Local governments will ensure their food security.

9. Women have the right to paid maternity leave and infant care from their place of employment, and paternity leave is also a right.

10. Any two people have the right to form a family. A marriage-like partnership between any two adults and being characterized by stability and monogamy produces a similar effect to that of a legal marriage.

11. Every parent has the right and obligation to care for, to feed, to educate their children while they are minors.

12. Children who are no longer minors have the right and obligation to assist their parents as necessary.

13. The law will ensure that no household with children shall live in poverty without the means to provide food and shelter. Families, society, and the State have the obligation of guaranteeing every child the right to harmonious development, including schooling and recreation. Besides schooling, the State will promote conditions conducive to the active participation of youth in the political, socioeconomic, and cultural life of the society.

14. Every senior citizen has the right to receive full protection by their family, society, and the State. The State will assist in ensuring that there are sufficient health and social services to meet the needs of the elderly through Social Security, Medicare, and other programs, and to oversee and regulate residential services for the elderly.

15. The State will formulate a policy for the treatment, rehabilitation, and integration into society of physically disabled and psychologically or sensorial impaired individuals. They are entitled to enjoy all the rights under the Constitution.

16. The State recognizes the right of everyone to freely and responsibly determine the number of children they plan to have, and will implement programs to ensure reproductive health and maternal health.

17. Everyone has the right to learn, to a comprehensive education conceived as system and process. Education is devoted to the full development of human personality and of identity, cognitive skills, and creativity. Schools will foster an environment where children and youth learn about their obligations in society and the importance of social solidarities as well as discover their own abilities. Schools will foster an inclusive environment and recognize the pluralistic backgrounds of students. Job training and life-long learning programs are also objectives of the educational system. Children of migrant workers are entitled to schooling.

18. Students have a right, if they wish, to religious instruction in a religion of their choice, coordinated with public education, but not part of public education. Charter, independent, and religious schools will meet Federal and State guidelines for educational purposes, and cannot discriminate on the basis of ethnicity or race.

19. Primary and secondary education, being essential for a free society, are universally free, and universities, whether private or public, will be established by Charter. The Federal and State governments will provide for scholarships, preferentially for students of need.

20. Health care is a human right, and is best advanced as a public good so that there is universal access. The Congress will maintain Medicare and Medicaid but additionally devise a national plan to ensure that all have health insurance and access to care and medical treatment. All people residing in the United States have access to medical care, including migrant workers and their families.

21. Victims of criminal acts and natural disasters have the rights of compensation as prescribed by law.

22. To guarantee the right to assemble and peacefully assemble, the law can only regulate this right for purposes of public traffic control and at certain hours to preserve the rights of others.

23. The death penalty is abolished.

VI. Media

1. Free expression and the freedom of the press, the dissemination of thoughts and opinions, without censorship, are guaranteed.

2. The structure and operation of mass media organization are subordinate to the State, and law requires that opportunities be given to all social and political sectors to guarantee a democratic and pluralistic access to media outlets. Public media channels will be exclusively devoted to providing coverage of congressional deliberations, meetings of congressional committees, and news conferences of the President, Vice President, and Cabinet leaders.

3. Advertisement will be regulated by law to protect the rights of consumers.

4. Peoples' right to receive true, responsible, and equitable information is recognized. Laws will require that anyone affected by the dissemination of false, distorted, or ambiguous information has the right to demand that the offending media organization rectify or clarify the report under the same conditions in which it was originally conveyed.

5. The transmission and programming of electromagnetic communication signals constitute public goods, and everyone has free access to the electromagnetic spectrum without limits except as those imposed by international regulations and technical rules. Government officials may not violate privacy rights in connection with the use of these signals.

6. Local, participatory democracy will be promoted in conjunction with universal access to broadband.

VII. Society and Social Policies

1. The Federal and State governments will promote all sports, especially amateur sports.

2. Hate crimes and hate speech are especially injurious because they target groups as well as individuals, and grow out of the same impulses that give rise to genocidal crimes. Governments will promote policies for tolerance and multicultural understanding, and the criminal code will be revised to punish and rehabilitate hate crime offenders and educate the perpetrators of hate speech.

3. Federal, State, and Local governments are the primary stewards of public goods—the environment, transparent government, peace, as well as resources such as air, water, and oil. National policies will protect these public goods from irresponsible business and private use. It is the responsibility of schools, churches, nonprofit organizations, and local communities to educate people about the importance of indivisible, publicly shared goods.

4. All citizens have the duty to pay taxes under the conditions prescribed by law.

5. Citizen surveillance is an invasion of privacy and erodes trust within society. Law will regulate the government's use of surveillance and a citizen advisory board will have authority to oversee government practices.

6. To promote the public good and cosmopolitan regard of young people for others, a one-year national or international service is required upon graduation from high school. This service requirement can be met working in schools in disadvantaged neighborhoods, in environmental protection or restoration programs, in health clinics, in a service program under the auspices of an NGO or governmental agency.

7. The protection of the natural habitat and the environment is necessary for peoples' enjoyment, preserving biodiversity, and ensuring a healthy ecosystem. Federal, State, and Local governments will coordinate plans for national parks, protected areas, and reserves, including coastlines, waterways, marshes, and forests. Private access and use will be strictly regulated.

8. Cooperatives, co-ownerships and workplace democracy will be encouraged, along with citizen participation in Local government.

VIII. Work as a Human Right and Public Good

1. All able, adult citizens have the right and the duty to work, the right to advancement through work, and the right to sufficient remuneration. Governments will monitor the cost of living and ensure that wages are sufficient to satisfy the needs of workers and their families. Through wage policies and social programs, poverty will be abolished.

2. Worker unions, associations of employees, and associations of employers will be internally democratic and open to qualified persons. No one may be forced to join such a union or association.

3. The right of workers to strike is recognized.

4. The law shall guarantee the right to collective bargaining between the representatives of workers and employers, as well as the binding force of agreements.

5. Safe and healthy working conditions are guaranteed by law.

6. Immigrant workers and their families will receive the same health benefits as U.S. citizens and resident workers.

7. The Federal and State governments will guarantee support of unemployed and underemployed workers through a nationwide program that extends to domestic workers and farmworkers.

8. Companies that close in order to move to enhance their profitability must pay compensatory wages or salaries, as determined by law, and may be required to pay the Local government in cases where the government has provided special tax breaks or infrastructural support.

9. Employment security is to be enhanced through job training programs.

10. Discrimination in employment is strictly forbidden, in hiring, promotion, and in wages and salaries.

IX. International Cooperation

1. The United States will contribute at least 1 percent of its GDP to direct foreign aid.

2. The United States will abandon its nuclear missile program, and its development of biological and chemical weapons programs.

3. The United States will cooperate with individual nation-states, with regional bodies, and with the United Nations to advance peace, abolish worldwide poverty, and globally advance development and environmental goals.

4. High priority will be given to the treatment of HIV/AIDS, and to eradicating it.

5. High priority will be given to the worldwide advance of women's equality.

6. High priority will be given to helping nations meet their goals for children's education and health needs.

7. In recognizing its global responsibilities, the United States will cooperate with other countries by, first, ratifying existing international treaties, and, second, by working cooperatively with other nation-states to implement them.

Notes

1. Adopted from Article I, 1791 Amendment.

2. Adopted from Article XIV of the 1868 Amendment, and Article XV of the 1870 Amendment.

3. Article IX of the 1791 Amendment.

4. Adopted from Article II of the 1791 Amendment.

5. Article III of the 1791 Amendment.

6. Adopted from Article V of the 1791 Amendment.

7. Adopted from Article VI of the 1791 Amendment.

8. Adopted from Article VII, ratified in 1791.

9. Adopted from Article VIII of the 1791 Amendment, and Article XV, ratified 1870; and Article XIX, ratified 1920.

10. Article X of the 1791 ratification.

11. Adopted from Article XI of the 1795 Amendment.

12. Adopted from Article XIII of the 1865 Amendment.

13. Adopted from Article XII of the 1804 Amendment.

14. A substitute for Article XII of the 1804 Amendment.

15. Adopted from Article XIV, Section 1.

16. Adopted from Article XIV, Section 3.

17. Adopted from Article XIV, Sections 4 and 5.

18. Adopted from Article XVI, ratified in 1913.

19. Adopted from Article XVII, ratified 1913.

20. Adopted from Article XVIII, ratified in 1918. Therefore, Article XXI is nullified.

Index

About the Authors

This volume is a sequel to Judith Blau and Alberto Moncada's Human Rights: Beyond the Liberal Vision. *Their American and European collaboration brings a fresh perspective to understanding how to promote equitable and just societies. Moncada was a founding member and president of Sociólogos Sin Fronteras, and Blau is president of the U.S. chapter of Sociology without Borders. This academic organization is committed to advancing human rights and raising consciousness among Western social scientists about collective responsibilities to Third World peoples.*

Judith Blau is professor of sociology at the University of North Carolina at Chapel Hill. Her earlier books include: *Race in the Schools*; *Architects and Firms*; *Social Contracts and Economic Markets*; *The Shape of Culture*; and she has edited *The Blackwell Companion to Sociology* and is coeditor of volumes on public sociology, urban sociology and urban planning, and sociology of art. She was editor of *Social Forces*, a journal of social research highlighting sociological inquiry.

Alberto Moncada has taught at the University of Madrid, Stanford, the University of Lima, Florida International, and Alcalá University. He was the cofounder and first president of the University of Piura, Peru. He has published nearly thirty books (in Spanish) on a wide range of topics, including the media, sociology of education, politics, sociology of culture and the arts, Latinos in the United States, and sociology of religion.